Bicycling the PACIFIC COAST

A COMPLETE ROUTE GUIDE ■ CANADA TO MEXICO

THIRD EDITION

Tom Kirkendall & Vicky Spring

 Published by The Mountaineers
1001 SW Klickitat Way, Suite 201
Seattle, WA 98134

© 1998 by Tom Kirkendall and Vicky Spring

First edition 1984
Second edition 1990
Third edition: first printing 1998, second printing 1999

Published simultaneously in Great Britain by Cordee, 3a DeMontfort Street, Leicester, England, LE1 7HD

Manufactured in the United States of America

Maps by Tom Kirkendall
All photographs by Kirkendall/Spring
Cover design by Watson Graphics
Book design and layout by Gray Mouse Graphics

Cover photograph: *Cyclist at Bandon, Oregon.* Back cover inset: *Cyclist on Highway 1 south of Monterey, California*
Frontispiece: *Highway 1 plunging into Russian Gulch*

Library of Congress Cataloging-in-Publication Data
Kirkendall, Tom.
    Bicycling the Pacific Coast : a complete route guide, Canada to Mexico / Tom Kirkendall and Vicky Spring. -- 3rd ed.
      p. cm.
    Includes bibliographical references (p.) and index.
    ISBN 0-89886-562-X
    1. Bicycle touring--Pacific Coast (North America)--Guidebooks. 2. Pacific Coast (North America)--Guidebooks. I. Spring, Vicky, 1953- . II. Title.
GV1046.P17K57 1998
917.904'33--dc21   98-10391
                                            CIP

 Printed on recycled paper

■ CONTENTS ■

⬯ CANADIAN HIGHWAY		人 HIKER-BIKER CAMPGROUND	
▭ US HIGHWAY		▲ CAMPGROUND	
◯ STATE HIGHWAY		⌂ HOSTEL	
⬯ INTERSTATE HIGHWAY		○ CITY OR TOWN	
▬▬▬▬ MAIN ROUTE		△ POINT OF INTEREST	
▬▬▬ ALTERNATE OR SIDE ROAD		✈ AIRPORT	
═══ FREEWAY		▬◨▬ TUNNEL	
▬► ONE WAY STREET		▬ ▬ ▬ FERRY	
▬···▬·▬··· GRAVEL ROAD		〜··〜··〜·〜 *RIVER*	
·············· BIKE PATH		▬▬ -- ▬▬ STATE OR COUNTRY BORDER	
╋ UNDERPASS		▬▬ - ▬▬ COUNTY BORDER	
OVERPASS OR CROSS STREET			

▪ PREFACE ▪

Why North to South?

If, in 1981, Tom had decided to ride the Pacific Coast south from Canada to Mexico, he would have had a great time, and this book would never have been written. However, in 1981 Tom decided to ride from Mexico to Canada, and the results are as follows.

I rode with Tom from Mexico to Santa Barbara, ending the short trip with a sunburn and a great enthusiasm for bicycle touring. As he continued to pedal on, I drove north, heading to a summer job, knowing that I was missing a great ride.

As a West Coast native, I am proud of our beautiful coast, and expected Tom to be as thrilled by the scenery as by the challenge of the ride. I was terribly envious. But something happened as Tom headed on by himself.

Coastal view south of Carmel

Rest stop at a small coastal town in California

North of Santa Barbara, he encountered stiff headwinds that blew the fun right out of his adventure. Scenery and the thrill of exploring became secondary to his daily battle with the wind. The wind created an invisible, never-ending hill that had to be constantly climbed. The wind beat dirt into his face, produced an annoying whistling through the air vents in his helmet, while attempting to push him back to Mexico. By San Francisco, riding had become a chore. In Oregon, 80-mile-per-hour winds blew him to a stop while going down a steep hill. In Washington, he had 3 hours of peace when a very wet storm blew through from the south.

When describing that trip, Tom will pull out his trip journal. The beginning of the journal is full of his thoughts and impressions; in the second half he wrote only of the wind. His journal describes how he got up early in the morning to avoid the winds that blew strongest in the afternoon. The journal describes the miles covered each day, the food he ate, and the interesting people he met along the way, but nowhere in the second half of that book is there any mention of beautiful vista points, magnificent redwood forests, sea otters, sea lions, lighthouses, sand dunes, and fascinating old forts. Nowhere is there any mention of the word *fun*.

The following summer, Tom and I rode back down the coast to prove it *can* be fun. It was an incredible trip. Oh yes, the wind was still blowing, but this time, it was pushing us south. Near the Sea Lion Caves in Oregon, I had to apply my brakes to stop on a steep uphill grade. The miles flew by, and we had plenty of extra time and energy to stop and explore the forest and beaches. We were surprised to note that the Highway Department expects cyclists to travel from north to south. We frequently enjoyed a good shoulder on the southbound side of the road while northbound cyclists had to dodge trucks and cars on a shoulderless roadway.

To help other cyclists avoid the disappointment of northbound travel, we spent the following year organizing this guide from Canada to Mexico. We may be biased but we believe that the magnificent and varied scenery, the temperate climate, and the numerous public facilities designed especially for cyclists make the Pacific Coast the best long-distance tour in the country. When you plan your first tour down the coast, take advantage of the tailwinds, head south, and leave yourself plenty of time to explore and enjoy your trip.

Vicky Spring
Seattle, 1998

▪ INTRODUCTION ▪

This book is a guide to the Pacific Coast Bicycle Route from Vancouver, British Columbia, south along some of the world's most scenic coastline to palm-lined beaches at the Mexican border. More than a route, this is an adventure that passes through two national parks, a national recreation area, several national historical monuments, innumerable state parks, museums, forts, and lighthouses. Along the route are friendly towns with bakeries and art galleries, huge bustling metropolises with fascinating museums and excellent restaurants, beautiful forests, lonely seacoasts, and wind-sculptured sand dunes. Included in the adventure are sea otters, sea lions, sea gulls, pelicans, elk, raccoons, chipmunks, deer, and an amazing cross section of people.

Nearly all types of road conditions, terrain, and weather may be encountered on a tour of the Pacific Coast. A few broad generalities, open to exception, can be drawn as follows: wind blows from the north in good weather and from the south in bad; the chance of bad weather decreases as you travel south; and the number of facilities for cyclists (and the number of cyclists) increases to the south.

The Pacific Coast Bicycle Route is 1,816.5 miles long, excluding side trips. Following the day-by-day descriptions, the entire route may be cycled in 35 days. Some cyclists will ride it in less time. Others will want more time for exploring areas of special interest, taking side trips, and enjoying leisurely rest days.

For the purpose of simplicity, the book is divided into three chapters: British Columbia and Washington, Oregon, and California. However, the text and maps are arranged so that users may pick out the portions that interest them.

No formalized bicycle route exists for the coast of British Columbia or Washington. However, Oregon and California both established coastal bike routes for the American Bicentennial in 1976, and unless safer or more scenic routes were found, the Pacific Coast Bicycle Route follows the established route. Oregon has made a commendable commitment to cycling and the Bicentennial Route is well signed. Due to economic and liability considerations, the state of California no longer maintains the Bicentennial Route, and when signs are stolen or otherwise removed, they are not replaced. The state of Washington is still trying to determine if people really ever ride bikes after the age of 16. And, naturally British Columbia

Harris Beach near Brookings

was never part of the Bicentennial Route, even though cycling is well supported in the province.

This book was designed for cyclists on a budget who plan to stay in campgrounds and cook their own food. However, credit card cyclists will find it easy to adapt the information to suit their own needs, as restaurants and motels are plentiful on the coast.

Pedaling Through the Pages

At the start of each chapter is a discussion of the weather, camping, road conditions, and any problems or conditions unique to that state or province. The chapters are then divided into day rides, starting and ending at campgrounds. The day rides average 52 miles but vary from 18.1 miles to 78.2 miles, depending on the availability of campsites and number of points of interest along the ride. If the days suggested are too short, cycle farther. If they are too long, shorten them. Most important, have fun in your own special way.

Each day's ride includes a discussion of highlights, road conditions, possible problems, and suggested alternative camping areas (if any); a map; and a mileage log listing road directions, side trips, and points of interest.

When traveling on a major highway, mileages are accompanied by a milepost number (mp). Mileposts are small signs along the road with

Left, an example of the milepost signs found in Washington and Oregon. Right, a California milepost sign noting highway number at the top, county name (abbreviated) in the center, and number of the miles from the county line below.

a number that indicates the miles from a county or state line. (Mileposts are used by the highway maintenance crews to accurately locate problems. They are not always spaced correctly and some are missing.) For the scope of this book, mileposts serve as another tool to aid in routefinding. They cannot be relied on in place of a cycle computer. In Washington and Oregon, mileposts do not list tenths or hundredths. We have added tenths to the mileage logs to help riders determine whether the point listed is before or after the milepost. In California, mileposts note mileages to the hundredth place. No mileposts were noted in British Columbia; instead we have given distances in both miles and kilometers to help riders correlate information with street signs.

Maps

Additional up-to-date maps and information are always handy. We suggest you obtain maps of all the major cities you will be visiting (if following the entire route, this means Vancouver, Victoria, San Francisco, Los Angeles, and San Diego). Trace the bike route on these maps to get a better idea of where you are going before you head into the city. Automobile clubs such as AAA are good sources for city street maps.

The internet and major chain stores such as REI and Performance can be helpful in locating other maps and publications.

Hiker-Biker Sites

A hiker-biker site is a special area in a campground set aside for people traveling alone or in small groups using nonmotorized forms of transportation. Maximum stay is two nights unless otherwise noted. These camps vary in size and fee charged. Some may lack certain conveniences, such as nearby water or restrooms. Space is available on a first-come basis.

The hiker-biker system of campsites is well organized in Washington, Oregon, and California. In these three states, there is virtually no need to worry about full campgrounds or finding a place to stay on busy summer weekends. The fee is moderate, and space is available for a large number of cyclists. Hiker-biker sites may be found in state parks, some forest service campgrounds, and a few county parks.

Hiker-biker sites are a great help to cyclists. When using these sites PLEASE remember they are a privilege and not a right. The fee is modest, so pay it. The campground officials are not raking in a profit from hiker-biker sites, so help out by keeping the sites clean. Hiker-biker areas may be eliminated if too much upkeep is involved. Most important, let the campground officials know how much you appreciate having sites like these available.

If you are traveling in a group of four or more, a regular campsite will always be less expensive than a hiker-biker site. If you are traveling with a support vehicle, you are required to use a regular campsite. For state park

Heceta Head Lighthouse

reservations in Washington and Oregon, call (800)452-5687. In California, call the individual campgrounds to make a reservation.

In southern California, the hiker-biker sites have become favored hangouts for transients. In response to this serious problem, the official hiker-biker sites have been closed in some campgrounds. No cyclists will be turned away; however, you may be moved from one site to another until the official site for the day is chosen.

Hostels

Twenty-five hostels are located on or near the coast route. Hostels are considerably more expensive than campsites, but a lot cheaper (for one person) than a motel. If you run into a streak of wet weather, you may be glad to spend a night indoors. For current information about hostel locations and charges, write to: American Youth Hostels, P.O. Box 37613, Washington, D.C. 20013-7613.

Getting Ready to Tour

Before starting a long bicycle tour, it is important to get your body and bicycle into the best shape possible. Numerous excellent books thoroughly cover the subject of how to tour, so we will not pursue it here. (See Recommended Reading.) These books are available at bookstores and most bicycle shops. A fairly complete catalog of all books and maps pertaining to bicycle touring is available from Adventure Cycling Association, P.O. Box 8308-AN, Missoula, Montana 59807; (406)721-1776; e-mail: http://www.adv-cycling.org

Riding Safely

The first time you ride your fully loaded touring bike is a shock, even to the most seasoned rider. When loaded with an extra twenty to thirty pounds of gear, a lightweight bike behaves like a lopsided tortoise on level ground, and what it does on the uphills defies description. Of course, on the downhill, it takes off like a locomotive. Start off slowly, and take an hour or so to readjust your balance to the extra weight.

On the road, a cyclist's first line of defense is to be visible to motorists. A bright-colored helmet, brilliantly colored clothing and/or bright fluorescent vests or fanny triangles, and eye-catching touring bags will greatly increase the chances of being seen from a distance, giving motorists a chance to slow down or move to another lane.

Along the Pacific Coast, a cyclist has the same rights and obligations as the driver of a motor vehicle, which means riding single file except to pass, having one hand on the handlebars at all times, obeying stop signs and traffic signals before turning or stopping, and moving as far off the road as possible for rest or repairs.

Large trucks are intimidating to many cyclists, with good reason. An 80,000-pound truck cannot stop quickly or swerve as sharply as a small car if it unexpectedly comes upon a cyclist in the middle of the road. As a large truck passes, its slipstream pulls the relatively lightweight bicycle in toward the center of the road. The following suggestions were made by a logging truck driver: Do not ride in the center of the lane; ride as far to the right as possible, preferably on or to the right of the white line. When traveling in a group, do not string out in a long line down the road; break up into groups of two or three, and keep at least a quarter of a mile between groups to allow trucks time to swing out to pass riders then get back into their lane. When the driver tries to pass a long group, he may be forced to swing in close if he meets oncoming traffic.

Cyclists should be especially cautious in popular tourist areas. Many people are unfamiliar and uncomfortable with the large mobile homes they drive. Unlike commercial truck drivers, they are less likely to move over when passing, and much more likely to panic in an emergency.

The Necessities

Three necessities are universal to all touring cyclists: food, restrooms, and water. Travel tends to degenerate into a constant search for one or all of these basics. Public restrooms and water are easily found at numerous parks along the coast. However, in some areas, you are faced with long stretches without any kind of facility at all. Do not plague the small stores and gas stations along the route by begging for water or attempting to leave some. When necessity forces the use of private facilities, try to incorporate into this stop the acquisition of the first necessity: food. Do your best to leave a good impression or the next group may be faced with a NO CYCLISTS sign.

Leaving Valuables Behind

The Pacific Coast is a popular area for vacations and a prime location for thieves. It takes only a second for a thief to grab a touring bag—or your entire bike—and throw it into the back of a truck. There is no perfect answer to this problem. Some cyclists never leave gear unattended,

Cyclist resting at hiker-biker camp

always leaving one person with the bikes while the others explore. Others leave their bikes, then worry about them the entire time they are away. Groups having the most fun are those who take reasonable precautions, then concentrate on having a good time. If leaving your loaded bike, take valuables—money, credit cards, camera—along. Carry a good bike lock and always use it. In camp, get to know your neighbors and watch out for each other.

Stashing gear when heading off the main route on a side trip is common, though potentially risky. When stashing gear, make sure no one sees the hiding place, then check to make sure the gear is not visible from the road.

The First Principle of Bicycle Touring

The first and foremost principle of bicycle touring is to have fun. If the days suggested in this book are too long, shorten them. If they are too short, ride farther, take more side trips, or go for a hike. Take rest days when you feel like it. Just be sure to have FUN.

A Note About Safety

Safety is an important concern in all outdoor activities. No guidebook can alert you to every hazard or anticipate the limitations of every reader. Therefore, the descriptions of the roads, trails, routes, and other features in this book are not representations that a particular place or excursion will be safe for your party. When you follow any of the routes described in this book, you assume responsibility for your own safety. Under normal conditions, such excursions require the usual attention to traffic, road conditions, weather, terrain, the capabilities of your party, the quality of your gear, and other factors. Keeping informed on current conditions and exercising common sense are the keys to a safe, enjoyable tour.

—The Mountaineers

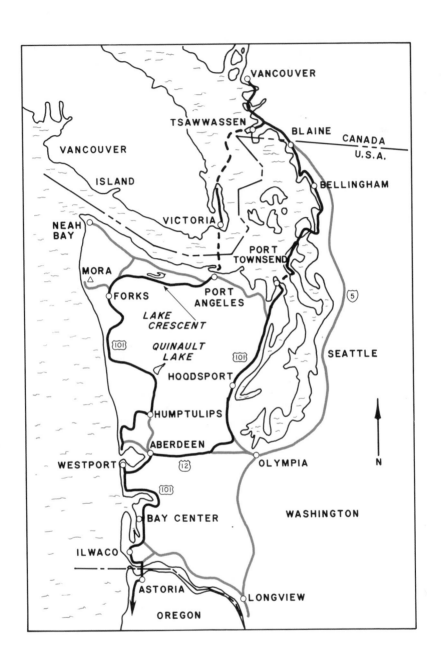

VANCOUVER

TSAWWASSEN

BLAINE   CANADA
U.S.A.

VANCOUVER

ISLAND

BELLINGHAM

NEAH
BAY

VICTORIA

MORA

PORT
TOWNSEND

FORKS

PORT
ANGELES

*LAKE
CRESCENT*

*QUINAULT
LAKE*

101

101

SEATTLE

HOODSPORT

HUMPTULIPS

ABERDEEN

OLYMPIA

N

WESTPORT

12

101

BAY CENTER

WASHINGTON

ILWACO

ASTORIA   LONGVIEW

OREGON

Lake Crescent near Fairholm

Green forests, lush vegetation, lakes, rivers, inland waterways, rugged coastline, and glacier-capped mountains are all part of the very fabric of the northern portion of the Pacific Coast. If you think that all the verdant growth, the abundant water, and large glaciers are indicators of a very cool and very moist climate, you are correct. The rain falls generously and frequently from September through mid-June. Luckily there are, on an average, 60 days a year when the sky is a sparkly blue, and the great snow- and ice-covered peaks of the Coast, Cascade, and Olympic Ranges gleam brightly over the open waterways and forested foothills. Bring your rain gear, but don't forget your sunglasses.

Vancouver, British Columbia is a natural starting point for a tour of the Pacific Coast. (If, for economic reasons, you choose to start your tour in Seattle, see directions at the end of this section.)

Vancouver is the hub of all commerce on the west coast of Canada and has excellent transportation facilities. The city has an intense vibrancy and vitality. Everyone has an outdoor activity: rollerbladers cruise along with cyclists on the crowded bike paths, boats of all sizes and shapes clog the busy city waterways, errant hockey pucks whiz under wheels, packs of joggers are everywhere, and sunbathers crowd the beaches. You will not see this amount of enthusiasm for the outdoors again until you reach Southern California.

Studies in Vancouver have convinced city planners that bike lanes are dangerous. Riders are therefore expected to ride aggressively out in traffic. This is fine for the veteran riders, but very stressful for novices and the timid. A law requires that all cyclists wear helmets. This law is well publicized, but generally ignored. If you are not Canadian, come prepared to obey all laws, and that means bring a helmet!

Despite being the northernmost section of the Pacific Coast ride, temperatures are mild, averaging 64 degrees Fahrenheit (16 degrees Celsius) in the summer, and rainfall is just under 40 inches a year. Riding is best

Rialto Beach

from May through September, when rainfall is at a minimum and daylight hours at a maximum.

United States residents entering Canada should carry some identification establishing their citizenship. Technically, this means a birth certificate, passport, or voter registration; however, a driver's license is usually all that is needed. Carry sufficient money ($200 per person per day) or a major credit card. Other foreign visitors should always carry a valid passport.

Getting to Vancouver is easy. There is a large international airport as well as a train and bus station. If plane tickets are cheaper to Seattle, you can take advantage of the daily Amtrak rail service between downtown Seattle and downtown Vancouver. (Make train reservations ahead of time, as space for bikes is limited.) Of course, riding from Seattle to Vancouver is also an option.

Before arriving in Vancouver, take time to decide whether you prefer to ride the Peninsula Route across Vancouver Island, then around the west side of the Olympics, or the Inland Route along the byways of the Puget Sound. These two routes divide on the south side of the George Massey Tunnel and do not rejoin until you reach the southern half of Washington. The Peninsula Route and the Inland Route are designed for riders with different goals. The Peninsula Route is for those who wish to explore. Riders on the Peninsula Route should not plan a quick dash down the coast. A day should be set aside just for exploring the museums, parks, and scenery of Victoria. In Washington, it is necessary to take side trips to high alpine meadows, explore tide pools and beachcomb the wilderness coast, then follow forest roads inland to appreciate the amazing biodiversity of the rain forests. Weather plays an important role on the Olympic Peninsula and riders should be prepared for heavy fogs and rain (over 140 inches of rain fall each year in the Hoh River valley). US 101 (the only road around the peninsula) is narrow and busy. Grocery stores, restaurants, and motels are few and far between, and showers are nonexistent. National park campgrounds are the most reliable source for campsites. These well-maintained facilities are available on a first-come basis, and cyclists are advised to arrive by midday to secure a site. When the areas are full, you may have to ride long distances to find a campsite or be prepared to free-camp in the forest.

If you are not interested in long side trips or miles of clearcut forest and you prefer your route to be dotted with bakeries and ice cream shops, then the Inland Route is the way to go. Points of interest are easily accessible from the main route. Riding conditions are generally good, and the climate is much drier. In addition to numerous state parks, old forts, and Victorian towns, riders can expect to enjoy beautiful scenery and an occasional classic Northwest view. Moderately rolling terrain and moderately good roads make this route enjoyable for all cyclists.

Riders beginning their tour in Vancouver are faced with several challenges. The nearest campsites are the destination points for the first day's ride out of Vancouver. It is best to make advance reservations, if possible before leaving home. For Birch Bay State Park call (800)452-5687 from 11 months to 2 days in advance (2 months in advance is strongly recommended). For lodging in Vancouver, you may check in at one of many hotels or motels or stay at a hostel.

In Washington, all state parks are supposed to have primitive campsites for cyclists (Birch Bay State Park seems to be an exception). These sites are small, with trail access to the water and restrooms. Cyclists are charged per tent (or tarp), rather than per person. These sites do not require reservations but may fill up during the summer. Most park employees are somewhat sympathetic to the needs of cyclists and will help you find an alternate spot.

Most national park campgrounds are open year-round. Forest service camps are closed mid-September through May. State parks encountered on the Pacific Coast Bicycle Route are open all year.

Due to the moist climate, fenders and rain gear are recommended. Take a tent or heavy-duty tarp and a stove, so you can cook at least one hot meal each day when it's raining. However, it's a documented fact that if you load up on rain gear and forget your sunglasses, you will have excellent weather the entire time you are in the north.

Distances in the trip logs for the British Columbia portion of the ride are given first in miles and then in kilometers. No kilometer posts are noted. Mileposts in Washington decrease from north to south, and only whole numbers are indicated. Tenths have been added to the mileage logs to increase accuracy. For cyclists heading south, if the milepost number reads 25.7 in the mileage log, the point indicated will be passed 0.7 mile before milepost 25 (or 0.3 mile after milepost 26).

If ending your trip at the southern end of Washington, it is best to cross the Columbia River to Astoria, Oregon, then ride Highway 30 inland to Portland. You may box the bikes (if you can find a box) and take a Greyhound bus to Seattle or Portland. A bicycle shop is a possible source of bike boxes for bus travel. See the introduction to the Oregon section of this book for bike routes to the bus and train stations and airport in Portland.

Directions from Seattle-Tacoma (SeaTac) International Airport

Cyclists choosing to start from SeaTac International Airport (located south of Seattle) are faced with a maze of freeways. You may start at the airport or find a bus or taxi to carry your gear to your chosen ferry dock or downtown accommodations. If riding from the airport, avoid the downtown area by heading to the Fauntleroy ferry. Pick up bikes and gear at baggage claim, pack up, then head out along the sidewalk or road, following the flow of the traffic. At the end of the terminal buildings, the road passes a bus loading and parking area. Ride to the end of the bus area to find a city bike route sign that leads you to a sidewalk. Follow the sidewalk 0.1 mile to International Blvd. (Highway 99). Cross the road and head left (north), either on the road with the traffic or on the wide sidewalk. At 0.8 mile, turn left on S. 170th St. and ride under a freeway. Turn right on Air Cargo Road at 1.1 miles and ride north through a complicated intersection. At 2.3 miles, cross S. 154th St. and go straight on 24th Ave. S. Make a left turn on S. 136th St. at 3.5 miles and ride west for 1.8 miles. At 5.3 miles turn right on 4th Ave. S.W. (Note: Do not turn on 4th Ave. S., which is passed right after you cross over Highway 509.) After 1.9 miles, go left on S.W. 108 St. and head west. When S.W. 108 St. ends, jog right on 12th Ave. S.W., then take the first left on S.W. 107 St., which will turn into S.W. 106 St. At 9.8 miles S.W. 106th ends. Go right on Marine View Dr. S.W. for 0.8 mile. At S.W. Wildwood, turn left and descend to reach the small Fauntleroy ferry dock, 11 miles from the airport. Be sure to catch a ferry going all the way across the Puget Sound to Southworth.

Once on the west side of Puget Sound, follow Highway 160 west. After 3.7 miles, pass the turnoff to Manchester State Park. (This small state park, located 2.5 miles off the route, has limited camping. Call ahead to reserve a site before leaving home.) Highway 160 merges with Highway 16. Shortly after, at 11.7 miles from Southworth, head west on Highway 3 for 7.4 miles to Belfair (there is an excellent state park just 3 miles off the route). Continue east on Highway 106 for 19 more miles to join the Inland Route just south of the town of Potlatch. If cycling up to Port Angeles, head north on Highway 3 to the Hood Canal Bridge, then west on Highway 104 to US 101; the shoulder is excellent the entire way.

For cyclists heading to the center of Seattle to catch the train to Vancouver, the ferry to Bremerton or Winslow, or simply to spend some time in the downtown area, continue straight on 24th Ave. S. until it ends, 4.8 miles form the airport. Turn right (east) on S. 116th Way and descend 0.5 mile. Make a left turn onto (unsigned) Pacific Highway S. After 0.7 mile, reach a confusing intersection. Go right and after a few cranks of the pedal, take another right on Airport Way, which loops through a narrow canyon then heads north along Boeing Field. At 6.7 miles from SeaTac, pass an entrance to the Museum of Flight (one of Seattle's finest museums). When riding through Mill Town at 10.1 miles, stay right and cross the overpass above the train tracks. Turn left on Royal Brougham at 12.9 miles and head west. (Expect detours and other confusions here for the next ten years while the new stadiums are being built.) To reach the train station, turn right at 13.5 miles on Occidental, then 0.4 mile beyond, turn right again on S. King St. Go straight to the train depot. For the Bremerton, Bainbridge, or Victoria, B.C., ferries, follow Royal Brougham to its end, then go right on Alaska Way South (also called Highway 519) and follow the signs.

Vancouver to Peninsula and Inland Routes (38.2 Miles/ 61.1 Kilometers to McDonald Provincial Park and 60 Miles/96 Kilometers to Birch Bay State Park)

Vancouver is a beautiful city, and one of the most challenging to bicycle through on the entire Pacific Coast. With no major freeway to take the brunt of the traffic through the downtown area, the narrow city streets are exceptionally busy. Cyclists in Vancouver—and there are a lot of them—ride well out in the center of the lane and seem oblivious to traffic. As a first-time visitor, you probably will not be able to achieve that kind of confidence in the drivers. You will also be faced with routefinding on streets that wind over rolling hills and around bays, requiring careful attention to book and map. If you get off-route, ask a local cyclist.

The route described through Vancouver is neither the shortest nor straightest. In order to avoid the more congested streets, you will ride bicycle paths and roads along the coastline and through miles of parkland. A short section of city streets must be traversed through the heart of Vancouver's fascinating Chinatown. Don't be surprised if you find yourself desiring to linger and explore.

Seaside Bike Path in downtown Vancouver

As Vancouver is the starting point of the Pacific Coast Bicycle Route, most cyclists will arrive by bus, train, or air. As the combined bus and train station is the farthest point north, the trip description and mileage log start from there. For those arriving by air, the trip is 17 miles (27.4 kilometers) shorter. If you arrive late, the youth hostel at Jericho Beach Park (telephone (604)224-3208) is a convenient place to spend the night. The hostel is located on the route between the bus and train station and the airport.

Vancouver lies on the giant delta of the Fraser River. This area is cut by bays and arms of the river strung together by numerous bridges. Most bridges have broad shoulders or sidewalks for cyclists. However, the George Massey Tunnel under the main channel of the Fraser River has neither and is completely closed to bicycles. A free shuttle takes cyclists through the tunnel from June 1 until Canadian Labour Day (usually the first weekend in September). Weekend-only service is offered in May and from Labour Day to Thanksgiving (late October in Canada). When in operation, the shuttle runs once an hour from 8:00 A.M. to 7:00 P.M. (You will need to unload your bike.) City bus #404 is an alternative to the shuttle. The bus can take two unloaded bikes per run. If you cannot arrange your travel schedule to secure yourself a ride through the tunnel, you must ride east for 5 miles on River Road and use the Alex Fraser Bridge on Highway 91, then either follow the River Road back west or (if heading to Blaine) continue east to intercept King George Highway.

Before starting on this ride you must decide which route you intend to use on your trip south through Washington State: Inland Route or Peninsula Route. If you really cannot make up your mind, or wish to sample a bit of Victoria's English elegance before heading to the Inland Route, follow the Peninsula Route to Tsawwassen and spend a night at either McDonald Provincial Park or Royal Oak Park. After touring Victoria you may return to the Inland Route via the very scenic Sidney-to-Anacortes ferry (this service may be cancelled in the future), or take the Coho ferry from Victoria to Port Angeles and head east on US 101 to join the route at Quilcene.

Camping in the greater Vancouver area is very difficult. If arriving after midmorning, it is best to plan a night at a hostel or motel, get your gear organized, and be ready for an early start the next day.

For Peninsula Route riders, the day includes a 90-minute ferry ride from Tsawwassen to Swartz Bay on Vancouver Island. British Columbia ferries are a treat, more like fancy cruise ships than public transportation. The ride is scenic and food and souvenirs are available on board. Once across, you will barely have time to warm up before arriving at McDonald Provincial Park. When this campground is full you must continue south to the commercial Royal Oak Campground.

Cyclists following the Inland Route have a longer ride. They must weave through farm fields and then climb out of the Fraser River delta to cross

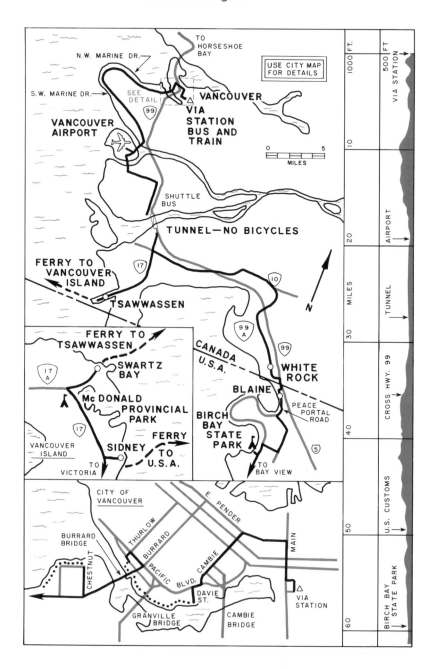

the Canadian–U.S. border at Blaine. The ride continues south on narrow roads for another 10 miles before reaching the day's destination, Birch Bay State Park. This campground often fills, so call ahead a minimum of two days before you start your trip to secure a site, (800)452-5687.

Mileage Log

0.0 mi/0.0 km Via Station and Bus Depot. If arriving by train or bus this is where you will start your trip. Wheel your bikes out to the main entrance, load up, then head north (left) and start your Pacific Coast odyssey with a ride along the tree-lined Station Rd.

0.1 mi/0.1 km Take the first left off Station Rd. onto National Ave. and ride 1 block to Main St. Go right on Main, a busy, 4-lane road, and grit your teeth. Luckily, the road is so busy that traffic moves slowly as you climb through Chinatown.

0.6 mi/0.9 km Go left on E. Pender. (When traffic is too heavy to allow for an easy merge to the left, use the pedestrian crosswalk. This is highly recommended at the start of any tour when you may be searching for your balance.)

1.1 mi/1.7 km After cresting a short, steep hill, make a left turn on Cambie, a one-way street heading southwest. After a short climb, the road descends, passing the B.C. Dome on the left.

1.8 mi/2.8 km Cambie St. ends. Go straight across Pacific Blvd., then head right (west) on a bike route that follows the sidewalk for 1 block to Davie St.

1.9 mi/3.0 km At Davie St. go left and descend. Ride onto the Seaside Bike Path and head right along the shores of False Creek.

2.6 mi/4.2 km The bike path passes under Granville Bridge, then heads through an apartment complex.

2.9 mi/4.6 km Follow the path as it passes under the Burrard Bridge then take the first right on Burrard St. Go up 1 block, then turn left on a busy 2-lane road.

3.2 mi/5.1 km Go right on Thurlow for 1 block to Pacific Blvd. and go right again.

3.3 mi/5.3 km Take a right onto Burrard Bridge and ride the shoulder over the marina-filled inlet.

4.0 mi/6.4 km Turn right on Chestnut and descend into Vanier Park, location of the Vancouver Museum, Maritime Museum, and Planetarium.

4.3 mi/6.9 km Time for a choice. You may stay on the road by turning left on Ogden Ave. or follow the waterfront bike path, which is very scenic, meandering, and frequently crowded.

4.5 mi/7.2 km If following the road, turn left and head up Maple. The bike path flows from Vanier Park to Hadden Park to Kitsilano Park as you head around English Bay.

Vancouver, BC

4.6 mi/7.4 km On the road, turn right on McNicoll Ave., and a few feet beyond go left on Arbutus St.

4.8 mi/7.7 km Road riders should now grit their teeth and head onto the bike path by turning left into the Kitsilano Beach parking area. Follow the bike path for the next 0.4 mile (0.6 kilometer).

5.2 mi/8.3 km Bike path returns to the streets. Continue straight on Pt. Grey Rd. and ride along the coast.

5.6 mi/8.9 km Stay with the signed bike route as the road bends left and heads up to cross Cronwall. After 1 short block, turn right on York for 1 block.

5.7 mi/9.1 km At Stephens Rd., go left.

5.9 mi/9.4 km Go right on W. 3rd Ave. and get set to cruise some narrow streets.

7.1 mi/11.4 km W. 3rd Ave. ends at Wallace St. Here you have a choice. A right turn leads to a bike path that may be ridden to Jericho Beach. When the bike path is busy (that is, every day it is not raining), go left for several cranks of the pedals, then take a right on 4th Ave. Follow 4th Ave. for the next 0.4 mile (0.6 kilometer).

7.5 mi/12.0 km Reach a major intersection. Continue straight on N.W. Marine Dr. and descend steeply back to the shore of English Bay.

7.9 mi/12.6 km Jericho Beach Park and hostel. The hostel is located in a white, three-story building on the right. The park is a popular sailboarding area; rentals are available.

8.3 mi/13.3 km The route now parallels the coast along the Spanish Banks. If you are still on the bike path, this is a good time to return to the road.

9.6 mi/15.3 km Pass a sign noting the official end of the bike route. N.W. Marine Dr. picks up a shoulder here.

10.0 mi/16.0 km Pacific Spirit Regional Park; beach access only. Beyond the park, the road climbs into the University Endowment Lands. Cyclists are supposed to use the narrow sidewalk as they head up the narrow road.

10.9 mi/17.4 km Intersection, go right and continue on N.W. Marine Dr.

11.1 mi/17.7 km Pass the entrance to the Museum of Anthropology on the left. If you have time for just one stop in Vancouver, make this beautiful museum your goal. The museum has one of the world's best collections of Northwest Coast art, such as totem poles, feast dishes, and canoes. Beyond the museum, N.W. Marine Dr. passes the university. The road is narrow and frequently very busy.

12.4 mi/19.8 km N.W. Marine Dr. widens to 4 lanes with a shoulder. Settle in for 6.6 miles of steady riding.

14.0 mi/22.4 km Pass a historical site where an information board explains the exploration of the Fraser River, once mistaken for the Columbia River.

19.0 mi/30.4 km Suddenly you will find yourself on 70th. At the first intersection go right and return to S.W. Marine Dr. and begin your approach to the Arthur Laing Bridge with a downhill glide.

19.2 mi/30.7 km Follow the road as it bends to the left. Just ahead the road divides; you need to merge left 1 lane.

19.4 mi/31.0 km Ride over the North Arm Fraser River on a wide shoulder. Use caution when passing the freeway-style entrances and exits on the south side of the bridge.

20.3 mi/32.5 km Pass the main airport entrance, and follow signs to Richmond and South Terminal. Once off the bridge, continue straight on

Russ Baker Way, which has a comfortable shoulder. Riders starting from the airport will join the route here. (*Airport Route.* From Vancouver International Airport, cycle the shoulderless main road [Grant MacConache Way] out of the terminal area. Go straight, following signs to Vancouver and the Arthur Laing Bridge. Just before riding under the overpass, exit right to Richmond and join the route on Russ Baker Way.)

21.4 mi/34.2 km At Gilbert Rd. go left and cross the Point Dinsmore Bridge. Once over, continue straight, crossing some train tracks before you reach downtown Richmond.

22.3 mi/35.7 km Turn left on Westminster Hwy. and head east on an unpleasantly busy 4-lane road without shoulders.

23.6 mi/37.8 km Start of a wide shoulder.

24.8 mi/39.7 km Richmond Nature Park lies on the left (north) side of the 4-lane highway. The park has running water, toilets, a small nature center, marsh, trails, and viewing platforms for bird-watching.

24.9 mi/39.8 km Go right on No. 5 Rd. and head south. This is a busy 4-laner with no shoulder. The wide sidewalk can serve as an escape route if the road is unpleasant.

27.6 mi/44.1 km Cross Stevenson Hwy. and continue straight. (Note: If planning to take the city bus through the George Massey Tunnel, go left on Stevenson Hwy. 0.3 mile/0.2 kilometer. Go right down the entrance ramp to the freeway, then after a few feet turn left to the bus stop.)

28.1 mi/44.9 km Turn left on Rice Mill Rd.

28.4 mi/45.4 km Go left to a large sign near the old Toll Plaza and check information sign for next shuttle. You will be let off on the south side of the tunnel at the Town and Country Inn on the northeast side of the Highway 99 freeway. When ready, ride out of the parking lot and head west on Highway 17. Use caution as you weave your way across the overpass and pass the freeway entrances. The shoulder is good as you head west.

29.7 mi/47.5 km Intersection with Highway 10 (Ladner Trunk Rd.). At this point the Peninsula and Inland Routes divide.

Peninsula Route

29.7 mi/47.5 km From the intersection of Highway 10 and Highway 17 continue straight, riding the comfortable shoulder to Tsawwassen. This well-designed road crosses the nearly level delta, passing broad farm fields. The only climb is over a railroad overpass. If you need to make a stop to buy food for the night, go left at 56th St. and head into town.

35.5 mi/56.8 km Ride onto a narrow, artificial spit.

37.1 mi/59.3 km Entrance booths. Bicycles are directed to cross traffic at a pedestrian crossing, then proceed to the booth on the far left. Your destination is Swartz Bay. Once off the ferry continue south on Highway 17. Shoulders are good.

38.2 mi/61.1 km Take your time for a cautious left turn off Highway 17 to McDonald Provincial Park: camping, picnicking, water, restrooms, and beach access. (If the park is full continue south 12.7 miles/ 20.4 kilometers to Royal Oak Campground.)

Inland Route

29.7 mi/47.5 km Go left off Highway 17 onto Ladner Trunk Rd. (Highway 10). It is best to use the pedestrian crossing for this turn. This busy road starts off without a shoulder; however, in 0.4 mile (0.7 kilometer) Highway 10 narrows to a 3-laner with shoulder. The road heads across an old river delta and the nearly level land is covered with farms.

34.3 mi/54.9 km Stay with Highway 10 as it bends left and crosses the freeway. The shoulder is narrow for the next 2.2 miles (3.5 kilometers).

37.3 mi/59.7 km Intersection with Highway 91. Go straight on Highway 10, ride across an overpass, then climb a forested hill on a freeway-type road with good shoulder.

38.5 mi/61.6 km At the top of the hill, Highway 10 shrinks back to a busy 2-laner with a very passable shoulder.

41.1 mi/65.7 km Go right and descend to intersect the King George Highway (also referred to as Highway 99A). Head south on a 4-lane road with wide, though frequently rough, shoulders. In less than a mile (1 kilometer) the road crosses the Serpentine River on a very narrow bridge. Wait for a break in the traffic or use the sidewalk.

43.7 mi/69.9 km Use caution as the King George Highway crosses the Highway 99 freeway. The entrances and exits are dangerous. Shortly after the overpass the road crosses the Nicomekl River on a narrow bridge (sidewalk is an option) then heads up a steep hill. The shoulder remains wide but gets rougher as you go.

45.5 mi/72.8 km Enter White Rock. If you have extra Canadian money, this is a good place to pick up a few supplies for the night.

48.9 mi/78.2 km Go straight down the Highway 99 freeway entrance and head south on the broad shoulder toward the border.

49.2 mi/78.7 km Once on the freeway the road enters the border area. Ignore the bike signs and continue straight with the cars, riding past the Peace Arch. This border is set up for motor vehicles and you may have to stand in the fumes for a while.

50.2 mi/80.3 km U.S. Customs; have your identification ready. You are now on Interstate 5. You will see it again at the Mexican border.

51.1 mi/81.7 km Turn off Interstate 5 at Exit 276 and go straight through the small town of Blaine on Peace Portal Rd. Once out of town the

Tsawwassen ferry terminal

road heads around Drayton Harbor. Shoulder will come and go, mostly go.

53.3 mi/85.3 km Following signs to Birch Bay State Park, go right on Bell Rd.

53.5 mi/85.6 km After crossing a narrow bridge the road becomes Blaine Rd.

54.8 mi/87.7 km Blaine Rd. bends sharply to the right. No shoulders, moderate traffic.

58.4 mi/93.4 km At Bay Rd. go right.

59.4 mi/95.0 km Turn right on Jackson Rd. A convenience store and deli is passed just before the park entrance.

60.0 mi/96.0 km Entrance to Birch Bay State Park. This large campground is totally lacking in hiker-biker facilities. Hopefully you followed the advice given earlier and made reservations. Be sure to mention how helpful a cyclist site would be for tourists. Park amenities include beach, hiking trail through a marsh, and showers. Inland Route continues on page 54.

Peninsula Route: McDonald Provincial Park to Victoria (18.1 Miles/29.1 Kilometers)

This is a very short ride, designed to include plenty of time to explore downtown Victoria. The city, often accused of being more English than England, is easily accessible to bicyclists. Points of interest are all located within a few blocks of each other, and there are several scenic rides through beautifully maintained parks. Popular attractions include the Maritime Museum and Provincial Museum (hours can be spent here), Thunderbird Park, the Empress Hotel, Parliament buildings, and Beacon Hill Park, which has beautiful gardens and an excellent view. During the summer tourist season, minstrels stroll along the waterfront, and music is everywhere. Small coffee and tea shops are inviting. Stop at any Information Centre for a city map and advice.

A little farther out of town are the spectacular Butchart Gardens, open year-round. The 35-acre gardens display almost every known variety of flower in such exotic settings as the Sunken Garden, English Rose Garden, Japanese Garden, and Italian Garden.

The Royal Oak Campground is within easy riding distance of the downtown area and Butchart Gardens. This private facility has showers and walk-in tent sites. In downtown Victoria, you may stay at the hostel located on 516 Yates St. Call ahead for reservations, (604)385-4511.

The only way off Vancouver Island is by ferry. Most riders will be heading south to Port Angeles and the Peninsula Route through Washington State. (You may also reach the Inland Route by riding east on US 101 from Port Angeles.) While exploring Victoria, take time to stop at the Coho ferry dock and pick up a current schedule.

Mileage Log

0.0 mi/0.0 km From McDonald Provincial Park, you must recross the busy roadway before heading south on the broad shoulder of Highway 17.

1.1 mi/1.7 km Tourist Information. Stop here to pick up a map of downtown Victoria and the entire Saanich Peninsula.

2.3 mi/3.7 km Sidney exit. A left turn leads to ferry service through the San Juan Islands to Anacortes and the Inland Route.

3.3 mi/5.3 km Turnoff to Mill Bay ferry. This ferry connects Mill Bay with Brentwood (on the Saanich Peninsula).

5.2 mi/8.3 km Butchart Gardens exit; admission charged. Follow the road signs. The gardens may also be reached from Royal Oak Campground, a few miles ahead.

9.7 mi/15.6 km Elk/Beaver Lake Regional Park, a large day-use area with picnicking, swimming, restrooms, and water.

10.3 mi/16.5 km Beaver Lake Park and Royal Oak exit. Use this exit if you are planning to camp. Parallel Highway 17 for 0.3 mile (0.5 kilometer) to Royal Oak Campground and hot showers. If planning to explore Victoria, set up camp, drop off your gear, but be sure to bring your lock and wallet so that you can tie up your mount when exploring museums or splurging on high tea.

11.7 mi/18.8 km Royal Oak Dr.; second and last access to Royal Oak Campground. From this point on, the traffic volume increases and

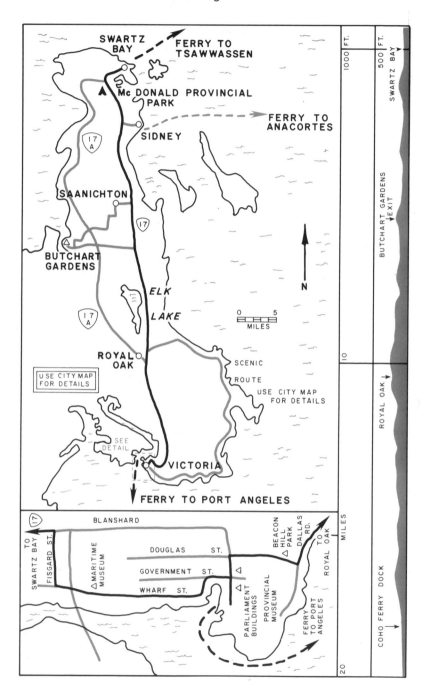

The Parliament building in Victoria

the shoulder dwindles. To reach the center of town, follow Highway 17 until it becomes Blanshard St., then turn right on Fisgard St.

17.1 mi/27.5 km Turn right on Fisgard St. and cycle through Victoria's Chinatown.

17.3 mi/27.8 km Fisgard St. ends; go left on Store St. and follow it until Wharf St. joins on the right. The Victoria Hostel is on the corner of Wharf and Yates Sts.

17.5 mi/28.1 km Continue straight on Wharf St., paralleling the Inner Harbor. At the end of the next block is Bastion Square, location of the Maritime Museum of British Columbia.

17.9 mi/28.8 km Wharf St. ends; go right on Government St.

18.0 mi/28.9 km Intersection of Government St. and Belleville St. The Provincial Museum is the large building across Belleville St. on the

Totem Pole Park in downtown Victoria

---

left; the Parliament buildings are on the right. To reach the Coho
ferry to Port Angeles, go right on Belleville St. for 1 block.

18.1 mi/29.1 km Coho ferry terminal. The dock is nearly overshadowed
by its large neighbor, the twice-daily ferry to Seattle.

Victoria Scenic Tour

After visiting the center of town, take a scenic ride along the shores of
the Strait of Juan de Fuca. Starting at the Parliament buildings, head east
on Belleville St. for 1 block to Douglas St. and Trans-Canada Highway 1.
Go right (south) and parallel the park until you near the waterfront. Turn
left (east) on Dallas Rd. and cycle through Beacon Hill Park to a spectacular viewpoint over the Strait of Juan de Fuca to the ice-clad Olympic
Mountains. Lock up the bikes and walk the park trails through immacu-
late gardens to the world's largest totem pole.

For cyclists with energy for a few extra hills and a good city map in hand, try this alternate route from Beacon Hill Park back to Royal Oak Campground. Follow Dallas Rd. east along the shores of the strait for 3.4 miles (5.5 kilometers) past scenic Clover Point and Gonzales Bay to reach Crescent Street. Turn right, following the SCENIC MARINE DRIVE signs back to Royal Oak Dr. Head west to Highway 17 and Royal Oak Campground.

Peninsula Route: Port Angeles to Fairholm Campground (28.8 Miles)

The Coho ferry from Victoria takes 90 minutes to cross the Strait of Juan de Fuca and dock in Port Angeles, the starting point of the Washington State portion of the Peninsula Route. During the summer months, the first ferry arrives midmorning, so this day's ride is intentionally short.

In good weather, adventure-minded riders may prefer to linger in Port Angeles and spend the afternoon riding to Hurricane Ridge, one of the state's scenic highlights. The ridge is part of Olympic National Park (a designated World Heritage Site) and the only place a cyclist may sample the alpine aspect of this diverse area. The ride up Hurricane Ridge is long and difficult. Only strong cyclists will find pleasure in the climb which gains 5,300 feet in just 18 miles. However, everyone who reaches the top will enjoy the view and the screaming descent. If the ride is more than you wish to tackle, consider an alternative, shorter, and easier side trip to the Olympic National Park Visitor Center.

The Elwha River valley, located 9.8 miles west of Port Angeles, offers a second opportunity to leave the main route and explore more of the national park. This lowland valley has campgrounds, numerous trails (including one to Hurricane Ridge), a large lake, and, if you go far enough, a hot springs.

Heading south of the Elwha River valley, you will encounter a notorious section of US 101 in the Lake Crescent area. The road around this beautiful lake has minimal shoulder, with blind corners and fast-moving auto and truck traffic. If ever there was a place to install flashing lights to let motorists know when cyclists are on the road, this is it. The state has placed signs at each end of the lake, recommending riders take one of the rare public buses around the lake.

The Storm King area, located about halfway around Lake Crescent, is the one easily accessible national park feature along this portion of the route. Along with the obvious attractions of restrooms, picnic tables, and running water, Storm King has several short trails to explore. The 2-mile round-trip walk to Marymere Falls is one of the not-to-be-missed highlights of the park and the nearby nature trail is an excellent

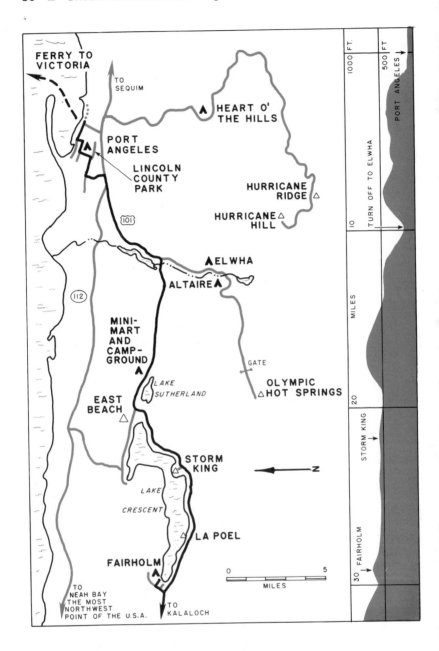

introduction to the lowland forest community. Maps can be picked up at the ranger station, open summer only.

The day's ride ends at Fairholm Campground, a relatively small, 87-site facility that fills up almost every night during the summer and always on weekends. Cyclists are encouraged to arrive as early as possible to secure a site.

Mileage Log

0.0 Trip starts from the Victoria (Coho) ferry dock in Port Angeles. Everyone (that includes cyclists planning to ride up to Hurricane Ridge) should turn right on Railroad St. and follow it along the waterfront. (As Port Angeles has the last large grocery stores before Fairholm, anyone who needs to stock up on food should take a side trip into town. Follow the signs for US 101 south to the supermarkets at the upper end of town.) ***Side Trip***. For a quick look at the Port Angeles area, go left after you exit the ferry and ride a short 0.1 mile east along the waterfront. When the road turns, continue straight ahead to a parking area. Lock up your bikes and wander the dock area. The Arthur D. Fiero Marine Science Laboratory is an excellent facility designed for children (perfect for most touring cyclists) with a large touch tank. When in port, you may take a tour of a Coast Guard

---

Downtown Port Angeles.

vessel (afternoons only) or climb the viewing tower for a look across the Strait.

0.1 Railroad St. bends left and the name changes to N. Oak.

0.2 The road divides; stay to the right and continue along the waterfront on Front St.

0.4 Bear right on Marine Dr. (also called W. 1st St.).

0.6 Intersection; continue straight (trucks go left).

0.7 Turn left on Tumwater St. (this is the first left after the truck route), and gear down for a 0.3-mile climb.

1.5 Tumwater St. turns into W. 5th St.

2.3 Turn left on I St. and head inland.

2.6 I St. ends; go right on W. 16th St., which takes you past the fairgrounds and magically turns into 18th St.

2.9 Take the first left on L St.

3.2 Go right on W. Lauridsen Blvd. If planning to make the side trip to Hurricane Ridge or if you just need a convenient place to spend the night, go left 0.2 mile to Lincoln County Park Campground: hiker-biker area, water, restrooms, and small store across the road (open for camping summer only).

3.3 When the road divides, stay to the right on Edgewood Dr. This road twists and turns through a rural, residential area for 2.7 miles.

6.3 **(mp 242.9)** Go right on US 101, which is blessed with a comfortable shoulder except at bridges.

6.6 **(mp 242.4)** Highway 112 branches off to the right; watch for turning traffic.

7.9 **(mp 241.1)** Pass a viewpoint overlooking the Elwha River valley. US 101 now descends.

9.8 **(mp 239.5)** Turn off to Elwha River valley and campgrounds on the left (east), and combination gas station–store on the right (west). *Side Trip*. Cycle up the Elwha River valley to Olympic National Park on a narrow road that passes through cool, shady groves of moss-covered maples. The first campground, located 3 miles off US 101, has running water and walk-in campsites. Shortly beyond is a ranger station, then a second campground. The road is gated 4 miles before its end at Olympic Hot Springs. Bicycles may continue on up the rough road to a primitive camp area near the hot springs; pick up a backcountry permit at the ranger station if interested.

16.7 **(mp 233.0)** Gas station with a mini-mart and an adjoining private campground. Tents are welcome. As you climb, Lake Sutherland is visible through the trees to the left.

17.8 **(mp 231.9)** Pass turnoff to East Beach, Piedmont, and Spruce Railroad Trail.

18.4 **(mp 231.3)** Shoulder narrows as US 101 leaves Olympic National Forest and enters Olympic National Park. The road descends steeply

Winding around Lake Crescent on Highway 101

toward Lake Crescent. Tighten your grip—the next 10 miles are nerve-racking and the road is often rough.

18.5 (mp 231.2) Sign warning cyclists about hazards ahead and a note about the bus service. (Where is the sign for *motorists* to use caution over the next 10 miles?) Viewpoints allow you to pull off and let traffic by, if needed. Watch for grooved pavement on the corners.

21.7 (mp 227.9) Barnes Point–Storm King turnoff. ***Side Trip***. Go right 0.1 mile to Storm King Ranger Station: restrooms, water, picnic tables. This busy area is the starting point for several short trails. Highly recommended is the easy 2-mile round-trip hike through stately old trees to beautiful Marymere Falls. The trail starts in front of the ranger station. The Moments in Time Nature Trail leads to a view of the lake and is an easy 1-mile round trip. Find the trailhead by walking through the picnic area, then across the boat launch road.

26.0 (mp 223.7) La Poel Picnic Area: running water, vault toilets, and limited lake access.

28.5 (mp 221.0) Fairholm Grocery: limited groceries, deli, and boat rentals. Shoulder widens as US 101 begins to climb away from the lake.

28.7 (mp 220.8) Fairholm Campground; go right (west) on Camp David Jr. Rd. Ride past the lake access and boat launch.

28.8 Turn right and descend into the campground. The walk-in sites along the lake shore are scenic and often vacant after the rest of the sites are full. The campground has restrooms, running water, and a boring nature trail. Small boats may be rented from the Fairholm Grocery. There is a designated swimming area at the boat launch. (When

Hurricane Ridge in Olympic National Park

this campground is full, you may continue on US 101 to Klahowya, Walhgren, or Tumbling Rapids Forest Service Campgrounds. Or, cook your dinnner at Fairholm, then ride on and find a free campsite on national forest land.)

Hurricane Ridge Side Trip

Pack plenty of warm clothes, shoes for walking, lots of food, a couple quarts of water, and a set of bike lights for the tunnel. Food service is available during the middle of the day.

0.0 Once you have unloaded your bike at the Lincoln County Park campground, retrace your route back to the waterfront. Carry plenty of warm clothing and food for the trip.

2.5 Stay on Marine Dr., which becomes W. 1st St. Once across Lincoln St., W. 1st St. joins US 101; continue east for 0.8 mile.

3.6 Turn right (south) on Race St., following signs to Hurricane Ridge. From this point, it's all uphill to the ridge. Buy groceries before leaving town.

4.6 Olympic National Park headquarters: park and weather information, restrooms, and water.

10.6 Park entrance. If you did not bring your own lights, you will be loaned one for the ride through the tunnel. Just beyond the entrance station is Heart o' the Hills Campground, elevation 1,957 feet. The road above Heart o' the Hills is steep and narrow, with numerous turnouts, all on the left side.

21.5 Hurricane Ridge Visitor Center: restrooms, water, and information. The views from the top are unforgettable, extending over the Strait of Juan de Fuca, Vancouver Island, the Cascades, and Mount Olympus. The roadside meadows burst with colorful wildflowers mid-July through mid-August. For your own safety, make the descent to the campground before dark. If the weather turns bad, head back immediately.

Peninsula Route: Fairholm Campground to Kalaloch Campground (61.2 Miles)

From the clear blue waters of Lake Crescent, the Peninsula Route heads south to the popular beaches of the Kalaloch unit of Olympic National Park. The route follows US 101, heading south through stump-covered clearcut forests and stump-covered pastures to the town of Forks. Beyond town the terrain becomes increasingly hilly and the countryside increasingly forested as the road winds its way out to the coast. Shoulders are mostly good in this section, disappearing at bridges. With only an occasional view of the mountains over massive clearcuts to distract you, the miles fly by.

The Kalaloch area beaches are easily accessed from the main highway. Ruby Beach has a couple of large sea stacks and most resembles the wilderness beaches of the northern sections of the park. Fourth Beach has excellent tide pools on the near-shore rocks and is the scene of daily naturalist talks. Kalaloch and South Beaches are great for barefoot strolls through the sand.

The day ends at Kalaloch Campground. The 177 campsites usually fill by noon. Luckily, there is an overflow campground at South Beach, just 3 miles to the south. Because there is no water or garbage pickup service at South Beach, no fee is charged. You may find it convenient to set up camp at South Beach, then ride back to the Kalaloch Campground and cook your dinner at a picnic area.

Kalaloch is a full-service area with a small grocery store, accommodations (usually booked months in advance), a coffee shop, and a restaurant.

This day's ride will take you by three major national park access points. To visit any of these areas requires a full-day excursion off the main route. If you have the time or inclination to explore one or more of these areas, your efforts will be rewarded with incredible scenery. Just 1.5 miles south of Fairholm Campground is the Sol Duc Hot Springs turnoff. The hot springs are located in a beautiful rain forest and reached by a 12-mile ride along the edge of the Sol Duc River. In the spring and early fall, when

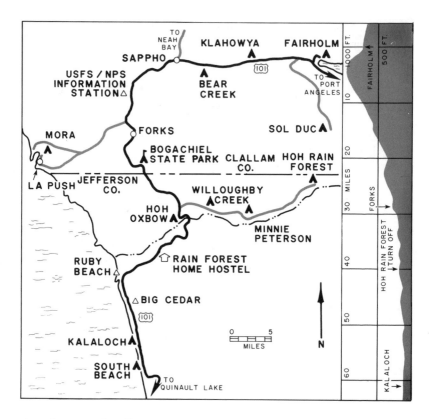

the salmon are heading upstream to spawn, their incredible journey can be watched from the overlooks along the river. Sol Duc Hot Springs have been commercially developed with a beautifully maintained swim area and hot pools for soaking. A substantial admission fee is charged. You may stay at the Sol Duc campground (which usually fills by noon) or rent a cabin (expensive) and eat at the restaurant. Other than the hot springs, the area's chief attraction is a beautiful falls that is reached by a 0.9-mile walk through the rain forest.

The second national park access passed on the day's ride is the Mora area, where you will find miles of wilderness beaches to explore. Several of the beaches are reached by well-maintained forest trails; however, for the cyclist, Rialto Beach offers the easiest access. Here you may hike past giant drift logs to towering sea stacks, and walk through the Hole-in-the-Wall. The tide pools are teeming with life and bald eagles are often spotted. Nearby Mora Campground is an excellent place to spend the night (usually fills by early afternoon). WARNING: When hiking on wilderness beaches, pay attention to the tides.

The third park access is the Hoh River valley, which lies at the western

Third Beach, Olympic National Park

edge of the Olympic Mountains and receives more rainfall than any other spot in the continental United States. Although a rain forest might seem to have little to attract cyclists, you should not bypass the Hoh. The rain forest is a world colored in green, from the lush vegetation of the forest floor to the giant trees covered with lacy moss. Vegetation grows at fantastic rates and trees grow to record heights. Elk, deer, and a multitude of small forest animals thrive in this environment. The large national park campground is an ideal location to spend the night (fills by noon) and a great base for exploring the nearby nature trails. The small, cozy Information Center is an excellent place to browse for an hour on a wet day.

Mileage Log

0.0 From Fairholm campground, ride back to US 101.

0.1 (mp 220.8) Go right (south) and start the climb away from Lake Crescent on US 101. The road has 3 lanes and a decent shoulder for grinding up the hill.

1.6 (mp 219.3) Crest of the hill and start of an easy riding section over gently rolling terrain. *Side Trip* to Sol Duc Hot Springs begins on the left. The scenic road up the Sol Duc River valley climbs gradually for 12 miles to the hot springs resort and campground, then continues on another 0.9 mile to end at the Sol Duc Falls Trailhead.

8.9 (mp 213.9) Klahowya Campground: restrooms, running water, and nature trail.

14.7 (mp 205.8) Bear Creek Campground (on the left side of US 101): restrooms, running water, and three short walks along the Sol Duc River.

16.2 (mp 204.3) Enter Sappho: a small cafe and a good-sized bar.

16.6 (mp 203.8) Pass turnoff to Neah Bay.

16.9 (mp 203.5) Tumbling Rapids Rest Area: restrooms but no running water; often closed.

20.1 (mp 200.4) Lake Pleasant Grocery.

24.2 (mp 196.2) Olympic National Park and National Forest Information Station.

27.2 (mp 193.2) *Side Trip* to Mora Campground and Rialto Beach. If planning to explore the wilderness beaches of Olympic National Park, go right (west) toward La Push. Follow this narrow road 7.9 miles to a junction with a small, but very complete, grocery store on the corner. Go right for a final 3.8 miles to Mora Campground: restrooms and running water. Once you have set up camp, grab your best bike lock and ride on the final 2 miles to the end of the road at Rialto Beach. Walk the beach north as far as time and tides will allow.

28.3 (mp 192.1) Enter Forks, a logging town with full tourist facilities as well as two large supermarkets and a private campground with hot showers. At the south end of town there is an Information Center and the Timber Museum.

33.0 (mp 186) Bogachiel State Park: a campground with running water, restrooms, covered cooking areas, and two hiker-biker (primitive) sites set in a grove of stately trees. This is a popular fishing area.

34.5 (mp 184.5) Leave Clallam County and enter Jefferson County.

40.4 (mp 178.9) *Side Trip* to the Hoh Rain Forest. Turn left (east) off US 101 on Hoh River Rd., heading inland to the rain forest. The road is narrow and winding. Use the turnouts to let traffic pass or to stop for a breather. The road passes through ugly clearcuts, then peaceful forest. Wear bright, visible clothing to help motorists see you. Terrain is rolling and some of the short hills are steep.

40.5 (mp 178.8) A forest display explaining the topography of a clearcut, located on the left side of the road.

41.5 (mp 177.7) Turnoff to Cottonwood Recreation Area, a private campground.

41.8 (mp 177.4) Hoh-Oxbow Campground, a private facility on the right.

42.7 (mp 176.0) Turnoff to Hoh-Clearwood State Forest (campgrounds are miles away from US 101).

43.2 (mp 175.5) Small store and RV park with cabins.

49.3 (mp 169.3) Rain Forest Home Hostel; open all year. Call ahead for reservations, (360)374-2270.

51.0 (mp 167.6) Hoh Tribal Center turnoff.

51.8 (mp 166.8) Enter Olympic National Park. The road runs through heavy forest with occasional views over the ocean.

53.9 (mp 164.7) Ruby Beach; views over the rugged Pacific Coast, beach access, and vault toilets.

55.2 (mp 163.4) Destruction Island viewpoint. A small turnout with information board relating the not-so-happy history of the island.

56.0 (mp 162.6) Beach 6: vault toilet, whale watching area, and beach trail.

56.4 (mp 162.2) Big Cedar, a very old and abused tree located ¼ mile off US 101 on an easy-to-ride dirt road.

58.3 (mp 160.3) Beach 4: parking lot, restrooms, and path to the beach. This is an excellent place to stop and explore tide pools. Park naturalists are often here at low tide to explain the complexities of inter-tidal life.

59.1 (mp 159.5) Beach 3: another beach access.

61.2 (mp 157.8) Kalaloch Campground: restrooms, running water, nature trail, and beach access. A small grocery store can be reached by a ½-mile trail from the campground.

Peninsula Route: Kalaloch Campground to July Creek Campground (33.6 Miles)

This is a short ride, designed with plenty of time for exploring the temperate rain forest environment. If you rode right past the roads to the Elwha, Sol Duc, and Hoh, do not miss this opportunity to regenerate your mental and physical energies with a walk through the fertile forests surrounding Quinault Lake. The greens are intensely pervasive. Noise is muted by the vegetation. A feeling of growth and vitality permeates the air. It's a wonderfully healthy break from the dirt and grime of the road.

After Kalaloch US 101 turns southeast, leaving the coast and heading inland through miles of forest and logging clearings. Without the distraction of views or points of interest, this is a good section to just cover some miles. Shoulders are just barely adequate and the terrain is gently rolling.

The day's ride ends back in Olympic National Park at a campground at the edge of Quinault Lake. This is rain forest area with lush, green forests, fern-filled canyons and moss-covered trees. At the end of the mileage log is a tour guide to the Quinault area.

Mileage Log

0.0 (mp 157.8) Leaving Kalaloch Campground, head south along the coast on US 101. The road has a good shoulder.

0.5 (mp 157.4) Kalaloch Resort: small store, cabins, coffee shop, and beach access.

0.7 (mp 157.2) Olympic National Park Ranger Station: information.

1.6 (mp 156.1) Beach 2: parking area with a path to a sandy beach.

2.5 (mp 155.2) Beach 1: beach access and restrooms.

3.5 (mp 154.3) South Beach campground and picnic area. The primitive campground is an overflow area for Kalaloch Campground, open midsummer only. Beyond the campground, US 101 leaves the national park and turns inland to bypass a section of the coast owned by the Quinault Indians. The ocean is not seen again until Copalis Beach, 61.4 miles south. Terrain is mostly level. Expect some truck traffic.

6.1 (mp 151.8) Queets. A very small grocery store is located on the left, 0.5 mile off US 101.

6.5 (mp 151.4) Leave Jefferson County and enter Grays Harbor County. The terrain remains almost level as the route makes its way inland through acres of clearcuts and stumps with occasional views of the Olympic Mountains.

10.0 (mp 148.0) Leave Grays Harbor County and reenter Jefferson County.

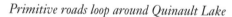

Primitive roads loop around Quinault Lake

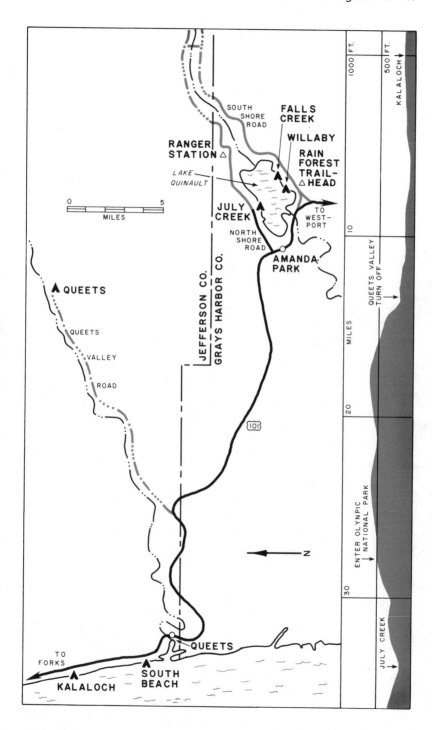

13.6 (mp 144.4) Queets Valley turnoff. This very primitive access to Olympic National Park is reached by a 14-mile gravel road. The road end campground is without potable water and the main trail up the valley to a beautiful grove of trees begins with a difficult ford of the Queets River.

13.8 (mp 144.2) Leave Jefferson County and reenter Grays Harbor County. The shoulder width varies here from 0.5- to 1.5-feet wide. For scenery you have a vast array of clearcuts in different stages of regrowth and a few decrepit lumber and shake mills.

27.8 (mp 130.2) Enter Olympic National Forest.

29.2 (mp 128.8) Pass a small gas station–store on the left.

29.9 (mp 127.9) Turn left (east) off US 101 on North Shore Rd. A small grocery is located here. (If this store is closed, another is located 1.7 miles south.) Follow the narrow and shoulderless road into Olympic National Park.

33.6 July Creek Campground, a walk-in-only area with restrooms and running water located on the shores of Quinault Lake.

Elk grazing in meadows near Quinault Lake

Exploring Quinault Lake—North Side

0.0 Starting from July Creek Campground, go right and continue east, along North Shore Road. The road is narrow, winding, and heavily shaded from both the sun and the rain.

6.5 Quinault River Ranger Station. This is one of the best places to see the rain forest. The ranger station has a small visitor center with displays of the rain forest environment (open summer only). A self-guiding nature trail makes a ½-mile loop through a glade of stately old maples, fancifully draped in long streamers of moss. Chances of seeing deer are very good. You may even see an elk. Consider walking the loop at least twice.

Although the scenery is good for the remainder of the distance around the lake, pavement ends in another 2.4 miles. If you would like to sample more of the rain forest scene, now is a good time to turn around and ride the pavement to South Shore Road. (Note: If your bike is equipped for rough roads, the entire lake loop is just 27 miles long.)

Exploring Quinault Lake—South Side

0.0 From July Creek Campground, head left, back to US 101.

3.7 Go left on US 101 and descend along the west side of the lake.

5.4 Ride through Amanda Park, passing a small grocery store.

5.7 Go left on South Shore Rd.

6.9 Junction; stay left.

7.3 Go right into a large parking lot with running water, restrooms, and picnic tables. This is the Quinault Rain Forest Trailhead. You may choose trail combinations that vary in length from a ½-mile nature loop through the big trees to a 10-mile ramble past waterfalls and fern grottos. Be sure to lock up the bikes before heading out.

If you wish to ride farther, 0.3 mile east is the little community of Quinault, which has a small grocery store, a large lodge, and Forest Service Information Center.

Peninsula Route: July Creek Campground to Twin Harbors State Park (55.6 Miles)

This ride depends on a small passenger ferry across the narrow mouth of Grays Harbor Bay between Ocean Shores and Westport. Unfortunately, the boat is seasonal, running a regular schedule from the fourth week of June through Labor Day, only. It departs once every 90 minutes between 11:00 A.M. and 6:00 P.M. The ferry runs on weekends only from the fourth week of May to the fourth week of June, and from Labor Day through the third week in September. If you have questions, call ahead to the Silver King Motel in Ocean Shores, (360)289-3386.

When the passenger ferry is not running, you must follow US 101 through the twin cities of Hoquiam and Aberdeen, then head west on Highway 105, winding around Grays Harbor Bay to Twin Harbors State Park. The off-season route is 10 miles longer than the summer route, uses congested roads, and is monotonous.

No matter which route you follow, the day starts with a good warm-up on US 101. The highway passes through alternating clearcuts and small bands of second-growth timber. Expect considerable truck traffic for these first 22.6 miles.

At Humptulips, the summer route leaves US 101 and heads west to

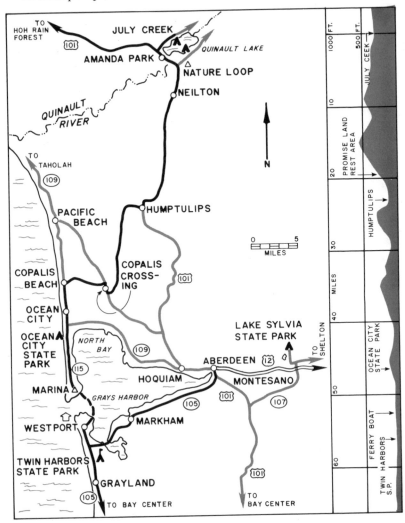

Westport marina

reach the salt-tanged air of the Pacific Ocean at Copalis Beach. Grocery stores, motels, RV campgrounds, restaurants, beach cabins, and tourist shops abound. Some of these long, sandy beaches are open to motor vehicles. Clam digging, kite flying, and sunbathing are popular activities.

Once the route reaches the ocean, it turns south, paralleling the coast. The terrain is level, the roads often shoulderless. After riding through several small towns, reach the tip of a sandy peninsula where the small passenger ferry to Westport is located. The ride continues south from Westport for another 3 miles to Twin Harbors State Park. For Peninsula Route riders, hot showers are the most notable feature of this destination (the first showers encountered in Washington—enjoy!). Twin Harbors State Park is the junction of the Peninsula and Inland Routes. The route continues south on page 72.

Mileage Log

0.0 From July Creek Campground, head back to US 101 on North Shore Rd. and bid your final adieus to Olympic National Park.

3.7 (mp 128.4) North Shore Rd. ends. Head left and continue your journey south on US 101. The first hills encountered are steep, shoulders adequate.

5.4 (mp 126.9) Amanda Park: grocery store.

5.7 (mp 126.6) Pass South Shore Rd. and access to the Quinault Rain Forest nature loop trails.

6.7 (mp 125.1) Pass second turnoff to Quinault. As you continue up, the road enters the Quinault Natural Area, a deeply shadowed virgin forest.

8.8 (mp 123) Neilton: small grocery store.

14.1 (mp 118.1) Leave Olympic National Forest.

19.8 (mp 112.3) Promise Land Rest Area. A large gazebo at the edge of a salmon spawning pond lets you hide from the rain or dodge the sun.

22.6 (mp 109.5) Humptulips: small grocery store.

22.7 (mp 109.4) Summer Route heads right, following signs to OCEAN BEACHES. Be sure your food supplies are in good order; no towns for 12.6 miles. (See end of this log for off-season route description.)

23.2 Riverview Campground, a private facility with campsites and rental cabins. Beyond the campground, the road is narrow without shoulder.

24.2 After passing a large fish hatchery, the road climbs steeply.

24.8 Top of the hill; check out the view.

34.4 Enter Copalis Crossing: cafe.

34.6 Go right (north) on Copalis Beach Rd., following sign to BEACHES.

35.2 Turn left (west) toward BEACHES, passing a small mini-market on the right.

40.0 (mp 21.3) Intersection. Go straight on Highway 119 into Copalis Beach: grocery store, cafe, motels, and beach access.

Historic building in Hoquiam

40.4 (mp 20.9) Pass the first of many beach access roads. The beach, located 0.4 mile west, may be used as a highway for several miles south to Ocean City. Highway 119 is narrow and congested.

41.0 (mp 20.3) Pass a privately operated campground with beach cabins.

42.9 (mp 18.4) Ocean City: motels, grocery stores, and restaurants.

43.4 (mp 18.0) Beach access.

45.4 (mp 16.0 and mp 0.0) Intersection. Go right on Highway 115 and head to Ocean Shores. The wide shoulder offers a chance to relax.

46.3 (mp 0.9) Ocean City State Park: hiker-biker site, showers, beach access.

47.4 (mp 2) Highway 115 ends. Go left, following signs to PED FERRY. Enter Ocean Shores via a divided road. This small town has grocery stores and numerous tourist amenities. A small but complete bike shop, OLYMPIC OUTDOOR, offers parts and service. (This is the first bicycle shop south of Port Angeles and the last before Oregon.)

47.8 Intersection; continue straight ahead. The road turns into a 3-laner. The road name will soon change to Pt. Brown Ave.

51.9 Intersection; go right.

52.1 Stop at the Silver King Motel to buy tickets for the 30-minute ferry ride to Westport, then go left into the Marina. The ferry docks at Westport, located on a narrow peninsula, with the Pacific Ocean to the west and Grays Harbor Bay to the east. Near the tip of the peninsula is Westhaven State Park, a day-use area and popular surfing beach. The town is a resort for sport fishermen, with numerous hotels, motels, restaurants, and a grocery store. Seafood is readily available. Westport Dorm Hostel (open March 1 to September 30) overlooks the marina at Float 17. Call ahead for information, (360)268-0949.

52.3 Once off the ferry, go left for 2 blocks, then turn right.

52.5 Take a left on Harbor Blvd. and ride south passing a large grocery store.

55.5 Turn right on Highway 105.

55.6 Twin Harbors State Park: hiker-biker (primitive) area, hot showers, beach access, kitchen shelter, clam cleaning shed, hiking trails to the beach, and dune trail.

Off-Season Route

Continue south from Humptulips on US 101 for 20 miles to Hoquiam. Follow US 101 south through the congested downtown area. Shoulders disappear; however, traffic moves slowly through town. When crossing the Hoquiam River, cyclists may use the sidewalk on the left side of the extremely narrow, steel-grate bridge.

Hoquiam flows into Aberdeen, with more supermarkets and tourist facilities. Continue to follow US 101 as it makes a sharp bend to the right (south) and crosses the Chehalis River on a wide bridge. On the south side of the bridge, leave US 101 at a traffic signal and go straight on

Highway 105. (Two large supermarkets are located on the left side of the highway at this intersection.) Highway 105 (a Washington State Scenic and Recreational Highway) heads west for the next 18.2 miles along the tide flats of Grays Harbor. The highway is narrow, and shoulders vary from good to none.

Enter Westport 42.6 miles from Humptulips. The road skirts the edge of town. Grocery stores, restaurants, and ferry to Ocean Shores are located 2 miles north. Turn left to Twin Harbors State Park.

Inland Route: Birch Bay State Park to Bay View State Park (53.8 Miles)

Beyond a doubt, the ride south from Birch Bay to Bay View State Park is the most scenic of the Inland Route. This is a somewhat circuitous ride that follows narrow country roads along Lummi and Bellingham Bays. These bays are quiet areas with gigantic views that soar from the island-dotted southern reaches of the Strait of Georgia to the glaciated summit of a smoldering volcano.

The nearly level terrain makes for easy going on the first portion of the day's ride, leaving plenty of time to enjoy the monumental views. After wandering along the peninsulas and inlets, the route heads through

Country road north of Bellingham

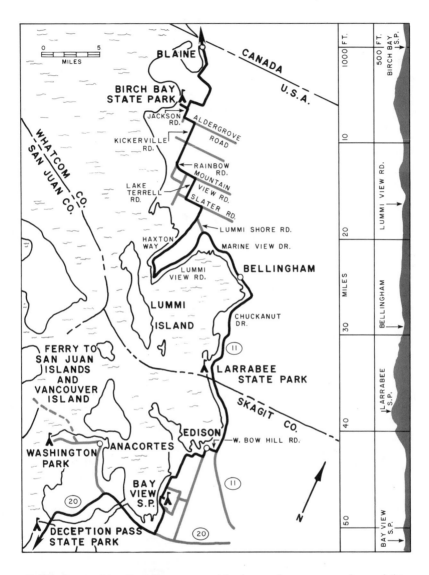

Bellingham, a friendly college town with plenty of museums and art exhibits as well as an invigorating enthusiasm for cycling and enjoying life.

Beyond town, the terrain becomes rugged and the road narrows, becoming a sculpted ribbon snaking along the cliffy flanks of Chuckanut Mountain, with more views of island-dotted bays and rocky inlets. Then after 9 challenging miles of riding, the terrain levels once again to cross a massive delta created by the Skagit River. The route weaves around the farm fields and estuaries to end at Bay View State Park.

The park has a welcoming, open feel. When the weather is good, walk the trail to the grassy banks of the beach and enjoy a restful hour of reading, people watching, and sunset gazing. For the eternally energetic, the park is a great base for exploring the nearby Padilla Bay National Estuarine Sanctuary. Just 0.5 mile north of the park is the Breazeale Interpretive Center which has well-designed displays explaining this rich and varied habitat. Just 0.8 mile south of the state park is the Padilla Bay Shore Trail, an old railroad grade converted into a walking and biking route along the water's edge. Look for cormorants, herons, ducks, and bald eagles.

The day's ride is fairly easy and the miles should speed by. However, if the weather is poor and, instead of view gazing, you are being whipped by wind and soaked by a penetrating mist, the ride may be shortened. (See mileage log entry 11.5 for directions.)

Mileage Log

0.0 Pass the entrance booth and leave Birch Bay State Park, heading east on Helweg Rd.

0.5 Reach a T intersection and go right on Jackson Rd., a 2-lane country road that receives only moderate use. On the left you will pass the lumps and knobs of an oil refinery.

2.0 Go left on Aldergrove Rd. and head east around the refinery.

3.8 Take a right on Kickerville Rd. and head south along the narrow shoulder. Watch for truck traffic.

Birds on a tide-washed beach

4.9 When you see a DEAD END sign, go left on Rainbow Rd. and ride along the border of the Lake Terrell Wildlife Area (make lots of noise in hunting season).

6.0 Merge left onto Mountain View Rd. at the entrance to the AL Smelter, and head east again.

6.4 Go right on Lake Terrell Rd. and descend south toward the Lummi Indian Reservation.

8.3 At Slater Rd. (S.R. 540) go left and head east on a well-used thoroughfare.

10.9 At the mini-mart, turn right on Haxton Way and head south again on a forested road with very little traffic and a narrow shoulder.

11.5 Road divides, stay right on Haxton Way. *Alternate Route.* When the weather is poor or if you are still hurting from the previous day's push through Vancouver, you may shorten your ride by 12 miles and skip the scenery. Angle right on Lummi Shore Rd. and follow it to Marine Dr. You will return to the mileage log at the 23.7-mile point.

15.7 Pass Lummi Island ferry dock on the right. Continue straight on Lummi View Dr. and head around Portage Point. The road name changes to Lummi Shore Rd. Across Bellingham Bay is the town of Bellingham, and beyond Bellingham are the Cascade Mountains with smoldering Mount Baker presiding over the lesser summits. To the west is Lummi, Portage, and the little Brant Islands.

23.7 Turn right on Marine Dr. and return to the serious, but less scenic, business of heading south to Mexico.

25.3 Leave Marine Dr. when it takes a sharp bend to the left and continue straight on County Lane.

26.0 Turn right on Bancroft Rd.

26.6 A left turn brings you back on Marine Dr. You are now heading into a residential area. Traffic picks up, but the shoulder remains on the missing list.

28.9 Enter Bellingham. Marine Dr. becomes Eldridge.

30.1 Cross Broadway and continue straight on W. Holly St.

30.7 Turn right on Bay St.

30.8 Go left on N. Chestnut, leaving the residential area and entering downtown. You will pass two bike shops in this section.

31.0 Turn left on N. State.

31.4 Go straight on Boulevard and stick with this road for the next 2.2 miles. The name will change to S. State.

33.6 Enter Fairhaven and go straight on 12th St. Fairhaven has numerous little coffee shops and assorted eateries. You will also pass a grocery store where you can stock up for the night.

33.8 Go left on Chuckanut Dr. (S.R. 11) and begin descending. Fairhaven Park is passed on the left: picnicking, restrooms, and running water.

38.6 Larrabee State Park: kitchen shelters, vault toilets, water, hiker-biker sites, hiking and biking trails, and beach access.

39.3 Leave Whatcom County and enter Skagit County.

39.6 Pass one of many viewpoints over Samish Bay. Take time to stop and soak up some of the scenery before continuing down the narrow road. Ride aggressively in your lane.

43.9 Shoulder returns as Chuckanut Dr. descends to the delta lands at the edge of Samish Bay.

44.3 Cross over railroad tracks then a small slough on rough old bridges before heading out through verdant fields.

46.8 Take a right on W. Bow Hill Rd.: narrow, shoulderless, and moderately busy.

47.6 Enter the small town of Edison. Stick with the main road as it bends left, crosses a creek, then winds through town. The road name will change several times. As you leave town you should be heading south on Farm to Market Rd.

48.3 Go right on Bay View–Edison Rd.

48.8 Cross the Samish River, then meander through the farm fields.

51.3 Climb a short, steep hill, then follow the road along a bluff overlooking Padilla Bay.

53.0 Padilla Bay Natural Estuarine Breazeale Interpretive Center: information and displays on left.

53.8 Bay View State Park Campground is on the left: restrooms, water, picnicking, beach access, and hiker-biker area.

Inland Route: Bay View State Park to Old Fort Townsend State Park (49.6 Miles)

This short ride can be one of the most enjoyable of the Inland Route, provided you are willing to stop and play along the way. The day's ride begins with a brief tour around the estuary of Padilla Bay then heads over a bridge to Fidalgo Island. After passing two very blue lakes the route follows Highway 20 across an airy bridge over Deception Pass to Whidbey Island.

On Whidbey Island you will follow a pleasing combination of rural roads and the main highway to the tiny town of Keystone where a ferry takes you on a scenic, 35-minute ride across Puget Sound to Port Townsend. The day ends at an isolated park on the edge of Port Townsend Bay.

The area between Bay View and Old Fort Townsend State Park is rich in history. Two of the towns, Coupeville and Port Townsend, were important seaports in the late 1800s and have beautifully maintained Victorian-style buildings. Port Townsend was settled in the 1850s, and was a thriving seaport until Seattle became the western terminus of the Union Pacific

Railroad in the mid-1890s. Today, the downtown and bluff area are a designated National Historic District with buildings dating back to the 1880s. Stop at the Information Center and pick up a free guide map to the historic buildings, art galleries, antique shops, and the Jefferson County Museum.

Three old forts are passed along the route. Two were designed to protect the Puget Sound from foreign invasion, the third to fight Indians. These massive structures were never tested in battle, which was fortunate, as they became obsolete almost as soon as they were built. The forts are fun to explore and great places to sit and watch the view. Fort Casey and Fort Worden also have lighthouses overlooking broad waterways.

You do not have to be a history buff to enjoy the pleasant, almost lazy atmosphere of this ride. The scenery is excellent and the beaches, especially in the Deception Pass area, are fun to explore. Bakeries, espresso

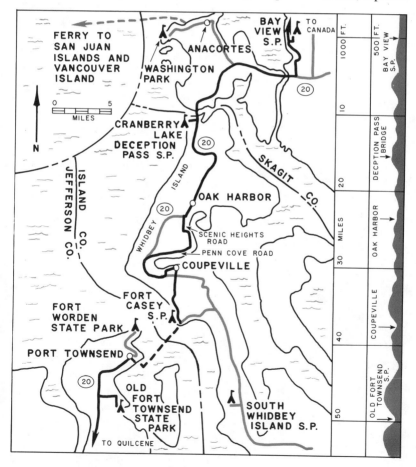

stands, and coffee shops abound. For the hungry cyclist on a budget, there are several supermarkets and lots of fast-food eateries.

Mileage Log

0.0 Head south from Bay View State Park, still following the Bay View–Edison Rd. Watch for owls, eagles, hawks, and herons in the marshy waters.

0.8 On the right is the start of the Padilla Bay Shore Trail which follows an old railroad grade through the estuary area and returns to the road in 2.2 miles. The trail is gravel, but very rideable. Loaded touring bikes will have trouble passing through the gated entrance.

2.9 Lower end of the Padilla Bay Shore Trail.

4.0 Cross railroad tracks to reach a busy intersection with Highway 20 at a traffic signal. Go right and ride west on the wide shoulder. For the hungry, there is a small market across the busy 4-lane highway.

5.7 Cross a bridge spanning the many arms of the Swinomish Channel to Fidalgo Island.

9.6 Descend a hill, climb again, then prepare for a difficult left turn at

Lunch stop on Pass Island in Deception Pass State Park

Dean's Corner. This is a major intersection and very busy. You may wish to pull over to the right and wait for a break in traffic to get across. Go left and head up a long hill on Highway 20.

11.5 The road divides. Stay left and continue to follow Highway 20 as it swings around Campbell Lake. Shoulder narrows.

14.4 Immediately after entering Deception Pass State Park, the road heads around Pass Lake.

14.9 At the west end of Pass Lake, the road divides. Stay left on Highway 20 as it heads into deep shadows, where the shoulder disappears. *Side Trip* to Rosario Picnic Area. From the intersection go right, then, almost immediately, take a left and descend to the shores of Bowman Bay. Lock the bikes before taking a scenic stroll south along Lottie Bay to Reservation Head and Lighthouse Point.

15.5 Cross Deception Pass Bridge. Turnouts on either end allow you to park your bike and gaze at the spectacle of small boats rushing to challenge the pass's amazingly strong currents.

16.4 Cranberry Lake Campground: wonderful hiker-biker site, showers, restrooms, marshes, cliffy beaches, lake for swimming, trails, and views. A small grocery store is located just 0.1 mile south of the campground entrance. Beyond the campground, Highway 20 widens to include broad shoulders. This is a settled area with farms and stores.

24.4 Oak Harbor: numerous supermarkets, a bakery, and a host of fast-food restaurants. Follow Highway 20 straight into town to a large intersection near the waterfront.

25.8 Stay with Highway 20 as it turns right (west) and heads uphill. *Side Trip.* To visit a windmill that looks like it came straight from the Netherlands, turn left at the intersection for 1 block.

26.2 About halfway up the hill, make a left turn off Highway 20 onto Scenic Heights Rd.

27.2 The road divides; stay right on Badla Rd.

28.5 Badla Rd. becomes Morre Beck Lane.

28.8 A right turn takes you back on Scenic Heights Rd., which soon descends into Penn Cove and changes its name to Penn Cove Rd.

32.5 Go right on Holbrook.

32.6 Turn left onto Highway 20 and ride around the end of Penn Cove on a good shoulder.

33.6 At the west end of the cove, leave Highway 20 by making a left turn on Madrona Way. Ride around the south side of Penn Cove, passing groves of madrona trees.

37.4 Intersection. Go straight and descend on Madrona.

37.5 At Cloveland, turn right and continue descending into the quaint town of Coupeville, with its renovated Victorian harbor and small museum. Explore the beach and waterfront before heading up N. Main St.

Fort Casey

37.8 Head steeply up N. Main St. to Highway 20.

38.4 Highway 20. Go straight across, passing a large grocery store. The road starts off narrow but soon gains a rideable shoulder.

42.2 Fort Casey State Park: campground, showers, trail, fort, lighthouse, and museum all located near the ferry dock. The first park entrance leads to the fort, lighthouse, museum. It is best to continue on to Keystone and check the ferry schedule, before coming back to explore.

42.3 Keystone ferry dock. After a 35-minute crossing, the ferry lands in Port Townsend. Go left on Water St. (which is actually Highway 20), passing supermarkets and an Information Center. The main historic area is located to the right on Water St.

42.9 After crossing Kearney St., Water St. turns into Sims Way, which in turn becomes Highway 20. The shoulder is good except at bridges. The interesting smell is from the nearby paper mill. ***Side Trip*** to Fort Worden State Park. Turn right on Kearney St. and follow the well-signed route 2.8 miles to the park. The park has a hiker-biker area, youth hostel, hot showers, hiking trails, old fort, lighthouse, and marine science center.

46.5 Cross a narrow bridge; no shoulder.
47.4 Turn left and follow signs east on a narrow road to Old Fort Townsend State Park.
49.6 Old Fort Townsend State Park: hiker-biker area, running water, restrooms, historical area, beach access, and hiking and mountain biking trails. Open May through mid-September only.

Inland Route: Old Fort Townsend State Park to Potlatch State Park (64.3 Miles)

Weaving south through the byways of the Puget Sound country, the Inland Route heads across a peninsula dividing the Strait of Juan de Fuca from the Puget Sound, then climbs the side of a steep mountain, before descending to the shores of Hood Canal. Hood Canal (a spur of the Puget Sound popular for scuba diving, clam digging, sail boarding, boating, shrimping, and fishing) is followed for the final 34 miles of the ride to Potlatch State Park.

Very little of the area's abundant scenery is visible from the road. Occasional glimpses of the Olympic Range highlight the pastoral areas and river valleys. Along Hood Canal, the hillsides rise steeply from the water's edge, climbing steadily to the crest of the Olympic Mountains. Vegetation is rich and abundant, growing with such enthusiasm it creates a nearly impenetrable wall and riders catch only an occasional glimpse of sparkling waters through the trees. The most entrancing views are seen when the highway dips into coves and the forest is replaced with low scrub at the edge of the mud flats. Birds abound in these tidal zones; herons and cormorants are common sights.

To really see the area, you must take a 5-mile side trip to the summit of Mount Walker. From the top you can look down on the bays, islands, and large cities of the Puget Sound. Unfortunately, this is a very difficult ride on a steep, gravel road and simply not for all bikes or all riders.

Several Olympic National Park access roads are passed in this section. These accesses are designed for hikers intent on exploring the miles of wilderness found in the park's interior, and are basically useless for a touring cyclist. If you wish to include the park in your itinerary, now is the time to turn east toward Port Angeles and the Peninsula Route.

In this section, the riding is fairly easy. US 101 receives considerable commercial use as well as tourist traffic. The shoulders vary from comfortable to nonexistent, disappearing just when they would be most appreciated. Hills are not much of a problem; many are steep, but except for the hill just south of Quilcene, most climbs are short.

Potlatch State Park, at the end of the day's ride, has a pleasant location on the edge of Hood Canal. Pick up groceries 3.7 miles north at Hoodsport.

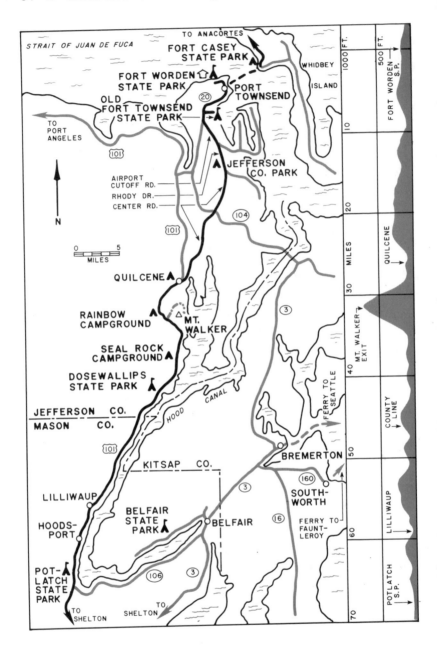

Mileage Log

0.0 From Old Fort Townsend State Park, ride back to Highway 20.

2.0 Go left on Highway 20. The shoulder is adequate except at bridges.

2.4 The road divides; stay left (east) on Airport Cutoff Rd. and watch for low-flying aircraft. Highway 20 heads west, toward Port Angeles and the Peninsula Route.

4.8 When Airport Cutoff Rd. ends, bend left on Rhody Dr. (no sign in 1997).

7.1 Pass Chimacum Jefferson County Park: limited camping, water, picnic shelter, pit toilets, and a somewhat abused dragon.

7.7 A 4-way intersection with a confusing sign for cyclists. Ignore the sign and take a right turn on Center Rd., heading toward the town of Quilcene on a wide shoulder. The Olympic Mountains form a dramatic backdrop for farmlands, clearcuts, and forest.

13.0 Intersection; continue straight on Center Rd.

14.7 Center Rd. passes under Highway 104.

22.9 (mp 294.5) Center Rd. intersects US 101 and ends at the small town of Quilcene: grocery store, campground, historical museum, and fast-food outlets. Quilcene prides itself on its oysters; the largest oyster hatchery in the world is located southwest of town on Linger Longer Rd. Go left and ride south through town on US 101. (Note: The mileage on mileposts in this section of US 101 increases from north to south. Shoulder width is narrow.)

23.3 (mp 294.9) Quilcene Jefferson County Park: campsites, picnic area, water, restrooms, and a Best tractor.

23.7 (mp 295.1) Quilcene Ranger Station offers information on campgrounds and upcoming attractions. Open weekdays only.

25.3 (mp 296.7) After crossing a shoulderless bridge, US 101 begins a steep climb over Walker Point, wandering in and out of Olympic National Forest. Shoulder width increases and logging truck drivers are adept at avoiding cyclists.

26.9 (mp 298.4) Falls View Campground: picnic area, water, and trail into Falls Canyon. No hiker-biker site.

28.3 (mp 299.9) Rainbow Campground, another forest service area offering campsites, water, and a hiking trail. No hiker-biker facilities.

28.4 (mp 299.9) Summit of the Walker Point climb. It's a downhill glide for the next couple of miles. *Side Trip.* From the highway summit, the gravel road on the left climbs 4 steep miles to the true summit of Mount Walker and two outstanding viewpoints over Hood Canal to the Cascades and to the Olympics. (Suitable for mountain bikes only, leave gear at the bottom. You may also reach the viewpoints by walking a 2-mile trail starting 0.2 mile from the highway.)

31.9 (mp 302.4) US 101 winds along the edge of the Hood Canal, climbing in and out of small bays. When the tide is out, the beach is lined with clam diggers. The sections of the canal marked with buoys are oyster farms. Enjoy the scenery, but remember to keep a sharp lookout for traffic; the shoulder varies from adequate to none.

34.1 (mp 305.4) Seal Rock Campground, a forest service area with campsites, picnicking, running water, and beach access. No hiker-biker facilities.

34.5 (mp 305.9) Brinnon, a small resort town with a general store, motel, and restaurant. Use caution when crossing the narrow, shoulderless bridge over the Dosewallips River at the south end of town.

35.6 (mp 307) Dosewallips State Park has camping on the west side of the highway, and beach access and a picnic area on the east. Amenities include a hiker-biker (primitive) site on the banks of the Dosewallips River, hot showers, running water, access to an oyster shell covered beach, beach viewing platform, hiking trails, and excellent mushroom picking in August.

38.9 (mp 310.3) Duckabush River bridge. No shoulder; use caution when crossing.

43.3 (mp 314.5) Triton Cove State Park; a day-use area with picnic tables, toilets, and boat dock.

43.4 (mp 314.6) Leave Jefferson County and enter Mason County.

View of the Olympic Mountains from US 101 north of Shelton

47.9 (mp 319) Eldon, a very small community with a restaurant and a mini-mart on the left. Use caution; the shoulder often disappears on the corners, making it difficult for drivers of big trucks to slow down or move over when suddenly encountering cyclists. Look back and check for traffic before heading around blind corners.

51.9 (mp 323) After passing an area where the road is etched into steep hillsides, the terrain moderates and the shoulder improves.

55.1 (mp 326.1) Public beach access with roadside parking.

56.2 (mp 327.2) Lilliwaup: small grocery store, motel, and restaurant. The town spreads south of the main commercial area with cottages butting right up to the edge of the highway, leaving little room for a shoulder.

60.5 (mp 331.3) Hoodsport, a resort town with a market, restaurants, bakery, motels, and even wine tasting. An Information Center for Olympic National Park and Olympic National Forest is located on the right side of the road. Pick up groceries for the night here.

62.7 (mp 333.6) Potlatch. This small town is the center of the Skokomish Indian Reservation; fireworks stands, shellfish, and smoked salmon are the specialties.

63.8 (mp 334.6) Tacoma Power Plant (right) and picnic area (left), over-look The Great Bend of Hood Canal.

64.3 (mp 335.1) Potlatch State Park has a picnic area and beach access on the east side of the highway, and a campground on the west. Amenities include a hiker-biker (primitive) area, hot showers, beach access, and two trails into the forested uplands west of the camp area. Oyster picking and clam digging are popular in season. Both activities require a license. Do not harvest out of season; these succulent mollusks carry a deadly virus for part of the year.

Inland Route: Potlatch State Park to Twin Harbors State Park (74.6 Miles)

This section of the Inland Route takes you through the southern reaches of the Puget Sound country, then turns west to the Pacific Coast. With no specific stops or side trips between Potlatch and Twin Harbors State Parks, you can concentrate solely on riding.

The ride is a long one; however, the terrain is rolling, with several short, steep hills interspersed by long, level sections where, if there isn't an on-shore wind, the miles seem to speed away. If you have just started down the coast and are not ready for a long ride, divide the ride into two parts and spend the extra night at Lake Sylvia State Park near Montesano. This will ensure plenty of time to get that rented surfboard waxed just the way you want it before braving the first wave at Westport. Or, if you are pressed

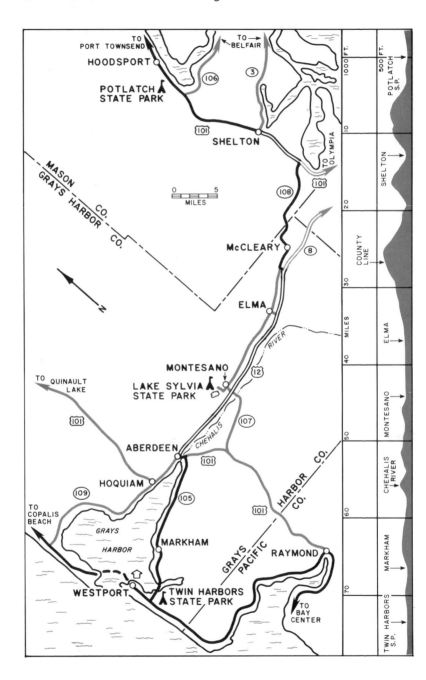

for time, you may take a shortcut on Highway 107 from Montesano to Raymond.

Scenery along the route varies from cooling towers of a defunct nuclear power project to blue herons fishing in the mud flats of Grays Harbor. At the end of the ride is Twin Harbors State Park, located on a thin peninsula between Grays Harbor, Elk Bay Harbor, and the Pacific Ocean (which is sometimes peaceful and sometimes not, but always interesting).

Twin Harbors State Park is located at Westport, a bustling resort town. It is a great place to spend an hour or a day, strolling the beaches and harbor. Watch kayakers and surfers challenge the waves, and, if you are brave and very warm-blooded, rent a board (and wet suit) and catch a few waves yourself. Check out the long fishing piers, watch the fishing boats, then work your way through the ice cream shops and bakeries. Top off the day with fresh oysters, crab, or salmon purchased from a little roadside stand.

Mileage Log

0.0 (mp 335.1) From Potlatch State Park, head south on US 101 paralleling the mud flats of The Great Bend of Hood Canal. The ride starts off on a 2-foot shoulder, which narrows somewhat as you go south.

2.0 (mp 336.8) Highway 106 branches off to the left, heading east to Bremerton and the Seattle ferries. This area is part of the Skokomish Indian Reservation; grocery store/smoke shops, fruit stands, and fireworks stands line the road.

4.5 (mp 339.5) Purdy Cutoff, an alternate access to Highway 106 and Bremerton. On the right is a turnoff to the Skokomish Valley Recreation Area. Campground and recreation facilities are a long way west of the highway. US 101 now climbs above the lowlands of Hood Canal and cruises through miles of Christmas tree farms.

10.2 (mp 345.3) First turnoff to Shelton (known as Christmas Town U.S.A. because of the large number of Christmas trees produced in the area). A large shopping center is located left (east) of US 101. Continuing south, US 101 is now a freeway. Use caution when crossing entrances and exits.

18.3 (mp 353.4) Exit US 101 and head west on Highway 108 to McCleary. A medium-sized grocery store, the last for 10 miles, is located near the exit. Highway 108 heads past farms, then through forest. The shoulder is narrow, and traffic is moderate. Expect an occasional logging truck.

26.3 (mp 4.3) Leave Mason County and enter Grays Harbor County. The road narrows.

27.5 (mp 3.1) Start shoulder.

28.6 (mp 2.1) Intersection. Still following Highway 108, turn left (south) and enter McCleary.

Lake Sylvia State Park

29.5 (mp 1.2) At the center of town, turn right (west) toward Elma. Ride past several small stores and restaurants, as well as a small city park with running water, restrooms, and a display of old logging equipment.

30.5 (mp 0.2 and mp 6.1) Intersection. Go left, still on Highway 108 for 100 feet to join Highway 8, a freeway. Head west. Shoulders are broad, traffic volume heavy, and the headwind frequently strong. Cooling towers of the abandoned Satsop nuclear plant are visible to the south.

36.6 (mp 0.0) Highway 8 merges with Highway 12. Continue west on Highway 12.

37.1 Elma, a small town with several grocery stores, a city park (no facilities), and fairgrounds (the fair takes place during the second week of August). If tired of the traffic on Highway 12, Elma is a good place to exit. Follow the McCleary-Elma Rd. west, through town, where it becomes the Elma-Montesano Rd. Beyond Elma, the shoulders are good.

39.8 Satsop: small grocery store to the right (north) of Highway 12.

44.8 Montesano: large grocery store, fast food, restaurants, historic county courthouse, and Lake Sylvia State Park. The state park is located on a forested lake 1 mile above town. To reach the park, ride to the center of town. At the intersection with Highway 107, continue straight for 3 blocks, then take a right on 3rd St. and follow the signs to the state park. The park has a hiker-biker area, hot showers, lakeshore campsites, boat rentals, swimming, hiking trails, and some interesting artifacts from the turn-of-the-century logging industry.

47.3 (mp 6.7) Wynoochee River bridge. Wait for a break in the traffic before crossing this shoulderless span.

49.4 (mp 4.6) Central Park: market on left.

54.5 Enter Aberdeen.

55.5 River Park: picnicking, restrooms, and access to historic waterfront area. The park is reached by making a lefthand turn just before a large shopping center.

56.0 Cross the Wishkah River on a narrow bridge. Follow the US 101 South signs and prepare for a lefthand turn 2 blocks beyond the bridge.

56.2 (mp 0.0 and mp 88.4) Turn left on US 101 and cross the Chehalis River on a wide bridge. Cyclists may use the pedestrian route.

57.0 (mp 87.8 and mp 48.8) On the south side of the bridge, go straight on Highway 105 (US 101 turns left here). Two large supermarkets, located on the left side of the highway at the intersection, offer an excellent opportunity to pick up your groceries for the night. Highway 105 (a Washington State Scenic and Recreational Highway) heads west, paralleling the tide flats on the south side of Grays Harbor. The highway is busy and shoulderless in town. Soon after passing a large shopping center, the road narrows from 4 to 2 lanes with a comfortable shoulder.

67.6 (mp 38.2) Markham, home of Ocean Spray fruit juices. No tasting room or retail outlet.

72.0 (mp 32.4) Bay City, a small town with a grocery store. Shoulder comes and goes in this area.

74.5 (mp 30.0) Westport, a resort town with charter boats, salmon fishing, aquarium, museum, ocean beaches, campground, grocery store, motels, restaurants, ferry to Ocean Shores, tourist shops, bakeries, and kite shops. Grocery stores and restaurants are found 2 miles north in the center of town. A small market is located at the turnoff. Continue straight ahead on Highway 105 for 200 feet, then turn left to reach Twin Harbors State Park.

74.6 Twin Harbors State Park: hiker-biker (primitive) area, hot showers, beach access, kitchen shelter, clam cleaning shed, nature trail through the sand dunes, and hiking trails to the beach.

Twin Harbors State Park to Bush Pacific County Park
(52.8 Miles)

The Peninsula and Inland Routes join at Twin Harbors State Park and together head south toward the Columbia River and the Oregon border.

The southern coastline of Washington is broken by large bays which force the route to turn inland below Twin Harbors State Park. Cyclists can expect lots of tree plantations with occasional views of either the ocean or vast mud flats (depending on the tide) as the route heads southeast around massive Willapa Bay to rejoin US 101 at Raymond. If you can drag yourself away from the delightful views of artistically posed sculptures of deer and elk grazing along the road, you may escape the noise of the main highway by following a 2.5-mile bike path west along the Willapa River to South Bend.

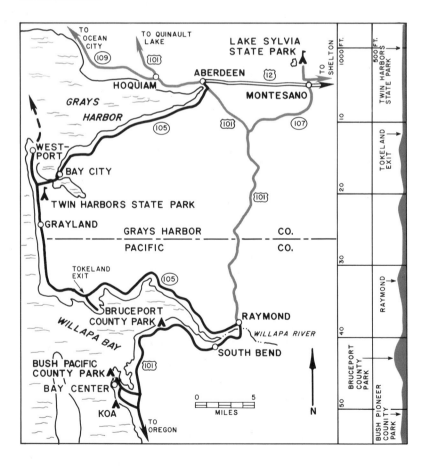

Surfers at Westport

Start the day with full water bottles and plenty of extra food; few stores or restrooms are found along the route. With little to break the rhythm of the ride, the miles tend to speed by. Cyclists arriving at Bush Pacific County Park may understandably be tempted to continue south another 33 miles to Fort Canby State Park near Ilwaco. Not a bad idea, if you use the time gained to explore the historically interesting and very scenic Columbia River mouth.

This is a quiet area. Both Highways 105 and 101 receive only minor traffic, allowing you to hear the surf and listen to the shorebirds. Shoulder width is good except for a short stretch as you enter Raymond and the final section to Bay Center.

The economy in this area is based on the forest industry, so be prepared for logging trucks on the highways. Always give these huge trucks as much space as possible, or get off the road to avoid being trapped in a squeeze play. Most drivers are very friendly to cyclists, but the trucks are big, heavy, and difficult to maneuver.

Mileage Log

0.0 (mp 30.1) From Twin Harbors State Park, head south on Highway 105. Shoulders are narrow, and traffic is moderate to light.

2.8 (mp 27.5) Grayland, a small resort town with motels, grocery store, and deli.

3.4 (mp 26.9) Beach access: toilets.

4.6 (mp 25.6) Turnoff to Grayland Beach State Park: water, restrooms, showers, hiker-biker sites, interpretive trails, and beach access. This park is oriented to the needs of campers with motorhomes.

4.7 (mp 25.5) Leave Grays Harbor County and enter Pacific County.

6.5 (mp 24) Pass the first of several beach access points.

7.9 (mp 22.3) North Cove, a very small town with a very small market.

9.8 (mp 20.6) Highway 105 parallels the edge of North Cove.

11.2 (mp 19.3) Enter the Shoalwater Indian Reservation. Groceries, motels, and fireworks may be found near the turnoff to Tokeland, a small community with a fishing dock and a rather plain-looking historic hotel. The highway turns east here, crossing a forested peninsula, then paralleling the shore of Willapa Bay. The bay is very shallow, and the ebbing tide exposes miles of tide flats. To the south lies Leadbetter Point (the northern tip of the North Beach Peninsula), as well as the objective of this day's ride: Bay Center. The route skirts around Willapa Bay for the next 63 miles.

20.4 (mp 10.1) After passing a commercial campground, the highway crosses North River, then Smith Creek. Across the bay, the mills of South Bend and Raymond come into view.

30.3 (mp 0.8) Raymond, a lumber town with art sculpture that will put a smile on your face. You will find just about everything for the touring cyclist here—except a good bike shop. There are motels, restaurants, a supermarket, and camping at the county park.

31.5 (mp 0.0 and mp 59.6) Highway 105 ends. Turn right on US 101 and cycle across the North Fork Willapa River.

32.0 (mp 59.1) Pass a city park on the left side of the highway: restrooms and running water.

32.5 (mp 58.5) Leave US 101 when it intersects Highway 6 at an intersection with a stoplight. Go straight across the intersection, then turn right and go up onto the sidewalk. Continue straight ahead, passing a sculpture of kayakers and cyclists, then cross the Willapa River. ***Alternate Route.*** Stay on US 101.

32.7 Go left and follow the bike route up a city street.

32.8 Find the bike path and follow it around the south side of the Willapa Market Place shopping center.

33.2 Bike path temporarily ends. Go straight down a well-signed street.

33.4 Return to the bike path. The path parallels US 101 along the Willapa River. (In the early 1900s, there were twenty working lumber mills along this portion of the river.)

35.6 Bike path ends. Take a left on Summit St. then right, to return to US 101 just as it enters South Bend, a small, charming town first settled in 1860. Many old buildings remain. Amenities include a city park, public restrooms, grocery store, tourist facilities, and an RV park that accepts tents.

Kite-flying on sand dunes near beach at Westport

37.2 (mp 54.0) Pacific County Museum, a small, friendly facility. Public restrooms are located on the north side of the street beyond the Information Center and parking area. Beyond South Bend, the road is level for several miles. The shoulder starts off comfortably, then gradually narrows.

42.7 (mp 48.6) Bruceport County Park: picnic area, campground, restrooms, running water, hot showers, and special rates for cyclists. Campsites overlook Willapa Bay and are available on a first-come basis.

45.3 (mp 46.4) Historical marker relating the story of Bruceport's origin.

47.5 (mp 44.0) Naipikipi River bridge.

48.7 (mp 42.6) Palix Creek bridge.

50.1 (mp 42.4) At Bay Center Dike Rd. turn right (west) and ride toward Bay Center and the campground. Cycle along the water's edge, passing huge piles of oyster shells; no shoulder.

52.5 T-junction at Bay Center. A small grocery store and park are to the right. A commercial KOA campground is to the left.

52.8 Bush Pacific County Park. This is a primitive park with campsites, picnic area, restrooms, and limited beach access. Generally, space can be found for all cyclists. If you prefer more amenities, try the KOA campground located just south of Bay Center on Bay Center Rd. (The KOA campground has hot showers, laundry, a shelter just for cyclists, and a store. Rates are reasonable.)

Bush Pacific County Park to the Oregon Border
(47.4 Miles)

The journey through Washington ends at the Columbia River, just a few miles inland from its terminus. This scenic area is rich in history. Indians lived and fished here for thousands of years before European explorer Captain Robert Gray charted the location of the river mouth in 1792. In 1805 Lewis and Clark ended their long western trek to the Pacific Ocean on the south side of the river near Astoria and wintered a few miles inland from the ocean.

The tricky sandbar at the Columbia River entrance caused many problems for early settlers, and over the years it has been the scene of numerous shipwrecks. Despite the building of lighthouses, the marking of the channel, and the taming of the waters by numerous upriver dams, the mouth of the Columbia River retains many of its navigational challenges. The designing of a very special Columbia River rescue boat gives testimony to the strength and danger of these waters.

The ride from Bush Pacific County Park to Oregon is an easy one, leaving plenty of time for exploring. Along the way you will pass the Willapa National Wildlife Refuge, inhabited by migrating ducks and geese in the spring and fall, and a host of shorebirds year-round. Two blinds for viewing and photographing the birds are situated near US 101 at the refuge headquarters. The next point of interest is the Long Beach Peninsula. Its most visible attractions are tourist-oriented: "World's Longest Driving Beach," innumerable restaurants, motels, and amusement centers.

At the southern end of the Long Beach Peninsula is Fort Canby State Park. The old fort is now the site of an excellent museum commemorating the Lewis and Clark Expedition. Museum exhibits lead visitors on an imaginary journey over the Lewis and Clark Trail. Two lighthouses, North Point and Camp Disappointment, are located within easy walking distance of the park.

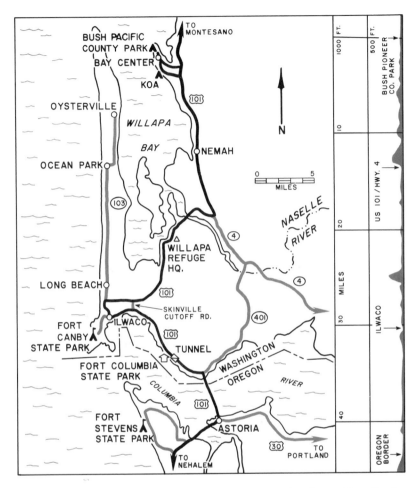

No public campgrounds are located at the state border, so Fort Canby State Park is the recommended overnight stop. The small town of Chinook, 5.3 miles from the border, has two commercial campgrounds that accept tents. During the summer months, you may also stay at the Fort Columbia State Park hostel, 3.1 miles from the border.

Mileage Log

0.0 The day starts at Bush Pacific County Park. Ride south on the shoulderless road through Bay Center and continue straight on Bay Center Road.

0.8 KOA, a commercial campground that is open year-round.

3.8 (mp 41.5) Bay Center Rd. ends. Head south (right) on US 101.

17.0 (mp 29.0) Junction of Highway 4 and US 101. The bicycle route follows US 101 as it turns sharply right (west). Shoulder is narrow to nonexistent. ***Alternate Route.*** Highway 4, in conjunction with Highway 401, may be used as a short-cut to Astoria, bypassing 11.1 miles of riding. No camping facilities or points of interest on this route.

19.4 (mp 26.4) Naselle River Bridge marks the return of a shoulder. Beyond, US 101 parallels the shore of Willapa Bay. The road is narrow and winding, with turnouts if you wish to stop and look over the sloughs and scenic mud flats.

22.0 (mp 24.1) The Willapa National Wildlife Refuge headquarters, on the left (east) side of US 101, has information on what to see and where to see it. Check out the bird blinds.

25.9 (mp 20.2) Green Head Slough.

30.9 (mp 15.2) Intersection of US 101 and Alternate US 101, called the Skinville Cutoff. The bicycle route continues straight on US 101 to the Long Beach Peninsula, Ilwaco, and Fort Canby State Park. The 0.2-mile-long cutoff shortcuts 6.1 miles of road, bypassing the Long Beach Peninsula and Fort Canby State Park.

33.3 (mp 13.6) Intersection of US 101 and Highway 103 at Seaview: grocery stores and complete tourist facilities. The bicycle route bears left (south), following US 101. Highway 103 heads right to the town of Long Beach and the northern end of the Long Beach Peninsula.

34.8 (mp 12.1) Enter Ilwaco. The town is located on the Columbia River and has tourist facilities and a grocery store.

35.3 (mp 11.6) ***Side Trip*** to Fort Canby State Park, lighthouses, and Lewis and Clark Trail Museum. Turn right (west) when US 101 makes a sharp turn left (east) in the center of Ilwaco. Go straight until the road branches. Either branch may be followed for the 3-mile ride to the park, where you will find hiker-biker (primitive) campsites, hot showers, beach access, lighthouses, museum, and hiking trails.

37.5 (mp 10.4) Intersection of US 101 and Alternate US 101 (the Skinville Cutoff Rd.). Continue straight on US 101 as it parallels the Columbia River through farmland. A commercial KOA Campground is located at the intersection.

42.1 (mp 5.6) Chinook, a small town with a grocery store and two commercial campgrounds. Beyond town, pass a county park with campsites for motorhomes only.

44.3 (mp 3.5) Fort Columbia State Park: picnic tables, trails, running water, restrooms, gun turrets, museum, and a hostel.

44.4 (mp 3.4) Pass through a short, straight tunnel. Before entering, set off the blinking light that warns motorists of your presence.

45.0 (mp 2.8) Lewis and Clark Campsite, a small area set aside to commemorate one of the expedition's overnight stops.

North Point Lighthouse

46.9 (mp 0.9) Intersection of US 101 and Highway 401 at the Astoria Bridge. Follow US 101 south across the bridge. The roadway is narrow, shoulderless, and difficult to ride when the wind is blowing. Take a deep breath and head across at a quick pace. Do not stop until you reach the other side.

47.4 (mp 0.0) The Washington–Oregon border is located on the Astoria Bridge over the center of the Columbia River.

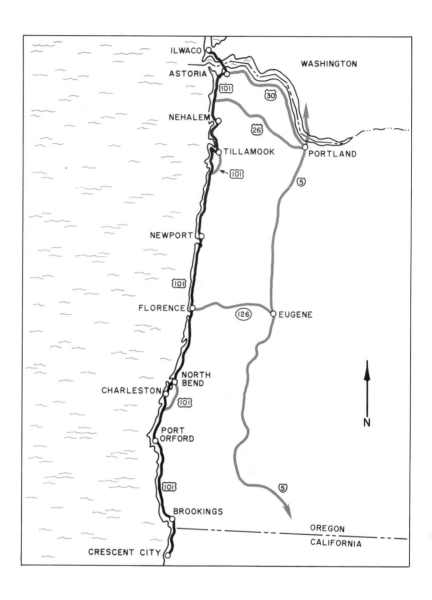

ILWACO

ASTORIA

WASHINGTON

[101]

[30]

NEHALEM

[26]

TILLAMOOK

PORTLAND

[101]

[5]

NEWPORT

[101]

FLORENCE

[126]

EUGENE

NORTH
BEND

CHARLESTON

[101]

N

PORT
ORFORD

[101]

[5]

BROOKINGS

OREGON

CALIFORNIA

CRESCENT CITY

Remains of the Peter Iredale *on the beach at Fort Stevens State Park*

The Oregon Coast Bicycle Route has 378 miles of spectacular ocean views, long beaches, sand dunes, wave-sculptured sea stacks, and rugged headlands. This is a popular tourist area, so finding food and lodging poses few problems. The Oregon Coast tour is good for everyone, from first-time cycle tourists to expert riders.

The Oregon Coast should be savored at a leisurely pace. Save the marathon days for a tour across the Great Plains. Slow down, hike, explore, or just sit and watch the sun set.

Cyclists on the Oregon Coast should carry waterproof gear for protection against long, rainy days. Bright, visible clothing and bike lights are essential for surviving the heavy, wet fog that can engulf the coast during the summer months. Fenders are a much-appreciated accessory when it rains, protecting you and your gear from the grime of wet roads. The months of July, August, and September are the driest. Expect heavy rains from October through June. Coastal winds gust up to 60 miles per hour in the summer months (most often from the northwest), and the winds are even stronger in the winter.

The Oregon Highway Department expects the majority of riders to be heading from north to south. Where the road is narrow, the southbound shoulder has been developed at the expense of the shoulder on the northbound side of the road.

Most key intersections have been marked with Oregon Coast Bike Route signs; unfortunately, these are popular home decorating items, so keep a close eye on the directions and map.

The two tunnels on the Oregon Coast cannot be avoided except by flying. Flashing signs, activated by cyclists before entering, warn motorists that bicycles are in the tunnels. Despite this convenience, tunnels are very hazardous, so be cautious. Strap on a light that will be visible to vehicles approaching from behind, then wait for a lull in traffic before starting out. All these precautions notwithstanding, the tunnels are nerve-wracking, so pedal fast.

Cyclist activating the warning light before entering Cape Arch Tunnel

The popularity of the Oregon Coast extends beyond the bicycling world. People flock to the coast in the summer, many driving oversized motorhomes—you know the kind—with picture windows, microwaves, showers, televisions, and toilets. Many of these vehicles are rental units, and drivers of these bus-size "camping" machines may lack experience in handling them. Ride defensively and try to anticipate the problems these drivers will have when they pass. Most of all, pray that the next gas shortage will send these "campers" back to hotels.

In Oregon, the milepost signs note miles in whole numbers, starting with 00 at the Washington border and increasing to the south. In the mileage logs, mileposts are noted in tenths for increased accuracy; a milepost number of 25.7 indicates that the point of interest is located 0.7 mile past (south of) milepost 25.

State parks provide sixteen hiker-biker camps for cyclists along the coast. The sites are primitive and generally tucked away from regular camping areas. Water, restroom facilities, and showers may be somewhat removed from the campsite. These areas are never full, no reservations are required, and the cost is reasonable. However, since the charge is per person, groups of four or more may find the regular campsites a better bargain. Larger groups should always reserve campsites ahead of time. The state parks have recently started building yurts in their campgrounds. As of 1998, eight campgrounds had them. These shelters are usually booked on weekends, but you will often find a vacancy during the week. If a regular campsite or yurt is desired, be sure to call ahead for reservations at (800)452-5687, Monday through Friday, 8:00 A.M. to 5:00 P.M., from 2 days to 11 months before your arrival date.

Between November 1 and mid-April, only eleven state park campgrounds are open. Oswald West, Umpqua Lighthouse, Sunset Bay, William M. Tugman, and Cape Blanco close during the winter.

Many of the state park day-use areas now charge entry fees. If you spent the previous night at a state park campground and have saved your receipt, you are exempted from paying a day-use fee. When no one is present to collect the fees, leave the receipt prominently displayed (taped) on your handlebars.

Portland has the closest major airport and train access to the northern Oregon Coast. The only form of public transportation from Portland to Astoria is the bus; bicycles must be boxed for the trip.

If planning to ride from Portland to the coast, Highway 30 (95 miles to Astoria with a good shoulder most of the way) or Highway 26 (80 miles to Cannon Beach with moderate shoulder, some freeway riding, and one tunnel) are recommended.

Neither route offers camping. Highway 30 is easier to reach from the airport, train, or bus station, and has numerous small towns with restaurants and motels along the way. To ride to Highway 30 from the Portland airport, follow the main road from the arrival area and merge right onto N.E. 82nd heading east. After 1.2 miles, go right on N.E. 82nd Way for 1.7 miles. When the road ends, head left on busy Highway 213 (also called 82nd), then take the first right onto N.E. Alberta St. Follow this road until it ends (it will turn to gravel) then take a left on N.E. 75th Way and follow it to the first major intersection. Go right on N.E. Prescott, which soon turns into an official city bike route. After 2.1 miles, jog left on N.E. 38th, then take the first right back onto Prescott for another 0.2 mile. Turn left at 33rd Ave. and follow it for a short 0.1 mile before going right on Skidmore St. Ride Skidmore for the next 1.1 miles until you reach 17th, where you take a short jog right, then return to Skidmore St. for another 1.7 miles. Go right on Concord Ave. and grind up the pedestrian over-pass. Once across, continue straight for 0.2 mile then take a left on N. Alberta. After 0.2 mile go right on N. Denver Ave. for 0.5 mile, then take a left on N. Ainsworth for 0.6 mile. Turn right on scenic Willamette Blvd. and follow it for 4 miles. Cross the Willamette River at St. Johns Bridge, and head west on Highway 30. (It is best to pick up a Portland map—AAA has them—before you leave home and trace your route through town.)

From the train or bus station (located next to each other in downtown Portland), head up 5th or 6th Ave. to Olisan and turn right. In 0.6 mile, turn right again on N.W. 18th. After another 0.6 mile, take a left on Raleigh and follow it for 1 mile, then turn right on 28th St. After 0.2 mile, go left on Thurman for 0.2 mile. Turn right on 29th St. for 0.3 mile to a major intersection. Go left here, onto Highway 30 (also called St. Helens Rd.). Traffic is heavy on weekends.

At the southern border of Oregon, riders leaving the coast route are once again faced with transport problems. The only public transportation in Brookings is the bus, and the trip to Portland takes 6 hours on the express. The alternative is to continue south 21 miles to Crescent City, California, and rent a car or take a commuter flight to larger cities inland (however, these small airlines may refuse to transport your bicycle).

Note: Cyclists have experienced difficulties in obtaining bicycle boxes in Brookings. To avoid hassles, have a friend ship you a bike box by bus.

Washington Border to Nehalem Bay State Park
(43.9 Miles)

The northern coast of Oregon is as excellent for bicycle touring as it is for sight-seeing. The Oregon Coast Bicycle Route starts high above the Columbia River on the Astoria Bridge and follows US 101 from the state border through farm country, past historical landmarks, to the wild and scenic coast.

View of Astoria Bridge and the Columbia River from the Astoria Column

---

US 101 is busy. The shoulder is good for the first 33 miles then disappears in Oswald West State Park. To add to the challenges, the first of the Oregon Coast tunnels is encountered. Use all precautions for tunnel travel suggested in the introduction to this chapter: Strap on a light, wait for a lull in traffic, activate the warning signals, and pedal like mad.

Although the ride is short, you can easily spend two days here checking out all the side trips and exploring the many state parks. The first side trip is into Astoria, where a collection of photographs and memorabilia at the Maritime Museum depicts the colorful marine history of the Oregon Coast, with emphasis on the problems caused by the turbulent entrance to the Columbia River.

The Lewis and Clark Expedition ended its westward journey near Astoria in November 1805. A couple of the expedition members spent the winter boiling sea water for salt at a place that is now called Seaside, while the main body of the expedition took shelter from the damp weather at Fort Clatsop. The second side trip leads to a national monument at the site of the fort.

More recent history is explored on a third side trip to Fort Stevens State Park, where the remains of the *Peter Iredale*, shipwrecked in 1906, lie just offshore. This once-mighty, four-masted British sailing ship is a reminder of the many ships that sank trying to enter the placid-looking mouth of the Columbia River. The fort can also be explored. The old structure has been abandoned for many years, but at one time it guarded the river entrance and was the only West Coast fort ever shelled.

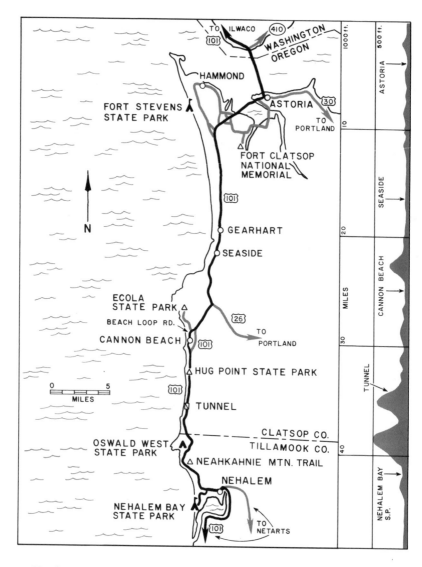

Farther south, at Hug Point State Park, a short beach walk leads to the remains of the first highway along the Oregon Coast. Most of this early roadway was right on the beach, and drivers had to schedule their travel for low tide. One exception was at Hug Point, where the narrow, single-lane road blasted into the side of a sea cliff can still be seen today.

Not to be forgotten is the tremendous scenery along the way. In Astoria, a side trip to the Astoria Column reveals sweeping views of the Columbia River, Pacific Ocean, Oregon's Coast Range, and parts of Washington. A side trip to Ecola State Park at Cannon Beach gives you a chance to enjoy a view of Tillamook Head Lighthouse (currently a mausoleum) and a broad vista over Cannon Beach. Farther south, the highway climbs over a large shoulder of Neahkahnie Mountain, with breathtaking views south over Nehalem Bay and beyond. Leave the bicycles and hike 2 miles to the summit of the mountain for an unforgettable 360-degree view.

The day ends at Nehalem Bay State Park, where long, sandy beaches provide an excellent opportunity to take a relaxing sunset stroll or a bike ride on a paved path out onto a long sand spit.

Mileage Log

0.0 (mp 0.0) Enter Oregon by following US 101 across the 4.2-mile-long Astoria Bridge over the mighty Columbia River. The Oregon Coast ride starts 0.5 mile from the north end of the bridge where you officially leave Washington and enter Oregon.

3.7 (mp 3.7) A stoplight marks the end of the bridge and the entrance to Astoria. The bike route heads right, following US 101 south across Youngs Bay. *Side Trip* to Astoria. To visit the Astoria Column, the Maritime Museum of the Columbia River, the bicycle shop, or one of Astoria's grocery stores, turn left (east) when you exit the bridge and follow US 30 for 1 mile into town. The road divides and becomes one-way. To reach the Astoria Column, take the first left on Commercial St. to 16th St., then turn right and head steeply up to the column. A left on 17th St. leads down to the Maritime Museum and the dock of the old lightship *Columbia*.

The bicycle shop is located at the eastern end of town, and markets and grocery stores are found throughout.

4.5 (mp 4.5) Youngs Bay bridge. Traffic is heavy; however, the shoulder is spacious.

6.3 (mp 6.3) Leave Youngs Bay. For the next 18.4 miles, US 101 travels over gently rolling terrain covered with large pastures and studded with small towns. A roomy shoulder provides relief from a constant flow of traffic.

6.5 (mp 6.5) First turnoff to Fort Stevens State Park; continue on US 101.

7.0 (mp 7.0) *Side Trip* to Fort Clatsop National Memorial. Exit left (south) off US 101. Cycle 0.3 mile to intersect US 101 Business, then turn left (east). After 1.9 miles, turn right on an unnamed road for the final 1.6 miles to the fort site. A fee is charged to enter the visitor center and reconstructed fort. Watch the movie, then wander through the interactive displays. Live demonstrations are conducted throughout the fort and the surrounding woods on weekends year-round, and every day during the summer season. The flintlock demonstration is particularly fun. Other monument amenities include a nature trail, picnic area, restrooms, and running water.

Park interpreter demonstrating a muzzle loader at Fort Clatsop National Memorial

---

Side Trip to Fort Stevens State Park. For a visit to Fort Stevens State Park, turn right off US 101 and cycle northwest 1.1 miles to Warrenton. Continue straight 2.3 miles to Hammond and a stop sign. Turn left on Lake Dr. and follow it south, passing two well-signed park roads before reaching the campground entrance at 0.8 mile. Here you will find hiker-biker sites, yurts, beach access, a nature trail, 9 miles of hiking trails, an 8.5-mile bike path, and lots of mosquitoes. Explore the park, hike, bike, swim in the lake, watch the sunset over the wreck of the *Peter Iredale*, wander through the old fort historic area, or browse the military museum. Maps of the park are available at the entrance booth.

16.1 (mp 18.3) Gearhart: motels.

17.3 (mp 19.5) Seaside: bike shop, several supermarkets, and surf shops. A side trip into this resort town leads to museums and several historic sites, such as the end of the Lewis and Clark Trail and salt mine. Directions to historic sites are well signed from US 101.

23.6 (mp 25) Junction of US 101 and US 26. Stay right on US 101 as it heads up a 2.2-mile hill. Once at the top, it's a downhill glide to Cannon Beach.

26.9 (mp 28.1) Turn right, leaving US 101 at the Cannon Beach exit. Continue downhill on Beach Loop Rd. for a scenic tour through Cannon Beach, one of the most photographed areas on the Oregon Coast. On weekends the roads through town are congested.

27.3 *Side Trip* to Ecola State Park. Two miles of steeply winding, narrow road through beautiful coastal forest lead to Ecola State Park, where you will be treated to fantastic views of Cannon Beach and Tillamook Head Lighthouse. Picnic tables, restrooms, and running water are available. It takes all day to thoroughly explore the long, sandy beaches and forested trails of the park. Unfortunately, no camping is allowed. A state park day-use fee is charged.

27.7 Cannon Beach, a very popular resort area with beaches, grocery stores, delis, and restaurants. Strolling on the beach and digging toes into the sand are the two most popular activities. As you ride through town, Beach Loop Rd. becomes South Hemlock. Continue south.

29.6 Tolovana Park, a small community with a store, beach access, restrooms, and water. Return to US 101 here. Heading south, the shoulders are moderate and the occasional ocean views excellent.

30.6 (mp 32.4) Arcadia State Park: beach access, ocean views, running water, and restrooms.

31.8 (mp 33.6) Hug Point State Park. A short, steep descent leads to restrooms, running water, picnic tables, and beach access. Walk the beach ½ mile north to a waterfall and small cave, then climb over a low headland on the remains of the original Coast Highway.

33.8 (mp 35.7) Cape Arch Tunnel runs uphill and bends to the left. Before entering, activate the flashing signal by pushing the button. At the south end, a turnout provides an opportunity to catch your breath while you enjoy the view. After the tunnel, the highway continues to gain elevation for several miles.

33.9 (mp 35.8) Enter Oswald West State Park. Campground, picnic area, and beach access are 4.3 miles south.

35.2 (mp 37.1) Leave Clatsop County and enter Tillamook County.

38.2 (mp 39.3) Oswald West Campground, a walk-in area reached by a ¼-mile paved trail (no hiker-biker sites). Wheelbarrows are provided to help campers transport their gear to the tent sites. To reach the picnic area, walk the trail for ¾ mile to Short Sand Beach. Beyond the trailhead parking area, US 101 climbs steeply over a shoulder of Neahkahnie Mountain.

39.1 (mp 40.2) Neahkahnie Mountain Trail starts on the left (east) side of the highway, opposite a turnout, and is marked by an unobtrusive wooden post. Beyond the trailhead, the shoulder on US 101 nearly disappears as the road climbs steeply for the next mile. *Side Trip*. Hide the bikes in the bushes and hike the steep 2-mile trail to unsurpassed views from the summit.

39.3 (mp 41.2) Top-of-the-hill viewpoint and start of a steep downhill.

39.8 (mp 41.6) Neahkahnie Mountain Trail, south side. This longer, less scenic trail also leads to the summit.

41.1 (mp 43.2) Manzanita Market, the last grocery store before Nehalem State Park, is easy to miss when zooming down Neahkahnie Mountain. The next grocery store is located 1 mile beyond the state park turnoff in Nehalem. For northbound riders, little to no shoulder exists for the next 15 miles.

41.9 (mp 43.9) Turn right off US 101 and follow the signs to Nehalem Bay State Park.

43.9 Nehalem Bay State Park: hiker-biker campsite, yurts, hot showers, beach access, and 1.5-mile bike trail to the south end of the Nehalem spit.

Nehalem Bay State Park to Cape Lookout State Park
(48.2 Miles)

The route continues south along the coast, following US 101 through small resort towns. The road is near the water's edge and the scenery is good for the first 21 miles. Shortly after passing through Bay City, the broad expanse of Tillamook Bay forces US 101 to turn inland, where it travels over a broad and nearly level plain covered with dairy farms and swamps. Miles are covered quickly, leaving you plenty of time to tour the cheese factory at the outskirts of the town of Tillamook. The self-guided tour leads to large viewing windows overlooking the almost entirely automated cheese-making process. A museum explains the history of cheese making, and a slide show illustrates the process. Finally, a snack bar answers any remaining questions.

At Tillamook, the bicycle route leaves US 101 and heads west on the Three Capes Scenic Route to spectacular ocean views, a lighthouse, and beach trails. (US 101 heads inland here to avoid the rugged coast.)

Most of the ride from Nehalem Bay State Park to Tillamook has ample shoulders. Once on the Three Capes Scenic Route, the shoulders end. The roads on this route are narrow and moderately busy. However, the scenery justifies the inconvenience.

Mileage Log

0.0 From Nehalem Bay State Park, pedal back to US 101.

2.0 (mp 43.9) Rejoin US 101 and head south. The shoulder is narrow and rough for southbound riders, and nonexistent for northbound riders.

3.1 (mp 45) Nehalem, a small town with a grocery store. US 101 makes a sharp right, then heads around Nehalem Bay.

3.8 (mp 45.7) Cross the Nehalem River on a bridge with a comfortable shoulder.

4.0 (mp 46) Road on right leads to a boat launch with public outhouses.

5.0 (mp 47) Wheeler: small market and tourist shops.

6.7 (mp 48.7) Shoulder narrows as the road enters a slide area. Mileposts are not accurate here.

7.9 (mp 49.9) The shoulder returns to a comfortable width as the highway enters a beach community.

9.6 (mp 51.6) Start another short section where the shoulder is less then optimal.

11.4 (mp 53.4) Manhattan Beach Wayside: restrooms, picnic tables, water, and a short trail to a sandy beach. A small market is located just across the road.

11.9 (mp 48.7) The town of Rockway Beach is entered after crossing a short, shoulderless bridge.

13.1 (mp 50.9) Rockway Beach Public Access: restrooms and beach. US 101 now heads inland, passing several small lakes.

16.1 (mp 53.9) Barview Jetty County Park. This trailer park is located at the North Jetty of Tillamook Bay. There is a small store at the

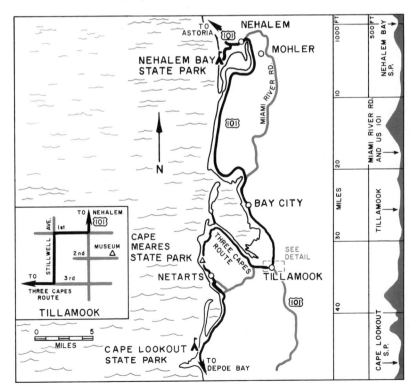

turnoff. Continuing south, US 101 follows the edge of the bay, passing a couple of small, twisted sea stacks just offshore.

17.0 (mp 54.8) Viewpoint: picnic tables.

17.2 (mp 55.1) Garibaldi: market, coast guard station, and an old train on display in Lumbermen's Memorial Park. On weekends there is train service to Tillamook.

20.6 (mp 58.5) Viewpoint over Tillamook Bay.

21.4 (mp 59.3) Bay City, a small town with a small market.

26.0 (mp 63.9) Tillamook Cheese Factory, located on the left (east) side of the highway. Signs, several busy parking lots, and a large sailing ship on the front lawn make this an easy attraction to spot. Admission is free; however, free samples are limited and the cheese is cheaper elsewhere. Check out the cheese curd, sold in small bags: it's very affordable and tastes great.

26.4 (mp 64.3) Tillamook: supermarkets, Laundromats, bicycle shops, and shopping malls. The Pioneer Museum is an interesting way to spend a half hour. To reach the museum, pass through the first stoplight then turn left (east) at the second stoplight. The museum is located 1 block up on 2nd St.

Fresnel lens inside Cape Meares Lighthouse

28.3 (mp 66.2) Three Capes Scenic Route. At the first stoplight turn right (west) off US 101 onto 1st St. and follow the signs to the Three Capes Scenic Route.

28.4 Turn left (south) on Stillwell Ave.

28.5 Go right (west) on 3rd St., which heads out of town, passing numerous cows busy producing milk for the cheese factory.

30.1 Turn right on the Three Capes Scenic Route. The old, bumpy, shoulderless road hugs the edge of Tillamook Bay. Keep an eye out for a variety of waterfowl.

35.5 Intersection. Following the Three Capes Scenic Route, turn left for a steep, 1.5-mile climb over Cape Meares.

37.7 Cape Meares State Park: picnic tables, restrooms, and water. Descend a short, steep road to the Octopus Tree, a large Sitka spruce, and the lighthouse. Once you have parked your bicycle, grab the binoculars for viewing birds nesting on the rocky cliffs as you walk ⅛ mile down to the lighthouse. You may climb the stairway to the top of the tower for a firsthand look at the prisms. The lighthouse is open daily during the summer from 11:00 A.M. to 5:00 P.M.

40.2 Oceanside State Park Beach: beach access and picnic tables.

42.2 Netarts. If spending the night at Cape Lookout State Park, this is your last chance to replenish your food supplies.

42.8 Turn right, following the Three Capes Scenic Route, and descend to the water's edge. The road then follows the shore of Netarts Bay. Road remains narrow. Traffic is heavy on weekends.

42.9 Netarts Bay Recreation Area: picnic tables and restrooms.

44.3 Stop sign and junction. Continue straight south along the water, still on the Three Capes Scenic Route.

48.2 Cape Lookout State Park: hiker-biker campsite, yurts, hot showers, picnic area, beaches, ¼-mile self-guiding nature loop, and hiking trails. If time allows, hike the trail to the end of Cape Lookout for terrific views of the coast.

Cape Lookout State Park to Beverly Beach State Park
(57.5 Miles)

This ride is dominated by three major climbs over three capes. The first climb, over Cape Lookout, begins as soon as you leave the campground. The second climb, over Cascade Head, occurs near the midpoint of the ride. The third climb is over the aptly named Cape Foulweather, and it awaits you at the end of the day. All three capes are forested and views are hard to come by. However, numerous highlights along the other sections of the ride ensure that you will not miss this area's outstanding scenery.

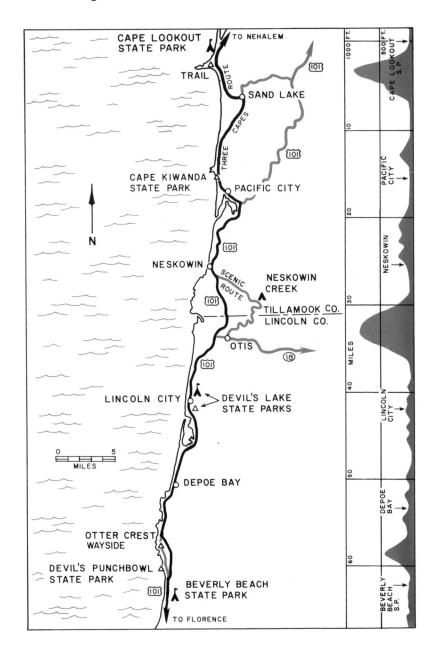

Plan an early start to allow extra time for a stop at Cape Kiwanda (the third cape on the Three Capes Scenic Route). The cape is a fascinating place; boats are launched directly into the surf, hang gliders take off from the sand dunes, and surfers challenge the waves. From the parking lot, a short walk over sand dunes leads to one of the greatest photography spots on the Oregon Coast.

After Cape Kiwanda, the road heads over several short hills before beginning the long, steep ascent of Cascade Head. You will return to the beach again at Lincoln City (a very congested area). The coast becomes wilder as you head south through Depoe Bay, a famous whale-watching area. The last major climb for the day is over Cape Foulweather. The top of the cape may be very windy, but the view is excellent.

The day ends at Beverly Beach State Park. The camp area is in the forest with access to a long, sandy beach. The best stores are located in Lincoln City.

Mileage Log

0.0 Heading south from Cape Lookout State Park on Three Capes Scenic Route, the day begins with a steep 2.7-mile climb over Cape Lookout.

1.1 Andersons Viewpoint. The turnout overlooks Netarts Spit and Bay.

2.7 Top of Cape Lookout (elevation 550 feet) and access to Cape Lookout Trail, a 5-mile round-trip hike through lush rain forest to a beautiful end-of-the-cape viewpoint. As the road heads down, watch for several sections of sunken road grade.

6.1 Junction. At the base of Cape Lookout, take the first right (south) to the community of Sand Lake, passing peaceful pastures, sleepy beach homes, and one small store. The lake is visible through the trees on the west side of the road. Beyond the intersection, the terrain varies from level to rolling. The road is narrow and traffic moderate, except on weekends when thousands of dune-buggy riders and tourists in huge vacation vehicles invade the area.

12.1 Unmarked junction. Stay right (west), paralleling the ocean.

13.6 Cape Kiwanda State Park: running water, restrooms, and beach access. Plan to stop here. The park is the scene of constant activity: dories launched directly into the surf from the beach, hang gliders, surfers, skim boarders, kayakers, sunbathers, children and adults sliding on sand dunes, cameras clicking and whirring. The famous photo spot can be reached by a short hike north. Climb a sand ridge to the viewing area. In fall and winter, people come from all over the world to photograph the waves as they crash against the sculptured cliffs. The summer visitor can enjoy a colorful display of layered sandstone as well as sliding on the steep sand dunes.

14.6 Intersection; the bike route turns left (east) and crosses the Nestucca

Waves breaking against the sandstone cliffs at Cape Kiwanda

River Bridge. **Side Trip** to Bob Straub State Park. Turn right at the intersection and pedal 0.5 mile south to a parking lot. Beach access.

14.7 Pacific City: several small stores. To continue, turn right (south) at the junction and follow the Nestucca River back to US 101. The road is rough and narrow.

15.6 Begin shoulder.

17.4 (mp 90.4) Return to US 101 and ride south. The traffic is heavy and the shoulders wide. After several level miles over open plain, the highway enters a small valley, climbs over a small headland, then returns to the coast. This is a very scenic but often windy area.

20.5 (mp 93.5) Oretown: no services.

21.6 (mp 94.6) Viewpoint.

24.4 (mp 97.4) Neskowin, a small town specializing in hotels and motels. A state park wayside gives access to a sandy beach.

25.9 (mp 98.9) The official Oregon Coast Bike Route turns left here and follows forest roads over Cascade Head. This is a delightful alternative route. However, the rarely used road is in poor condition.

26.1 (mp 99.1) US 101 begins to climb over Cascade Head. Shoulder narrows.

28.3 (mp 101.3) Forested summit of Cascade Head (elevation 704 feet).

30.0 (mp 103) Tillamook County–Lincoln County line.

32.0 (mp 105) Junction of State Route 18 and US 101. Use caution at the freeway-type intersections. Continuing south, the road is busy but has a good shoulder. Roadside development increases as you near Lincoln City. Mileposts make a mighty jump and resume some accuracy in town.

34.2 (mp 112) Cross the 45th parallel. You're halfway to the equator.

35.2 (mp 113) Enter Lincoln City, one of the chief tourist towns on the Oregon Coast. There are innumerable hotels, motels, restaurants, bakeries, curio shops, several state and beach parks, large supermarkets, and a bike shop. Traffic is heavy in the city area, and shoulders disappear in several sections of this very built-up, 5-mile-long strip.

35.9 (mp 113.7) Turnoff to Roads End Wayside State Park, accessed by a mile-long road that terminates in a steep descent to picnic tables and beach access. A large supermarket, located near the turnoff, offers a good opportunity to shop for the night.

37.9 (mp 114.7) Devil's Lake State Park campground, on the east side of US 101. The hiker-biker area is located on the left, just past the entrance booth, and is divided into two levels, forest and open grass.

38.1 (mp 114.9) "D" River Beach Wayside State Park, a popular area for kite flying. Restrooms and water. Take a quick look at "D" River, claimed to be the world's shortest.

38.8 (mp 115.5) Turnoff to Devil's Lake State Park picnic area. Picnic area, boat launch, restrooms, and water are located on Devil's Lake, 2 miles east of US 101.

41.8 (mp 118.5) Siletz Bay Park: picnic tables. This area is part of the Siletz Bay National Wildlife Estuary.

46.0 (mp 122.7) Turnoff to Gleneden Beach Wayside State Park. A 0.2-mile access road leads to picnic tables, restrooms, water, and a trail to a long, sandy beach. Several small markets are located along US 101 near the park turnoff.

47.3 (mp 124) Lincoln Beach.

47.8 (mp 124.5) Fogerty Beach State Park on left: picnic area, restrooms, water, and beach access. The park has two accesses off US 101, one on each side of a small creek. The two parking lots are joined by a paved path.

48.5 (mp 126.2) Boiler Bay Wayside State Park gets its name from the old ship's boiler that is visible at low tide. Restrooms, water, and picnic tables are available at this scenic overlook. This is a popular whale-watching area in season (see next mileage point).

49.6 (mp 127.3) Enter Depoe Bay, whose claim to fame is the world's smallest harbor. The bay is a popular whale-watching area from December through May. (Whales may occasionally be seen through the end of July.) Calm, cloudy days are the best for sighting whales.

52.0 (mp 129.5) Rocky Creek Wayside State Park, another popular whale-watching area: restrooms, water, picnic tables. Views from the park extend north over Whale Bay and south to Cape Foulweather.

52.2 (mp 129.7) Begin climb over Cape Foulweather. Shoulder is good in this section.

53.8 (mp 131.1) Turnoff to restaurant and gift shop located on the old road over Cape Foulweather. Hold on tight to bicycles; winds of up to 60 miles per hour are common.

54.0 (mp 131.4) Otter Crest Viewpoint. If you skipped the last turnoff, stop here and check out the view.

55.6 (mp 133) *Side Trip* to Devil's Punchbowl State Park and Marine Gardens. Go right on the 0.6-mile access road to a natural punchbowl that churns best at high tide, and a beach where shellfish gathering is prohibited to preserve the ecosystem.

57.5 (mp 135.1) Beverly Beach State Park campground, located on the left (east) side of US 101. The campground has a hiker-biker camp (located on the hillside beyond the group area), yurts, hot showers, and access to long, sandy Beverly Beach. Some groceries may be purchased near the park entrance. If you are looking for something to do at the end of the day, consider a ride to Yaquina Lighthouse. See the next section for details.

Beverly Beach State Park to Jessie M. Honeyman Memorial State Park (60.3 Miles)

With so much to see in the next 60.3 miles, expect travel time to be long and distances between stops very short. The first stop, Yaquina Lighthouse National Wildlife Refuge, lies just 3.5 miles south of Beverly Beach State Park. The obvious attraction here is the tall, white lookout tower on the windswept point, visible for miles up and down the coast. However, the real attention getters are the birds, nesting on rocky offshore islands clearly visible from a viewing platform at the lighthouse. Check out the visitor center, the tide pools of Lower Quarry Beach, then watch the surfers (long boarders mostly) take in the low, lazy waves. Avoid the temptation to linger; many other distractions lie ahead.

In Newport, the route leaves US 101 and heads through scenic residential streets along the coast to avoid downtown congestion and endless stoplights. The route returns to US 101 in time for a side trip to the Newport Marina, home of *Free Willy*, as well as the Oregon State University's Henry O. Hatfield Marine Science Center. The science center features fascinating interactive learning displays, and specializes in the economical and environmental aspects of the ocean. From sound waves to natural disasters to a computer game that sends you deep-sea fishing for a season, this is an extremely educational facility.

At Sea Gulch, stop and gawk at the world's largest collection of chainsaw woodcarvings. Artists often work along the side of the road. Their delicate expertise with a chainsaw is amazing to watch.

Among the many parks and waysides along the route, Cape Perpetua is the most popular. Trails lead to the Devil's Churn, tide pools, an old Indian camping ground, and a panoramic viewpoint. The visitor center offers displays and a movie on the area's history. A steep, 1.5-mile side road beckons cyclists up to one of the best views on the coast.

Sea lions are common along the coast but not always easy to spot. However, south of Cape Perpetua, at Strawberry Hill turnout, you have an excellent chance seeing these mammals take their daily sunbath on rocks just 100 feet offshore.

Farther south, the route passes Devil's Elbow State Park, location of the much-photographed Heceta Head Lighthouse. The park is near the Sea Lion Caves, a popular private enterprise where, for a price, you can ride an elevator down the cliffs to a colony of sea lions.

Yaquina Head Lighthouse

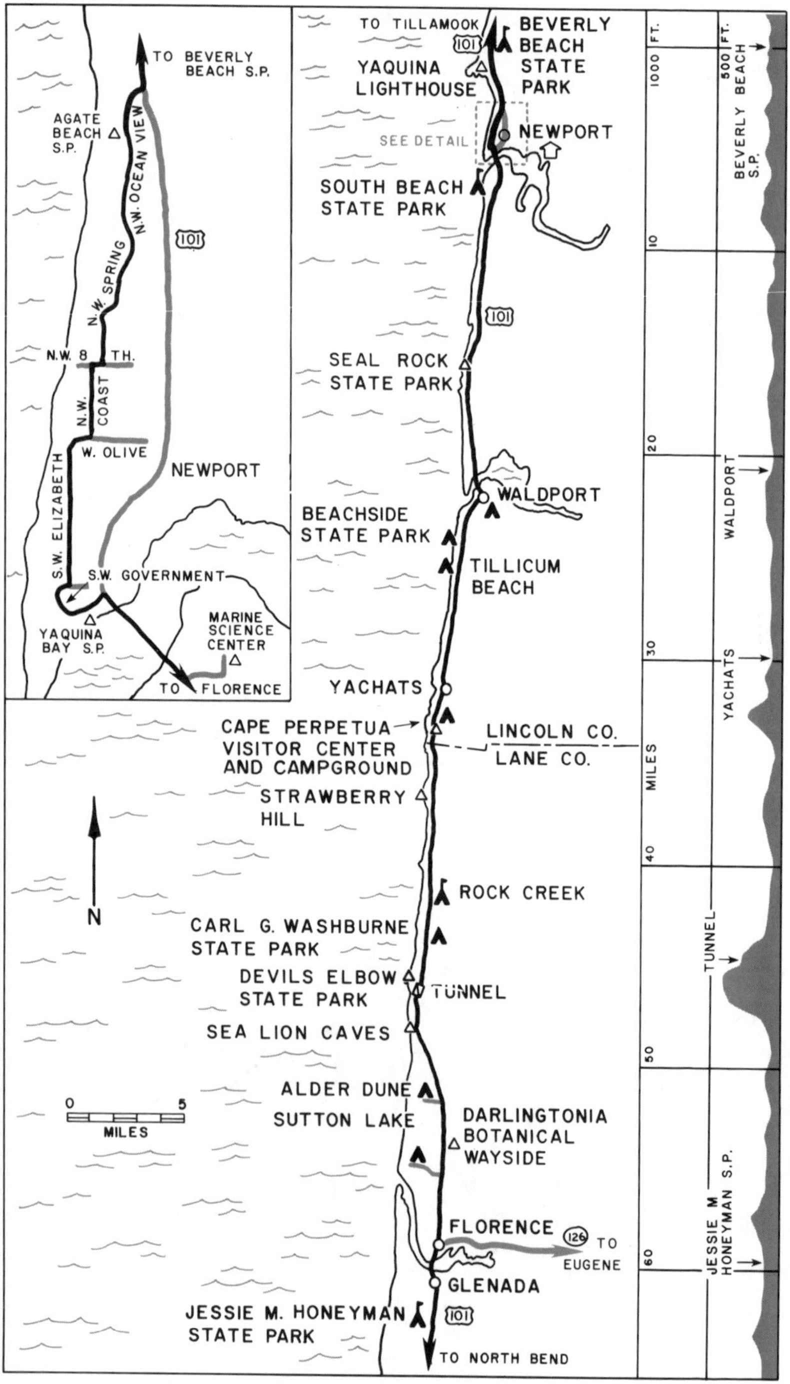

Detail map (inset, upper left):

TO BEVERLY BEACH S.P.

AGATE BEACH S.P.

N.W. OCEAN VIEW

N.W. SPRING

101

N.W. 8TH.

N.W. COAST

W. OLIVE

NEWPORT

S.W. ELIZABETH

S.W. GOVERNMENT

YAQUINA BAY S.P.

MARINE SCIENCE CENTER

TO FLORENCE

Main map:

TO TILLAMOOK

101

BEVERLY BEACH STATE PARK

YAQUINA LIGHTHOUSE

SEE DETAIL

NEWPORT

SOUTH BEACH STATE PARK

101

SEAL ROCK STATE PARK

WALDPORT

BEACHSIDE STATE PARK

TILLICUM BEACH

YACHATS

CAPE PERPETUA VISITOR CENTER AND CAMPGROUND

LINCOLN CO.
LANE CO.

STRAWBERRY HILL

ROCK CREEK

CARL G. WASHBURNE STATE PARK

DEVILS ELBOW STATE PARK

TUNNEL

SEA LION CAVES

ALDER DUNE

SUTTON LAKE

DARLINGTONIA BOTANICAL WAYSIDE

FLORENCE

126 TO EUGENE

GLENADA

JESSIE M. HONEYMAN STATE PARK

101

TO NORTH BEND

N

0   5
MILES

Right-side elevation profile:

1000 FT.

500 FT.

BEVERLY BEACH S.P.

10

20

WALDPORT

30

YACHATS

MILES

40

TUNNEL

50

JESSIE M HONEYMAN S.P.

60

Probably the most amazing sight on the entire coast is seen at the Darlingtonia Botanical Wayside, home of a group of very pretty and very carnivorous California pitcher plants.

The day's ride ends just south of Florence at Jessie M. Honeyman Memorial State Park. This park is located several miles inland from the ocean, separated from the beach by a broad expanse of sand dunes. In recognition of its uniqueness, the area has been designated as the Oregon Dunes National Recreation Area. Despite the large amount of motorized use on the dunes, this is a great place to spend an evening. The top of Honeyman Dune is an ideal location for watching the sunset, and an even better location to forget about the sunset and spend an hour sliding and climbing on the sand.

This section of the coast includes some of the best scenery and some of the narrowest sections of US 101. The shoulder disappears in the Cape Perpetua and Devil's Elbow areas. Southbound travelers also meet the challenge of the second and last tunnel on the Pacific Coast Bicycle Route.

Mileage Log

0.0 (mp 134.3) South of Beverly Beach State Park, US 101 parallels the ocean. A wide shoulder provides a comfortable buffer from the traffic. Yaquina Head Lighthouse is visible ahead. Moolack Beach parking area provides access to the beach.

2.5 (mp 136.8) Newport city limits: bike shop, supermarkets, restaurants, motels, youth hostel.

3.5 (mp 137.8) *Side Trip* to Yaquina Head Lighthouse. The access road is 1.5 miles long and a fee must be paid at the entrance station before proceeding to the visitor center, lighthouse, and beaches. At the lighthouse, walk to the viewing platform to look for cormorants, common murres, tufted puffins, and gulls nesting on the offshore islands. Whales are occasionally spotted in the bay below. A road descends to the shore where tide pools may be explored, and sea lions sunbathe on the rocks. Restrooms are available. The lighthouse is open for limited hours during the summer.

3.6 (mp 137.9) Pass parking for Agate Beach Wayside on right.

4.1 (mp 138.3) Start Newport bypass by exiting US 101 at Ocean Bay Dr. Cyclists looking for supermarkets or the bike shop must leave the posted bike route and brave the endless stoplights of the city.

5.6 N.W. Ocean View Dr. becomes N.W. Spring St. in a quiet residential neighborhood.

5.9 N.W. Spring St. ends; turn right (west) on N.W. 8th St.

6.0 N.W. 8th St. ends; turn left (south) on N.W. Coast St.

6.4 Turn right (west) on W. Olive St. which, in a few blocks, becomes S.W. Elizabeth St. Head south past summer houses, motels, and small shops. The City of Newport has built a small park along the headland overlooking the beach. Best feature of the Donald A. Davis Park is the small gazebo where you can temporarily escape the rain when needed.

7.3 When S.W. Elizabeth St. ends, turn right (west) on S.W. Government St. and follow it into Yaquina Bay State Park: restrooms, water, picnic tables, beach access, and a haunted lighthouse that may be toured for a small fee from May through September, 11:00 A.M. to 5:00 P.M. daily. Follow the road as it loops through the park, then returns to US 101.

7.8 (mp 141.4) Back on US 101, head south across the 0.5-mile-long Newport Bridge. Use the sidewalk when bridge traffic is heavy.

8.5 (mp 142.1) *Side Trip* to Newport Marina and the Marine Science Center. Take the first right (west) off US 101 after crossing the bridge. Northbound riders also exit right (east). Follow signs 1 mile to the huge marina parking lot (fee charged) then on to the science center (donations gratefully accepted); open daily 10:00 A.M. to 6:00 P.M. during the summer, and 10:00 A.M. to 4:00 P.M. the rest of the year.

9.7 (mp 143.3) South Beach State Park: hiker-biker sites, yurts, hot showers, beach access, ¾-mile self-guiding nature trail, hiking trail, and horse rentals.

13.5 (mp 147.1) Lost Creek State Park: picnicking and access to a sandy beach.

15.3 (mp 149.0) Ona Beach State Park: restrooms, water, and beach access. Stop and enjoy a shady picnic on a grassy lawn. Beyond the park, US 101 runs along the coast with glimpses of sandy beaches. Shoulder width is moderate.

16.6 (mp 150.3) Sea Gulch, the chainsaw art center, is on the east side of the highway.

17.0 (mp 150.7) Seal Rock State Park: restrooms, water, and beach access. Walk to the cliff's edge and watch the surf pound against a giant rib of rock. Despite the name, seals are rarely spotted.

19.2 (mp 152.9) Driftwood State Park: restrooms, water, picnicking, and a beach access.

21.0 (mp 154.7) Alsea Bay North Wayside, an off-the-road viewpoint of the bridge.

21.5 (mp 155.2) Enter Waldport at the southern end of a 0.5-mile-long bridge with a good shoulder. The town offers grocery stores, tourist facilities, and a private campground.

23.4 (mp 157.1) Governor I. L. Patterson State Park: restrooms, water, and a sandy beach.

25.3 (mp 159.0) Beachside State Park: a small campground with a hiker-biker camp, showers, and easy access to sandy beaches.

26.6 (mp 160.3) Tillicum Beach Campground, operated by the U.S. Forest Service. No hiker-biker site.

29.6 (mp 163.4) Enter Yachats. Every year in early July, the world's largest smelt fish fry is held here—perfect for hungry cyclists. Much of the smelt fishing takes place in the center of town at Yachats State Park. If you miss the fish fry, there are grocery stores nearby.

29.7 (mp 163.5) Smelt Sands State Park, as the name suggests, is a popular smelt-fishing area. The fishing is exciting to watch in the early months of summer.

30.9 (mp 164.7) Yachats Oceanic Wayside, a favorite beach spot for the locals: restrooms and running water. Some of the Oregon Coast's most spectacular scenery and steepest hills lie just ahead. Shift to low gear and pedal slowly to enjoy every possible view. The next 20 miles are the windiest on the coast; expect gusts up to 60 or more miles per hour. The shoulder width is narrow to nonexistent for southbound riders, and even less for northbound riders.

32.5 (mp 166.3) Cape Perpetua.

33.0 (mp 166.8) Devil's Churn Wayside. At high tide, rushing waves are forced into a narrow channel, where they churn into a white foam.

33.1 (mp 167.0) Cape Perpetua Campground and *Side Trip* to Cape Perpetua Viewpoint. This forest service campground has restrooms, running water, and walk-in campsites, as well as trails to the viewpoint, visitor center, and beach. The side trip to Cape Perpetua Viewpoint involves a very steep, 1.8-mile ride to the top of the cape, where you are treated to a spectacular panoramic view over 150 miles of coast. The viewpoint may also be reached by a hiking trail from the campground or visitor center. (If you don't wish to tackle the steep viewpoint road, check out the photographs at the visitor center.)

33.4 (mp 167.3) Cape Perpetua Visitor Center, open 9:00 A.M. to 5:00 P.M. daily, has restrooms and running water. The visitor center has many displays, including a 15-minute movie explaining the area's natural history. Trails lead to viewpoints and tide pools.

33.7 (mp 167.6) Leave Lincoln County, enter Lane County, and pass another nameless wayside.

34.5 (mp 168.4) Neptune State Park: restrooms, water, and picnic tables.

35.3 (mp 169.2) Strawberry Hill turnout. View sea lions and harbor seals on rocks just a few feet offshore.

35.9 (mp 169.8) Bob Creek Wayside: beach access.

37.0 (mp 170.5) Commercial campground and small market.

37.5 (mp 171.0) Stonefield Beach Wayside: picnic area and beach access. As the name implies, an intriguing stone-covered beach.

39.4 (mp 172.9) This is the halfway point between Washington and California.

40.1 (mp 173.6) Ocean Beach Picnic Area: picnic tables, beach access. No bathrooms.

40.5 (mp 174.1) Rock Creek Campground, a forest service facility open summer months only. Exit left (east) to reach the hiker-biker area. No hot showers.

41.6 (mp 175.2) Muriel O. Ponsler State Park, another scenic wayside with beach access.

42.3 (mp 175.9) Carl G. Washburne State Park. Exit left (east) off US 101 for camping with hiker-biker sites and hot showers.

44.5 (mp 178.1) Devil's Elbow State Park: picnicking, restrooms, water, and beach access. Descend a short, steep road to the park, then walk the scenic path to the much-photographed Heceta Head Lighthouse.

44.6 (mp 178.2) A short, shoulderless, uphill bridge with no sidewalk.

44.7 (mp 178.3) Enter Cape Creek Tunnel, the second and last tunnel on the Coast Route. The tunnel has an uphill grade, so strap on a bicycle light and activate the warning signal before entering. After the tunnel, the highway narrows, climbing steeply over a barren, windswept headland. Shoulder is narrow on the southbound side and nonexistent northbound. Check out the scenic turnouts with views of Heceta Head Lighthouse.

45.6 (mp 179.3) Sea Lion Caves. Admission fee covers the cost of an elevator ride down to a large cave inhabited by a colony of sea lions. Beyond the caves, the road winds over a second headland, then glides downhill for several miles with sweeping views over the coast.

50.1 (mp 183.5) Alder Dune Campground, a forest service area with restrooms and water but no hiker-biker sites.

51.8 (mp 185.2) Darlingtonia Botanical Wayside: picnic tables, restrooms, and water. Approximately 100 yards to the left (east) off US 101, a short path leads to a small marsh, where the rare and unusual California pitcher plants (*Darlingtonia californica*) flourish. These carnivorous plants thrive in nutrient-deficient soil by devouring insects. US 101 now widens to include a comfortable bike lane.

52.0 (mp 185.4) Sutton Lake Campground, a forest service facility with restrooms and water but no hiker-biker sites.

54.2 (mp 187.6) Florence. Supermarkets large enough to feed the hungriest of cyclists are located here, as well as a bike shop for those in need of repairs. Expect considerable traffic.

56.8 (mp 190.2) Junction of US 101 and State Route 126 (to Eugene and points far east). Continue straight on US 101.

57.8 (mp 191.2) Bridge with a slippery steel-grate decking. Cyclists are advised to use the sidewalk.

58.0 (mp 191.3) Glenada. This is your last chance to purchase groceries before Jessie M. Honeyman Memorial State Park.

60.3 (mp 193.7) Jessie M. Honeyman Memorial State Park: hot showers, hiker-biker camp, a small lake for swimming, a small store and restaurant, boat rentals, and access to the sand dunes. Try trail opposite site 11 in Loop I for easy access to Honeyman Dune.

Sand dunes at Jessie M. Honeyman Memorial State Park

Jessie M. Honeyman Memorial State Park to Sunset Bay State Park (54.9 Miles)

Miles of soft sand contoured by the wind and accented with ripple marks border the road from Florence to North Bend. Lie on it, walk through it, run over it, or slide down it; no matter how, take time to get to know this beautiful sea of sand known as the Oregon Dunes National Recreation Area. Very little of this fascinating area can be viewed from US 101, so plan one or more short side trips. For cyclists, the most convenient dune accesses and viewpoints are at Jessie M. Honeyman Memorial State Park and the Oregon Dunes Overlook. For a greater wilderness feel, try one of the short trails from Carter Lake, Tahkenitch, or Eel Creek Campgrounds. These trails are particularly attractive in May and June, when the native rhododendrons are in bloom.

After sticking with US 101 for the first 20 miles of the day's ride, get set for a brief tour of Winchester Bay, where back roads lead you past a

Sunset Bay

busy marina, Umpqua Lighthouse, a state park campground, and picnic area. The bicycle route leaves US 101 for a second time at North Bend for a tour of Coos Bay and Charleston, then ends the day at Cape Arago.

Cape Arago is magnificent. This unique area has three state parks along a 2.5-mile section of road. The first is Sunset Bay Campground, located on a broad bay with a narrow neck. The second park is Shore Acres Botanical Gardens, formerly a lumber baron's estate. The formal gardens, set on the lip of sculptured sandstone cliffs, are still beautifully maintained. The third park is Cape Arago, a picnic area next to knife-edged Simpson Reef. Background music for picnickers is provided by a noisy colony of sea lions living on the rocks. Trails from the park lead to nearby beaches and coves.

Mileage Log

0.0 (mp 193.7) From Jessie M. Honeyman Memorial State Park, follow US 101 south through forested countryside. Shoulder varies in width from 2 to 3 feet.

1.0 (mp 194.6) Dune City. Rent your dune buggy here.

3.4 (mp 196.9) Tyee Campground, a forest service area with restrooms and running water but no special hiker-biker facilities.

4.6 (mp 198.2) Turnoff to Siltcoos Dunes and Beach, a popular dune-buggy area. The Siltcoos Dune Rd. passes two forest service campgrounds and a trail to the beach, 2 miles west of US 101. (A trailhead parking fee is charged.)

5.1 (mp 198.7) Carter Lake Campground, a forest service area situated next to a deep-blue lake. A trail leads through the dunes to the beach. A trailhead fee is charged.

5.5 (mp 199.1) East Carter Lake Campground, another forest service area.

7.3 (mp 200.9) *Side Trip* to Oregon Dunes Overlook. A 0.3-mile road leads to a viewpoint overlooking the dunes, berm, and ocean. If time for dune exploration is limited, this is a choice spot. Just a few feet from the overlook, you can take off your shoes and run your toes through the sand. If you have time, hike a trail through the dunes to the ocean, or walk the entire 4-mile loop. The overlook has restrooms, water, and picnic tables.

8.9 (mp 202.5) Tahkenitch Creek Trail. A trailhead fee is charged to explore this interesting area.

10.0 (mp 203.6) Tahkenitch Campground, a forest service area with a 1-mile trail through rhododendron forest to the dunes. A trailhead fee is charged for parking.

14.8 (mp 208.4) Gardiner, a small town with a grocery store and large paper mill. The terrain levels as US 101 curves inland around Winchester Bay, a popular clam-digging area.

16.6 (mp 210.2) Smith River is crossed on a narrow bridge. Cyclists choose between a narrow sidewalk or a narrower shoulder.

17.4 (mp 210.9) Historical marker dedicated to Jedediah Smith.

17.5 (mp 211) Umpqua River Bridge. Cyclists may use the sidewalk for the 0.3-mile ride into Reedsport.

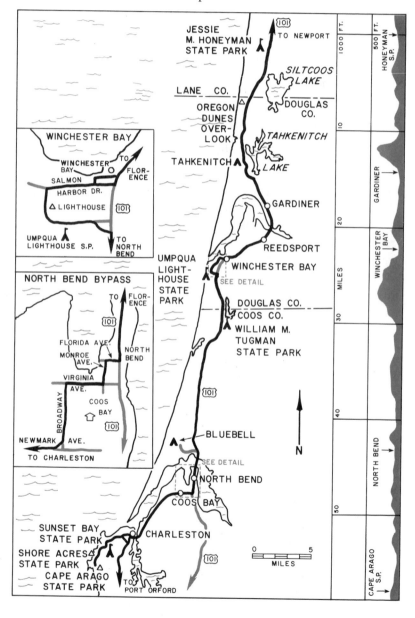

17.8 (mp 211.3) Reedsport: grocery stores, and headquarters of the Oregon Dunes National Recreation Area. Displays of dune formation and habitat are located on the right-hand side of the highway at the first stoplight after the Umpqua River Bridge. US 101 goes straight through the center of this small, congested town. No shoulders.

Beyond Reedsport, the road climbs a forested hill, then sweeps down to the town of Winchester Bay. Shoulder width varies from 2 to 8 feet.

22.3 (mp 215.8) Winchester Bay: small grocery store. Start Winchester Bay Scenic Tour. Take the second right (west) off US 101 and cycle the level, shoulderless road past the marina and Windy Cove County Park campground. The park has a nice tent area.

23.2 Take the first left (south) off Salmon Harbor Dr. and head uphill toward Umpqua Lighthouse State Park, passing the historic Umpqua Lighthouse and a coast guard museum. Near the lighthouse is a view over the breakwater and harbor entrance. Note how the surf is higher in the harbor entrance than on the surrounding beaches.

24.3 Umpqua Lighthouse State Park campground: hiker-biker area, hot showers, a small lake for swimming, beach access, and picnic area.

24.6 Beyond the park, the road heads up steeply to an intersection. Take the right (uphill) fork.

24.8 (mp 217) Return to US 101. The road climbs to the top of a forested hill, then cruises past Clear Lake.

25.0 (mp 217.2) Viewpoint of lighthouse and jetty.

29.0 (mp 221.2) Leave Douglas County and enter Coos County.

29.3 (mp 221.5) Pass William M. Tugman State Park campground on the left (east) side of US 101. Hiker-biker camp, located to the left of the entrance booth, has hot showers, lakeside picnicking, and swimming. Nearby food supplies are very limited.

29.5 (mp 221.7) Lakeside, a small tourist town with a small grocery store and commercial campground.

30.3 (mp 222.5) Eel Creek Campground, a forest service area with restrooms, running water, and trail through the dunes to the beach. Fee charged for parking. Beyond the campground, US 101 runs past a series of small lakes captured between large, forest-covered sand dunes. The road levels at about milepost 230 and swings inland around Coos Bay, where large mud flats attract hundreds of clam diggers.

30.5 (mp 222.7) Umpqua Dunes Trailhead: parking fee charged.

32.4 (mp 224.6) Spinreel Campground, a forest service area with running water and restrooms.

40.9 (mp 233) *Side Trip* to Horsfall Dunes, the southern end of the Oregon Dunes National Recreation Area. It's a 2-mile side trip to the forest service's Bluebell Campground, and 3 miles to a long, sandy beach. This scenic area is very popular for dune-buggy riding.

41.5 (mp 233.6) Coos Bay Bridge. Ride with caution: the bridge is narrow, traffic is heavy, vehicles are large, and crosswinds are often fierce. An ordinance makes it illegal to hold up traffic as you cross the bridge. This law is obviously aimed at getting cyclists up onto the narrow sidewalk. When crosswinds are strong, consider walking.

42.1 (mp 234.2) Enter North Bend.

42.5 (mp 234.6) South end of Coos Bay Bridge. No shoulder here, so ride with caution. Several lumber mills offer tours during the summer months in North Bend and its sister city, Coos Bay. Amenities include bike shops and supermarkets.

42.9 (mp 235.0) Tourist information, Pioneer Museum, old train engine, and a city park lie on the right (west) side of US 101. Running water and restrooms.

43.4 (mp 235.5) Turn right (west) off US 101 at Florida Ave. Cycle 1 block uphill, halfway around a large traffic circle, then continue down Florida Ave.

Cape Arago Lighthouse

43.6 Turn left on Monroe Ave.

43.7 Go right on Virginia Ave., a broad road without a shoulder. Watch for road signs to Charleston and state parks. Several large grocery stores are passed.

44.3 Turn left (south) on Broadway for 0.9 mile.

45.2 Go right (west), up a freeway-type ramp to Newmark Ave. A bike lane starts in 0.5 mile when the road enters the town of Coos Bay.

47.0 At the end of Newmark Ave., turn left (south) on Empire and follow it to Charleston. Bike lane is good in this section.

51.9 Cross South Slough on a wide bridge.

52.2 Charleston: two small grocery stores, the last until Bandon, 20 miles south.

52.4 Leaving Charleston, the road climbs a short, steep hill to an intersection. Stay right for Sunset Beach. The left fork climbs steeply up toward Seven Devils and Bandon. (You will return to this intersection in the next section.)

53.8 Turnoff to Bastendorf County Park: campsites, hot showers, and beach access.

54.6 The bike lane ends and road narrows; travel with caution.

54.9 Sunset Bay State Park: campground, hiker-biker sites, hot showers, hiking trails, picnicking, and swimming next to a bay that is almost enclosed by rock walls. This is also the starting point for the *Side Trip* to the tip of Cape Arago. Set up camp, then continue on along the narrow road for 1.1 miles to reach Shore Acres State Park, with its scenic overlooks, botanical gardens, picnicking, running water, and restrooms. Then ride on for another mile to Simpson Reef Viewpoint, where sea lions are often spotted sunning on the rocks. In 1997 the road was gated and the last 0.4 mile to Cape Arago State Park had to be walked, or ridden, due to a slide. At the end of the road are picnic tables and a trail to the beach.

Sunset Bay State Park to Humbug Mountain State Park (57 Miles)

Leaving Sunset Bay State Park, the route heads away from the rugged coast and climbs to the ridgetops to catch sweeping views of Oregon's coastal forest and South Slough Estuary. The tranquility of the ridgecrest is followed by a screaming descent back to sea level, where the route returns to US 101 after 18.9 peaceful miles—but not for long.

The bike route sticks with US 101 for just 2.7 miles before heading off again, this time for a tour along a spectacular section of sea stack-dotted coast at Bandon. Overlooks, state parks, and numerous access points to this unusual beach tempt riders to abandon their journey and explore.

Beyond Bandon, the bike route returns to US 101 and follows it over rolling, grassy hills, miles inland from the coast. This is prime rangeland for cows, horses, sheep, goats, and even llamas. It's also excellent riding country, and miles fly by without the distraction of waysides and scenic overlooks.

Humbug Mountain State Park, the day's destination, has a treat for saddle-sore cyclists: a 2½-mile hiking trail up Humbug Mountain. The trail is an excellent afternoon walk and the destination is a high vantage point with views south along the coast. Or you may walk north from the park on an abandoned portion of the Old Coast Highway. The road climbs up a small hill to a viewpoint of the coast and US 101, a great place to watch the sunset.

If you have any spare time during the day, consider a stop at Bullards Beach State Park, a tour of the old town of Bandon, or a visit to the cheese factory. The state park features a lighthouse and museum located on a long, sandy spit at the mouth of the Coquille River, and excellent views of Bandon and the fishing marina. The old section of Bandon has a delightful selection of shops designed to please a starving cyclist, such as a bakery, fudge factory, and restaurants. The cheese factory, the Coquille Valley Dairy Coop, is located on the north end of Bandon at 680 US 101 (2 blocks north of the old town), and is open to visitors from 8:00 A.M. to 5:00 P.M., Monday through Friday.

If you have lots of extra energy, take a side trip (5 miles each way) out to Cape Blanco State Park, a lighthouse, and 100-year-old Hughes House (open Thursday through Monday, May through September). The cape is such a beautiful, secluded area that once there, you may be tempted to stay.

Mileage Log

0.0 Leaving Sunset Bay State Park, ride back toward Charleston.

2.5 At the intersection just above Charleston, turn right (east) on Seven Devils Rd. (County Road 208). The road is steep for the first mile, steeper than most in Oregon, after which it levels off on a rolling ridgetop.

7.5 South Slough National Estuarine Reserve: interpretive center, views, nature trail, estuary trail, restrooms, and water. The South Slough cannot be properly explored without spending time hiking or boating the area; however, if your exposure to sloughs and estuaries has been slim or nonexistent the displays here illustrate the ecology and history.

13.3 Junction with unnamed road signed to Whisky Run Beach and Seven Devils Wayside. Turn right (west) and begin an exhilarating descent.

16.1 Junction with County Rd. 33A. The bike route turns left (south) heading back to US 101. *Side Trip.* To the right (north) County Road 33A descends 2 miles to Seven Devils Wayside: restrooms,

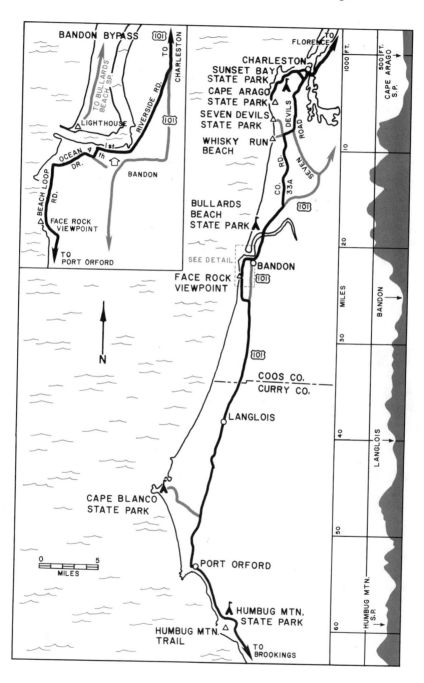

BANDON BYPASS

TO BULLARDS BEACH S.P.

TO CHARLESTON

RIVERSIDE RD.

101

LIGHTHOUSE

OCEAN DR.

1st.

4th

BANDON

BEACH LOOP RD.

FACE ROCK VIEWPOINT

TO PORT ORFORD

SEE DETAIL

TO FLORENCE

CHARLESTON

SUNSET BAY STATE PARK

CAPE ARAGO STATE PARK

SEVEN DEVILS STATE PARK

WHISKY RUN BEACH

CO. RD. 33A

SEVEN DEVILS ROAD

BULLARDS BEACH STATE PARK

101

BANDON

FACE ROCK VIEWPOINT

101

COOS CO.
CURRY CO.

LANGLOIS

CAPE BLANCO STATE PARK

PORT ORFORD

HUMBUG MTN. STATE PARK

HUMBUG MTN. TRAIL

TO BROOKINGS

N

0   5
MILES

1000 FT.

500 FT.

CAPE ARAGO S.P.

10

20

MILES

BANDON

30

40

LANGLOIS

50

HUMBUG MTN. S.P.

60

running water, picnic tables, and a long, lonely beach. *Side Trip.* Straight ahead (west), an unnamed road descends 1 mile to Whisky Run Beach: no facilities, just a sandy beach for strolling and beach-combing and views of huge wind turbines perched on a hill above. Just before the beach, a narrow dirt road branches off on the right, leading ¼ mile to a small interpretive center and viewpoint. (Unless you have a mountain bike, it's best to skip the interpretive center.)

18.9 (mp 257.4) Junction of County Road 33A and US 101. Turn right (south) on US 101 and start a long glide to Bandon. Shoulders are wide, making the brisk ride enjoyable.

20.8 (mp 259.3) Bullards Beach State Park: hiker-biker area, yurts, hot showers, 1½-mile hiking trail, beach access, and lighthouse with a museum featuring pictures of local shipwrecks (open summer months only). The nearest grocery stores are 1 mile south, off the main route, on US 101.

20.9 (mp 259.4) Narrow, shoulderless bridge over the Coquille River.

21.5 (mp 260.1) Start Bandon scenic route. Turn right (west) off US 101 on Riverside Rd.

22.1 Enter Bandon.

23.0 Turn right (west) on 1st St. and cycle past the marina. Views extend

Fishermen at Bullards Beach State Park

across the Coquille River to the lighthouse at Bullards Beach State Park. For grocery stores or a visit to the cheese factory, ride to the marina then return to US 101 and go left (north). Sea Star Traveler's Hostel is located on 2nd St., just off US 101.

23.5 After passing several factories, 1st St. bends left (south) and becomes Edison Rd., then climbs steeply for 1 block.

23.8 Turn right (west) on 4th St. S.W. and ride through a quiet residential area. Before long 4th St. becomes Ocean Dr., and soon after becomes 743rd. After a few more blocks the road bends left and becomes Beach Loop.

24.4 Coquille Point: viewpoint, nature trail, and beach access. Go left off Beach Loop to the large parking area with a view of the sea-stack studded bay. This is a bird-watching area, one of the most popular varieties for the layman being the tufted puffin.

25.2 Face Rock Viewpoint: restrooms and running water. Large sea stacks decorate the beach below. A trail descends to the beach, inviting exploration of these gigantic monoliths.

26.8 State park beach access: picnic tables and ocean view.

27.3 State park beach access: picnic tables and running water.

27.5 State park picnic area: no running water.

28.4 (mp 277.6) Junction of Beach Loop and US 101. Turn right (south), leaving the coast behind and exchanging the smell of salt for the scent of pine and grass. The shoulder is narrow but adequate.

31.1 (mp 280.3) Laurel Market is passed on the left.

36.6 (mp 285.8) Leave Coos County and enter Curry County.

38.7 (mp 287.9) Langlois: a small market and art shops.

39.2 (mp 288.4) Turnoff to Floras Lake County Park. Ignore bike route signs to the park, which is many miles off the main road.

40.2 (mp 290.2) Denmark: commercial campground but no other facilities.

40.5 (mp 290.5) Second turnoff to Floras Lake and Boice Cope Park: restrooms, picnic tables, and lake access.

46.4 (mp 296.4) *Side Trip* to Cape Blanco State Park, lighthouse, and Hughes House. The park is 5 miles west of US 101 on a steep, narrow, rough road. The motorhome-oriented campground, situated on a bluff above Cape Blanco Lighthouse, has hot showers as well as a hiker-biker area. Because of the park's isolation, buy food in Langlois or Port Orford. A small market at Sixes, 0.3 mile before the turnoff, can supply the basics when open.

49.7 (mp 299.7) Port Orford: last stores before Humbug Mountain State Park.

51.3 (mp 301.3) Battle Rock Historical Wayside: restrooms, ocean views, beach access, and picnicking. An information board explains the history of the area. Heading south, the road is carved along the steep hillside. Shoulder width varies radically with the condition of the road. Watch for sunken grades and nonexistent shoulders.

57.0 (mp 307) Turn left to Humbug Mountain State Park; hiker-biker sites, hot showers, hiking trails, and beach access. (The hiker-biker site is in the forest. It is very cool and full of bugs. If the park is not already full, you may want to join up with other bicyclists and share a regular campsite.) The trail up Humbug Mountain starts from the southwest corner of the park in the lower camping loop. The Old Coast Highway Trail starts to the right of the pay booth.

Humbug Mountain State Park to the California Border (56.2 Miles)

Saving the best for last, the Oregon Coast section of your tour ends with breathtaking scenery: long, sandy beaches, rocks carved into graceful arches, jagged sea stacks, and sheer cliffs. US 101 is etched on hillsides that drop nearly straight to the ocean. These wind-blasted hillsides are dotted with viewpoints, parks, and beach accesses. Highly recommended stops are Arch Rock, Thunder Rock Cove, Natural Bridge Cove, Whalehead Beach, and Harris Beach State Park. In late spring and early summer, flower-lovers should not miss Azalea State Park in Brookings.

The ride is relatively easy, with only one steep climb. You'll have more trouble with the level areas, which tend to be windy in the afternoons. Early morning starts are recommended to avoid the winds, logging trucks, and tourist traffic.

There is only one (short) opportunity to escape the noise of US 101 on this ride. This not-to-be-missed escape is on a section of the Old Coast Highway where the narrow and rarely used road winds along the coast through pastures and a small beach community.

Brookings, 6 miles north of the California border, is the logical endpoint for Oregon Coast bicycle tours. The chief source of transportation out of town is the Greyhound bus. All bicycles must be boxed for shipping.

Cyclists continuing south into California will find Harris Beach State Park a convenient and beautiful spot for an overnight stop. The next campground lies 27 miles south of the California border.

Mileage Log

0.0 (mp 307) From Humbug Mountain State Park, return to US 101. The road is narrow as it snakes its way over a shoulder of Humbug Mountain. Watch for rocks on the road.

0.7 (mp 307.7) Humbug Mountain State Park picnic area: restrooms, tables, and running water.

Harris Beach

3.0 (mp 310) US 101 turns toward the ocean, with views of the broken coastline. Humbug Mountain dominates the northern horizon.

4.7 (mp 311.7) Shoulder disappears, marking the start of a slide area. For the next 5 miles the road is rough and, depending on how the repair crew is doing, the shoulder may appear and disappear several times.

6.2 (mp 313.2) Dinosaurs leer at travelers from the side of the road, heralding a commercial campground and the Prehistoric Gardens. Admission is charged.

12.1 (mp 319.1) Ophir Rest Area: beach access, restrooms, and running water.

15.2 (mp 322.3) Geisel Monument State Park: a small wayside built to commemorate the burial site of the Geisel family, four of whom were killed by natives.

17.1 (mp 324.1) Watch closely, or you may miss the start of the escape

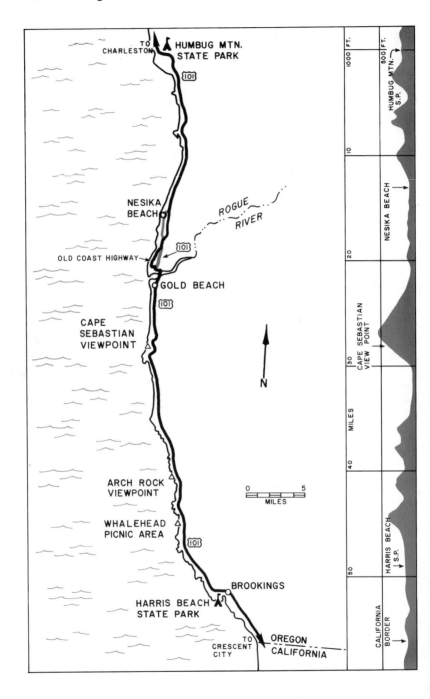

from US 101. Turn right (west) on Old Coast Highway. The road is narrow, little-used and very scenic. Pass several beach access trails and cross two cattle guards. Imagine what it was like when this was the main route along the coast.

17.3 Otter Point State Park. A 0.2-mile descent on a dirt road leads to beautiful beach with Coast Trail access.

19.0 The road improves.

19.8 (mp 326.3) Return to US 101 at the small community of Agate Beach.

21.0 (mp 327.5) Cross the Rogue River on a shoulderless bridge. Cyclists may use the narrow sidewalk.

21.3 (mp 327.8) Gold Beach, best known as the starting point for tours of the Rogue River. Billboards advertising jet-boat rides assault the senses as you approach town. Other features include an attractive boat harbor, a large grocery store at the south end of town, and the Curry County Museum featuring local history. Beyond Gold Beach, US 101 starts its climb over Cape Sebastian. This is a slide area, and shoulder width varies from comfortable to nonexistent. Northbound travelers have even less shoulder.

US 101 at Pistol River State Park

27.4 (mp 333.9) Summit of Cape Sebastian (elevation 712 feet).

28.6 (mp 335.1) Cape Sebastian Historical Marker describes the origin of the name.

28.7 (mp 335.2) Turnoff to Cape Sebastian Viewpoint. The viewpoint, reached by a very steep 0.5-mile access road, is somewhat overgrown.

30.9 (mp 337.4) Myers Creek bridge, short but lacking shoulders or sidewalk. Use caution when crossing this and subsequent bridges. US 101 is once again near sea level, and massive sea stacks dot the shoreline.

32.7 (mp 339.2) Pistol River State Park: beach access but no facilities.

37.1 (mp 344.1) Boardman State Park. This long, narrow park has three picnic areas, numerous viewpoints, beach accesses, and pullouts.

37.7 (mp 344.7) Arch Rock Viewpoint.

37.9 (mp 344.9) Arch Rock Picnic Area: views of the arch, picnic tables, and toilets. No water or beach access.

38.9 (mp 345.9) Thunder Rock Cove: awesome!

39.0 (mp 346) Natural Bridges Cove. Water enters this cove through rock arches. The area is exceptional when the tide is coming in. North Island Trail starts here and descends to the beach.

41.4 (mp 348.4) Thomas Creek bridge is 345 feet high, making it the highest bridge on the Oregon Coast. At the south end is a turnout and bridge viewpoint.

41.7 (mp 348.7) Indian Sand Trail Viewpoint. The viewpoint is overgrown. However, the trail leads to an elegant view of arched rocks.

42.2 (mp 349.2) Whalehead Beach Picnic Area: restrooms, picnic tables, running water, and beach access. The beach is reached by a steep, 0.2-mile descent.

42.8 (mp 349.8) Whalehead Trail Viewpoint.

44.3 (mp 351.3) Turnoff to House Rock Viewpoint.

45.2 (mp 352.2) Cape Ferrelo viewpoint access.

45.9 (mp 352.9) Lone Ranch Picnic Area, reached by a very steep 0.3-mile descent: restrooms, water, and tables. The scenic picnic area is located next to a sandy beach. The ocean is peppered with sea stacks.

46.9 (mp 353.9) Rainbow Rock Viewpoint.

47.4 (mp 354.4) Enter Brookings. The commercial section lies 3 miles south.

48.7 (mp 355.7) Turn right (west) for Harris Beach State Park and left (east) for the Oregon Tourist Information Center and Rest Area. The state park has complete facilities for day use and camping. The hiker-biker area is located behind the trailer dump station; the showers are really hot and the yurts really dry. A visit to the beach is a must. There are sea stacks of all sizes to climb, explore, and sit on while watching a lingering sunset. The nearest stores are 1.5 miles south in Brookings.

Harris Beach

50.0 (mp 357) Downtown Brookings: large supermarkets, and a bus station on Pacific St.

50.8 (mp 357.8) Azalea State Park turnoff: picnic area, restrooms, water, and azalea garden. To reach the park, turn left (east) off US 101 at North Bend Rd. and follow the signs.

50.9 (mp 357.9) US 101 crosses the Chetco River Bridge, marking the start of 5 nearly level miles through open country on an excellent shoulder.

56.2 (mp 363.3) California.

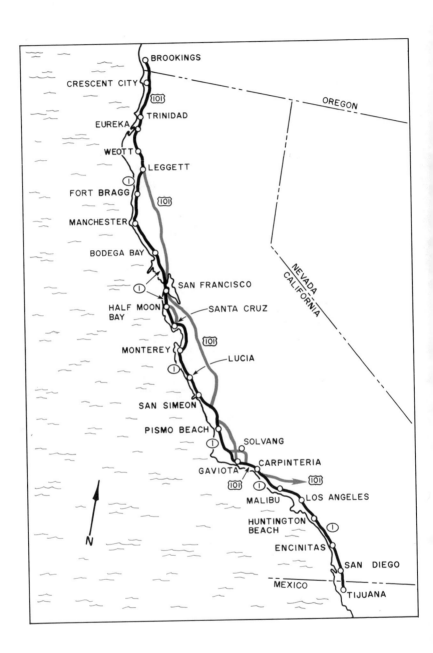

Highway 1 north of Ragged Point

The California Coast covers 1,038 miles, which is over half the length of the entire Pacific Coast Bicycle Route. The scenery is richly varied, with cool, foggy redwood forests in the north and gigantic cities and palm-lined beaches in the south. Some sections of the coast are ideal for riding and you can log impressive daily totals. However, speeding along is a waste, and if all you do is ride, you will not only miss the scenic grandeur of the coast, you will also miss the historic missions, lighthouses, marinas, beaches, and famous California ambiance.

Because the state is so long, it must be considered in three sections: north, central, and south. The northern section follows US 101 (the Redwood Highway) south for 208.9 miles from the Oregon border to Leggett. Much of the riding is through beautiful redwood forests, located just a few miles from the coast. Average yearly rainfall is high, up to 70 inches at Crescent City. September and October are usually the wettest months. Rain gear and fenders are recommended the entire year. Temperatures are

123

moderate along the northern portions of the coast, warming as you approach Leggett. The north has several sections of hazardous highway—fast, busy, and shoulderless—as well as long, steep hills. This portion is most enjoyable for experienced cyclists.

The central section of the California Coast Route follows Highway 1 for 492.7 miles, from Leggett to Pismo Beach. Except for a day spent riding through the San Francisco Bay area, this portion of the state is typified by lonely stretches of 2-lane highway etched into the cliffs overlooking the coast. The grades are frequently steep, the riding often demanding, the countryside beautiful, and the views outstanding—all in all, some of the best cycling on the entire coast. Traffic on Highway 1 is generally light, composed principally of vacationers. To avoid some of the traffic, early morning starts are recommended. The chance of rain is minimal in June, July, and August. On warm days, temperatures rise to the 70s or low 80s.

The central section of California is recommended for cyclists who have previous touring experience and who are in good shape.

If you are looking for the California mystique—beach boys, bikini-clad girls, surfers, suntans, palm trees, large cities, Mexican food, and Spanish architecture—the 336.4-mile-long southern section is the place to ride. The Coast Route loses its isolated feeling as it enters a long series of resort towns and massive, sprawling cities south of Pismo Beach. The terrain levels and the need for strength is replaced by a need for navigational skills through a network of city streets. Bicycles are a common mode of transport here, and motorists are the most courteous on the coast. Weather conditions for riding are good from April to mid-November. The southern section of the California Coast can be completed by all strong cyclists.

No matter where you are on the California Coast, be prepared for dense, wet blankets of fog that can last for several days. All riders should have bright, visible clothing and carry lights.

The Bicentennial Route, established in 1976, is followed most of the way through California. Caltrans (California Transit) has signed most of the key intersections throughout the state; however, signs have been stolen, so do not count on them. Mileposts in California show the miles from the nearest county line. The numbers decrease from north to south, reaching zero at the south end of the county. Each milepost notes at least three points of information: the road number, the county name (abbreviated), and the mileage to the hundredth.

Almost every winter, the California Coast is plagued by landslides, making Highway 1 the most costly road in the country to maintain. Caltrans sets up alternate routes whenever this occurs, creating very scenic, but sometimes long and arduous, detours. If in doubt about the route, contact the California Highway Patrol. The best source of information is other cyclists and tourists traveling in cars. Ask around.

The California Coast has only one tunnel, and it's for northbound cyclists only. The tunnel, on US 101 north of Gaviota State Park, is 0.3-mile-long, with an uphill grade and an 18-inch shoulder; expect a strong headwind.

The state and county park systems provide forty-six hiker-biker camps along the coast for cyclists. They are generally small, and may be very crowded. No reservations are required; you will never be turned away. Large groups (eight or more cyclists) should reserve regular sites ahead of time. Contact the state parks for details. Most state parks on the coast remain open year-round. Only Mill Creek Campground in Del Norte Coast Redwoods State Park, the farthest north, is closed after Labor Day. Future budget cuts may result in more closures; if planning an off-season tour, check ahead.

Campgrounds are not spaced evenly along the coast. In the northern and southern sections, you must cover long distances between public campgrounds. In several areas, private campgrounds were chosen to fill in the gaps between the state parks. The strength of the group should be the deciding factor as to whether the distance between campgrounds is too far. The rides through San Francisco and the Los Angeles area are extremely demanding. Plan ahead and use one of the many hostels, hotels, motels, and privately operated campgrounds along the coast if necessary. You may also shorten your city rides by calling a taxi or riding the bus across town.

In several locations advance reservations are a necessity. Call ahead and

Turnout, north of Westport

reserve your campsites as soon as you feel certain about your itinerary. Campsites that must be reserved ahead of time are: the hiker-biker site on the Marin Headlands overlooking the Golden Gate Bridge (see the Samuel P. Taylor State Park to Half Moon Bay State Beach section for more information), Malibu Beach RV and Newport Dunes Aquatic Park in the Los Angeles area (see the Leo Carrillo State Beach to Newport Dunes Aquatic Park section for more information). Hostels also require advance reservation.

South of Santa Barbara, transients pose a major problem at all the state park campgrounds, forcing many to close their hiker-biker sites. Some parks no longer have an official hiker-biker site. You will not be turned away from any campground; however, you may be required to pay full price for your site or end up sharing a site with the campground hosts.

The closest city to the northern California border is Brookings, Oregon (6 miles north of the border). Greyhound bus, from Portland, San Francisco, or Eugene is the only form of public transportation. Crescent City (21 miles south of the California-Oregon border) is the first major city on the California coast. It can be reached by Greyhound bus or small commuter airplane. Eureka is the first city with train access.

An easy escape from the maze of city streets that make up southern California is the Los Angeles International Airport (LAX). The bike route passes right by the end of the runway.

At the true southern end of California, San Diego International Airport and the Amtrak station are located right next to the bike route, and the bus station is only a few blocks away.

Oregon Border to Elk Prairie Campground (61.8 Miles)

Entering California may remind you of entering a foreign country. However, what appears to be an international customs inspection station is simply an agricultural inspection. Instead of pulling out a passport, you are required to pull out all fruit and vegetables from your touring bags and pockets. Any produce that might contaminate the native crops will be confiscated.

Once past the inspection station, the bicycle route escapes the busy and occasionally shoulderless US 101 and follows rural roads for the next 20 miles through Crescent City. You will pedal past open fields, cattle ranches, a state penitentiary, dense forests, and finally along a section of wild and beautiful coast.

At Crescent City the route parallels the rock-studded coast, passing one scenic vista after another, but missing the main shopping area. Potential stops include a visit to Battery Point Lighthouse, accessible at low tide only, and to the very small Redwood National Park Visitor Center

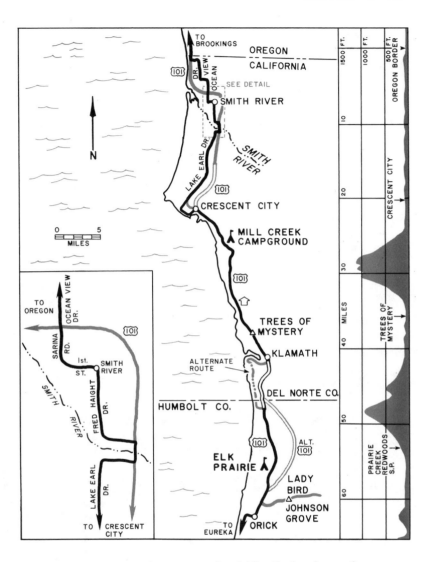

for an introduction to the country ahead. Finally, head out of town past the fishing docks, where, if lucky, you can watch fishermen unload their heavily laden boats.

South of Crescent City, ocean views give way to massive trees as the road climbs 1,100 feet over the triple summit of the Crescent City Hills. The road is narrow, truck traffic heavy, and shoulders nonexistent. Early mornings and weekends are best for traveling. To add a little melodrama and a lot of danger to the ride, the hills are frequently swathed in fog. Dress brightly and ride with a great deal of caution and courtesy.

After zooming down from the last summit of the Crescent City Hills, glide south past the Trees of Mystery, where an oversized Paul Bunyan and Babe, his giant blue ox, welcome the visitors to the world's largest collection of redwood carvings.

After several short miles of level travel, the highway climbs steeply over another hill, gaining nearly 900 feet in elevation. In the middle of this climb, the bike route leaves US 101 for a tour through the majestic redwood groves of Prairie Creek Redwoods State Park. Plan a stroll through this venerable forest before ending the day at Elk Prairie Campground, where a herd of Roosevelt elk graze year-round, occasionally wandering through the hiker-biker site. The elk may be there at any time, but are best viewed in the early morning and late afternoon when they are grazing. The park also has numerous hiking and mountain bike trails through the redwood forest: short trails to fern groves, longer trails to some of the world's tallest trees, and a 4-mile trail to a fern-covered canyon on the coast.

Harbor area at Crescent City

(1 mile)

Mileage Log

0.0 (mp 46.49) Oregon–California border. Enter Del Norte County on US 101.

0.2 (mp 46.29) California fruit inspection. Cooperate, and help protect California agriculture.

0.4 (mp 46.09) Take the first left after the fruit inspection on Ocean View Dr. (County Road D5). Shoulders are nonexistent, but traffic is light and travel pleasant.

6.1 Cross US 101 and continue straight on the nearly level Sarina Rd., passing small cattle ranches and large lily fields.

6.6 Intersection; bend left on 1st St.

7.3 Enter the small community of Smith River, also known as the Easter lily capital of the world. The surrounding fields produce over 90 percent of the nation's Easter lily bulbs. In July, a festival celebrates the harvest.

7.7 Turn right on Fred Haight Dr. (County Road D4).

10.8 Turn right (south) on US 101. Cross the Smith River on a shoulderless bridge then take the first right.

11.2 (mp 36.00) Exit right (west) off US 101 on Lake Earl Dr. (County Road D3), passing a small gas station and grocery store on the right. Follow Lake Earl Dr. to Crescent City. Traffic is light, and there is a good shoulder for over half the distance.

11.6 At an unmarked intersection, the route bends left, then heads past an old barn.

12.0 Cycle through the one-store town of Fort Dick.

12.5 Begin wide shoulder.

13.7 Pass a state penitentiary on the left.

14.5 Pass a road to Kellogg Beach Coast Access on right.

20.6 Major intersection. Turn right (south) and ride the wide shoulder along Washington Blvd., beginning a scenic loop around the commercial center of Crescent City.

22.3 Turn left on Pebble Beach Rd. and ride along the coast.

23.8 Pebble Beach: beach access. Picnic tables are located at the next turnout.

24.3 Crescent City limits: supermarkets, campground, motels, and restaurants.

24.5 Coast access road descends to a rocky outcropping.

24.6 Brother Jonathan Vista Point overlooking the rock-studded bay to Battery Point Lighthouse. City park with bathroom is located across the road.

24.9 Follow the coast road as it heads left up 5th St. for a block.

25.0 Go right on A St.

25.2 Cross Front St.

25.3 Turn left on Battery St. and ride through Crescent Park, which has

Big Tree in Prairie Creek Redwoods State Park

covered picnic tables, restrooms, and a hollow redwood tree. ***Side Trip.*** Before turning left on Battery St., go straight 0.2 mile to the often-photographed Battery Point Vista and Lighthouse. Admission charged to enter the lighthouse.

25.9 Turn left on H St.

26.0 Go right on Front St. and follow it to US 101. ***Side Trip*** to Redwood National Park Visitor Center and supermarkets. Follow Front St. for 3 blocks, then go left on K St. for 1 block to the visitor center. They can answer questions and suggest hikes through the giant trees. Supermarkets are found by continuing up K St. for 2 more blocks; turn right and ride until you reach the store and Laundromat.

27.1 (mp 26.20) Turn right on US 101.

27.3 (mp 26.00) Pass the Under Sea World aquarium. Admission is charged.

27.6 (mp 25.80) Turnoff to the Citizens Dock on the right. When the fish are running, the area bustles with activity. US 101 widens to include a shoulder as the highway heads out of town.

29.8 (mp 23.60) Base of the Crescent City Hills. Fog often engulfs these hills, so wear bright clothing and strap on a light that is visible to cars coming up from behind. Southbound travelers have 2 lanes (no shoulder) on the climb; northbound travelers have only a single lane.

30.8 (mp 22.70) Crescent City Vista Point offers a grandstand view of the city before the road enters Del Norte Coast Redwoods State Park. Although the road passes some magnificent trees, the ride is too hectic to really enjoy their grandeur.

33.3 (mp 20.31) After a short descent, pass the turnoff to Mill Creek Campground. A steep 2.2-mile road descends over 600 feet to the quiet campground nestled at the base of some giant redwoods: hiker-biker sites and hot showers. Food supplies must be brought from Crescent City. This campground is open summer only.

34.6 (mp 19.00) Summit of the first and highest of the Crescent City Hills, approximately 1,200 feet. Southbound traffic merges here into a single lane for a quick descent. The passing lane reappears when the road begins to climb again.

35.9 (mp 17.70) Summit of second hill; only one more to go.

37.3 (mp 16.22) Top of the third and last summit. It's all downhill for the next 3.5 miles. Sliding and slumping of the roadway has created some very challenging riding in this area. Stay alert.

37.7 (mp 15.80) Damnation Creek Trailhead: a scenic 4-mile hike to the beach.

40.1 (mp 13.4) Vista point with a view south.

40.9 (mp 12.53) The southern end of the Crescent City Hills is marked by a nice picnic area and sandy beach for relaxing. On the left side of the highway is the Redwoods Hostel (AYH). A narrow shoulder begins as the road skirts along a bay.

41.6 (mp 11.88) Coastal Trail access: restrooms and running water. The trail follows the coastline through Redwood National Park. The shoulder disappears.

42.6 (mp 10.86) Trees of Mystery and Klamath city limits. Rideable shoulders begin as you enter Klamath. Grocery stores, fast foods, and a commercial campground that accepts tents are just ahead.

45.5 (mp 8.15) Coast Trail access. The trail, picnic area, and scenic vista are reached by a steep road.

48.3 (mp 5.36) Klamath shopping center is located left of US 101 and has the best food selection for miles.

49.3 (mp 4.42) Golden Bear Bridge. Two golden grizzly bears, California's state symbol, stand guard at the entrance of a pair of shoulderless bridges over the Klamath River. After the second bridge, the good shoulders return as US 101 climbs over another major set of hills. Coast Road **Alternate Route.** Cyclists touring on mountain bikes may be interested in a 14-mile tour along the coast (8 miles are gravel). The road starts at the southern end of the Klamath River bridges and follows the river to the coast, then swings south to loop back to US 101; only moderately scenic.

52.4 (mp 1.20) Top of the first summit, approximately 500 feet in elevation.

53.4 (mp 0.0 and 134.89) Turn off US 101 onto Newton B. Drury Scenic Parkway, a scenic byway through the redwoods. At the base of the highway exit, go right and head uphill on a good shoulder. Leave Del Norte County and enter Humboldt County. Across the county line, the highway climbs uphill for several more miles to an elevation near 900 feet.

54.4 (mp 134.29) The Coast Road Alternate Route rejoins the bicycle route.

54.6 (mp 134.19) Enter Prairie Creek Redwoods State Park. Continuing uphill, the shoulder narrows as the heavily shaded highway passes under towering redwood groves.

55.1 (mp 133.67) Summit. It's all downhill to Elk Prairie Campground. The road passes several memorial groves with short (½-mile or less) trails into the forest. Stop at least once to look at the trees.

60.7 (mp 128.40) Cork Screw Tree turnout. Follow a short path to a twisted and deformed tree standing tall and proud.

Elk in prairie at Elk Prairie Campground

61.1 (mp 127.96) Big Tree. Exit left (east) to parking lot and walk to a tree over 300 feet tall and 17.7 feet in diameter.

61.8 (mp 127.24) Elk Prairie Campground: hiker-biker sites, warm showers, roaming elk, visitor center, and trails through the redwoods to the beach. The hiker-biker site has boxes for food storage for protection from bears and raccoons. If time allows, take an extra day to explore the park. The trail to the beach and fern canyon is a must. Elk may be seen on the beach in the mornings and late afternoons.

Elk Prairie Campground to Eureka KOA (46.3 Miles)

With the first major set of California hills behind you, the ride from Prairie Creek Redwoods State Park to Eureka will seem relatively easy. This should leave you plenty of time for side trips, exploring, or bicycle maintenance at the excellent repair shops in Arcata or Eureka.

This section sees the evolution of US 101 from a narrow country road into a busy 4-lane freeway. Riding on the freeway is legal (unless otherwise posted), and, thanks to a wide shoulder, generally safe. However, the noise and dirt is fatiguing, so be sure to take advantage of the two scenic escape routes off the freeway, as well as all the side trips.

The first suggested side trip is to the beautiful Lady Bird Johnson Grove. The grove has a mile-long loop trail through a forest of ferns and mammoth redwoods. The access road to the grove is very steep; hide the touring bags at the bottom, if possible.

The second stop of the day is at the Redwoods National Park Center, located just south of Orick. The displays are interesting, the building well heated, and the local population of banana slugs simply amazing.

Beyond the visitor center, US 101 heads around Stone Lagoon and Dry Lagoon (part of Humboldt Lagoons State Park). Winter storms can cause the lagoons to overflow and create deep channels where they empty into the ocean. To date, the surf has always repaired the lagoons. This is a very scenic section of highway.

Near Patrick's Point, US 101 widens into a freeway with wide shoulders and noisy traffic. After a couple of miles on the freeway, the bike route escapes to back roads and parallels the coast to the next "must" stop at Patrick's Point State Park. The park is situated on a rugged point overlooking the ocean. Trails crisscross the bluffs and climb to breathtaking views from sheer cliffs. The driftwood-covered beaches are fun to explore. Seals and sea lions live on offshore sea stacks; their constant barking echoes throughout the park.

In Trinidad, visit the Trinidad Memorial Lighthouse with its giant two-ton fog bell before heading south on US 101 to more excellent views of the coast. Leave the freeway (US 101) for a second time at Little River State Beach, and cycle along the beach road for a peaceful 1.8 miles before returning to the hectic rush of the highway. When riding on the freeway, use extra caution at the busy exits and entrances as you near Arcata and Eureka.

The day's ride ends a couple of miles north of Eureka at the KOA, the only campground in the area with a special site just for cyclists. Although a discount is offered to riders, it still isn't cheap. However, most other campgrounds in the Eureka area are designed for trailers; the managers generally do not accept tents. Alternate options include hotels, bed-and-breakfasts, and the Arcata Crew House Hostel in Arcata.

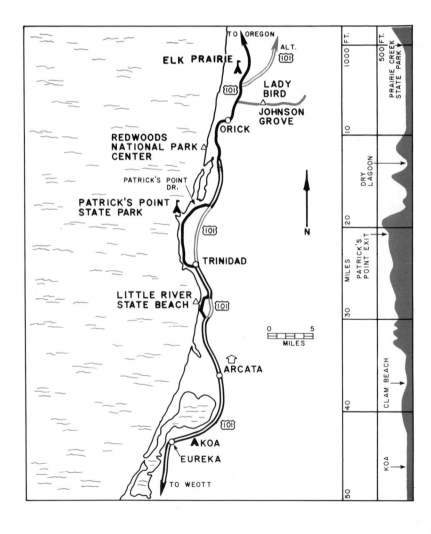

Mileage Log

0.0 Head south from Elk Prairie Campground on the Newton B. Drury Scenic Parkway. Elk can be spotted grazing in the open fields or resting under crab apple trees in the morning.

1.1 (mp 126.25) Newton B. Drury Scenic Parkway ends. Go right and return to US 101.

2.9 (mp 124.4) Lost Man Creek Mountain Bike Trail access on left.

5.1 (mp 122.31) *Side Trip* to Lady Bird Johnson Grove: restrooms. Turn left (east) off US 101 and cycle 2.3 miles up a narrow and very steep road to the 1-mile nature loop trail. This side trip is a must in May and early June, when the rhododendrons are in bloom.

5.6 (mp 121.87) Enter the town of Orick: grocery stores (the last before Patrick's Point State Park), restaurants, motels, and an assortment of tourist shops.

8.3 (mp 119.17) *Side Trip* to the Redwoods National Park Center and picnic area. The center, located 0.2 mile off the highway, has heated restrooms, warm water, beach access, and information. Beyond the park center, US 101 returns to its typical up-and-down motion, with little to no shoulder. The highway crosses a narrow sandspit between the ocean and Freshwater Lagoon, where the county provides a large parking area on the west side of the road. A tents-only area is located at the south end; no water.

10.2 (mp 117.38) Turnoff to Stone Lagoon, part of Humboldt Lagoons State Park.

12.3 (mp 115.28) Humboldt State Park Visitor Center, a small building with camping information. The tables outside offer an opportunity to picnic along the shores of Stone Lagoon. The shoulder ends here and riders should give themselves a generous amount of room to keep cars and trucks from trying to squeeze by on this narrow, rough road.

13.3 (mp 114.28) Turnoff to Dry Lagoon: beach access, restrooms, lots of driftwood, but no water is found 1 mile west of US 101. Beyond the park, US 101 climbs over two small hills, then descends to parallel Big Lagoon before widening into a 4-lane freeway with good shoulders.

19.6 (mp 108) Big Lagoon Beach County Park exit: scenic campsites near the beach, water, and restrooms. No hiker-biker campsites.

21.3 (mp 106.30) Exit US 101 on Patrick's Point Dr. The road is narrow and shoulderless but has less traffic than US 101. Watch for sections of rough road and occasional short, steep pitches. After passing motels and an RV campground, the road slips along steep, open hillsides overlooking the ocean.

24.0 Patrick's Point State Park entrance: hiker-biker sites, hot showers, beach access, and hiking trails. *Side Trip.* To visit the park, take a

Lady Bird Johnson Grove

right at the entrance and descend to the toll booth. Purchase an inexpensive park map, then follow the road toward Agate Beach. To reach the hiker-biker site, take a left turn off the Agate Beach Rd. toward Wedding Rock, and follow that road to its end.

27.5 Trinidad, a small town with a grocery store and fast-food restaurants. ***Side Trip.*** Before returning to US 101, make a short 0.5-mile side trip to Trinidad Memorial Lighthouse. Follow Main St. to its end, then turn left on Trinity St. for 0.2 mile. A state beach with picnic tables, restroom, running water, and beach access is located off Stage Coach Road.

27.6 (mp 100.50) At Trinidad, return to US 101. Shoulders disappear on bridges.

31.5 (mp 97.13) Exit US 101, following signs to Little River State Beach for the second scenic escape. This is a confusing exit; watch for the truck weigh station, then take the road that goes above it. At the end of the exit, go right and follow the state park road which parallels US 101 for 2.3 miles, passing several beach access areas. Return to US 101 at Clam Beach County Park: camping, restrooms, no water.

33.3 (mp 95.70) Little River State Beach Rd. returns to US 101.

34.6 (mp 94.38) Vista point overlooking the Clam Beach–Little River area: no facilities, and no access for northbound travelers.

39.5 (mp 89.77) Mad River Bridge: little shoulder and no sidewalk.

40.4 (mp 89.00) Arcata. Use extreme caution at all freeway exits and entrances. Those wishing to visit stores, a bike shop, Humboldt State University, or simply escape the hassles and dangers of riding a free-way through town should exit here. As a bonus, riders who go through town will see some carefully maintained Victorian build-ings. The Arcata Crew House Hostel is located on 14th and I Sts.; call ahead for reservations, (707)822-9995.

42.1 (mp 87.30) Humboldt State University and City Center exit. Once past the center of Arcata, US 101 swings around Arcata Bay. Be prepared for strong winds as the level road sweeps across the open countryside.

46.3 (mp 83.40) The KOA campground lies on the left (east) side of US 101, requiring a hazardous crossing of this busy highway. Be patient and wait for a break in the traffic. The campground has a small store, endless hot water for showers, small cabins to rent if the weather is bad, and laundry facilities.

Eureka KOA to Marine Garden Club Grove (51.2 Miles)

The day begins with a tour through Eureka. This is a beautiful old Vic-torian town with meticulously tended period buildings. The bike route leaves US 101 in town and runs through a residential area, passing fifty or more of these Victorian masterpieces. If that's not enough, you can take a short side trip to the ornate Carson Mansion and the Old Town area. Fort Humboldt, at the southern end of town, has an excellent indoor and out-door logging museum.

Beyond Eureka, the route rejoins US 101, which returns to its free-way status at the southern end of town. The shoulder is wide, the road nearly level, and miles speed by. If freeway riding is not your idea of a good way to see the country, take advantage of three alternate routes. The first is a loop through the town of Loleta where you may want to stop at the cheese factory and try a sample or two. The second alternate route swings out to the Victorian tourist town of Ferndale, then follows farm roads back to the freeway. This variation will add 11 extra miles to the day's total. The little town of Scotia provides the third escape. In Scotia, visit the Pacific Lumber Company Museum. While there, pick up a free pass for a self-guiding walking tour through the lumber mill and factory, which takes you on a catwalk overlooking the largest redwood mill in the world (open weekdays only).

The scenic portion of the ride begins when the route exits the freeway at the start of the Avenue of the Giants. This road is a section of the Old Coast Highway that winds through a narrow corridor of majestic redwoods. Explore the numerous groves, hike the trails, and spend some time

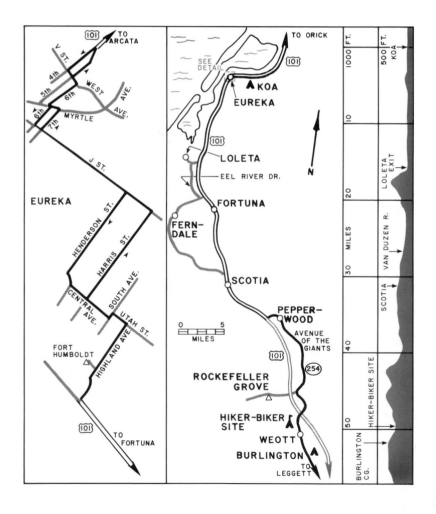

pondering these magnificent trees. The avenue is narrow and generally deeply shaded. Wear bright, visible clothing.

The day ends at the Burlington Campground hiker-biker site, located 1.8 miles south of the main camp area among the giant redwoods of the Marine Garden Club Grove. The site is primitive, without hot water or showers, but the scenic layout more than compensates for any inconveniences. Showers may be taken at the main campground.

Mileage Log

0.0 (mp 83.40) The first challenge of the day is to return to the west side of the freeway. Once across US 101, head south over a level plain along the edge of Arcata Bay. Riding is easy on the wide shoulder.

2.4 (mp 81.1) Enter Eureka.

3.6 (mp 79.95) The narrow bridge over Eureka Slough, with sidewalks but no shoulders, marks the entrance to downtown Eureka. Once across the bridge, the freeway ends and the bike route bypass of Eureka begins. Eureka has a supermarket and bike shop located on the bike route at the south side of town.

4.1 (mp 79.45) Turn left (east) on V St. for 2 blocks to 6th St. *Side Trip* to Carson Mansion and Old Town. Take 6th St. to M St. and head right (west) for 3 blocks to the mansion. Cyclists must be content with viewing the structure from the outside; the mansion is now an exclusive men's club. You can begin a tour of Old Town from the mansion. Cycle west on 2nd St. to C St., go left for 1 block, and head back up 3rd St. to M St.

5.0 Turn left on J St. and follow it for 1.3 miles to Henderson St.

6.3 Go right on Henderson St. for 1.4 miles through a commercial section of town. Look for the bike shop here. Eureka has spent time and money making this road appealing to cyclists; a bike triggers the stoplights as easily as a car.

7.4 When Henderson bends, take a left on Central Ave.

7.7 Jog left on Utah St. for 0.1 mile.

7.8 Turn right on Highland Ave. and continue straight to US 101.

8.3 Fort Humboldt State Historic Park: restrooms, running water, picnic tables, as well as an indoor/outdoor logging museum and excellent views of Eureka from the old fort site.

8.4 Go left on US 101 (known as Broadway in this section of town).

9.0 (mp 75.5) Freeway and good shoulder resume as US 101 leaves Eureka and heads through open country along Humboldt Bay. Use considerable caution when cycling past the exits and entrances to this busy freeway.

11.9 (mp 72.5) Fields Landing exit. On the east side of the freeway is a commercial area with a grocery store.

13.4 (mp 71.02) College of the Redwoods exit.

Carson Mansion, a Victorian masterpiece in Eureka

16.4 (mp 68.0) First Loleta exit, and start of the alternate route. Beyond the exit, the next 1.4 miles are spent climbing a steep hill. The freeway broadens into 3 lanes with no shoulders. ***Alternate Route*** through Loleta. At the end of the off ramp, turn right (west) on Hookton Rd., then take the first left on Eel River Dr. If the Loleta cheese factory is on your itinerary, turn off Eel River Dr. at Main St., and ride through the center of town. Go left on Loleta Dr. and cross the railroad tracks. The alternate route returns to the freeway at the Ferndale exit.

18.2 (mp 65.8) Top of the hill; freeway narrows to 2 lanes, with a shoulder on the southbound side. The northbound corridor widens to 3 lanes without shoulders.

19.6 (mp 64.59) Ferndale exit. ***Alternate Route*** through Ferndale begins here. From the exit, go straight on a shoulderless road. In 0.7 mile go right and cross the narrow Eel River bridge. Once across, the road widens to include a shoulder as it heads south through farmlands. At 4.7 miles from US 101 reach Ferndale. Ride through town and explore (on foot or wheels) some of the side streets to see the showpiece houses that have made this area famous. When you are ready to continue, head east from the town center on Washington St. After 0.5 mile take a right on Lincoln St. for 0.4 mile to Grizzly Bluff Rd. Head east through the farm fields where there are more dogs and chickens on the road than cars. Climb a steep bluff 7 miles from Ferndale and at 12.9 miles return to US 101.

21.6 (mp 62.6) This is the halfway point between Vancouver, B.C., and the Mexican border.

22.2 (mp 62.0) Fortuna exit. US 101 passes the west edge of town; the supermarkets are 1 mile east of the freeway.

27.2 (mp 57.0) Van Duzen River Bridge marks the start of the gradual ascent to the redwood forests. The bridge is narrow, with little shoulder and no sidewalk.

30.4 (mp 53.80) Rio Dell exit. A readily accessible market is located on the east side of the freeway. Ferndale Alternate Route returns to US 101 here.

32.2 (mp 51.97) Scotia exit and the third opportunity to briefly escape the freeway. Scotia is a company town and the company is Pacific Lumber, which claims to operate the largest redwood mill in the world. Summer visitors may tour the mill and factory or browse through the logging museum (weekdays only, closed daily from 10:30 A.M. to 1:00 P.M.). Off-season visitors may view the outdoor park section of the museum, and stock up on food at the grocery store. When you are ready to leave, parallel the freeway north, cycling past the lumberyard, and return to the freeway when the road enters Pacific Lumber land.

37.1 (mp 47.0) Vista point exit. Gaze over the Eel River from a large parking area.

38.1 (mp 46.0) Exit US 101 and go left to ride the Avenue of the Giants, a narrow, winding road with no shoulder. Traffic varies from moderate to heavy. *Side Trip* to the Pacific Lumber Demonstration Forest: water, restrooms, picnic tables, and nature trail. At the base of the freeway exit, go right for 0.2 mile to the parking area. This is a great chance to compare a logged redwood forest with the trees on the Avenue of the Giants.

38.2 Humboldt Redwoods State Park. Auto Tour maps are available on the right side of the road. Don't strain your neck looking up at all the trees.

40.1 Enter Pepperwood: small tourist shops but no grocery store. Just south of town, two short nature trails, Drury Trail and Percy French Loop, wander through redwood groves.

43.2 Immortal Tree, growing on the east side of the highway, shows marks of floods, fire, ax, and wind. This is a testimonial to the incredible ability of the redwood trees to survive.

44.7 Redcrest, a small tourist town whose principal attraction is the Eternal Tree House. In the tree house (actually a hollowed stump) is a register where you can check the number of international visitors this area receives. Restaurant but no grocery store.

48.6 No. 8 on the Auto Tour is a rest area with picnic tables and chemical toilets.

48.7 Avenue of the Giants brushes along the edge of US 101. *Side Trip* on Bull Creek Flats Rd., which branches right and ducks under the freeway. This road offers an excellent ride through tall stands of ivy-wrapped trees. At 1.3 miles take a short walk through Rockefeller Grove before heading back the way you came.

48.9 Turnoff to Founders Grove. The grove and ½-mile nature loop are located just 200 feet left (east) of the Avenue of the Giants. They provide an excellent introduction to the life of the forest. Giant redwoods, notably the Foundation Tree and Dyerville Giant, are located only minutes from the road.

51.2 Marine Garden Club Grove of Humboldt State Park: hiker-biker camp, picnic tables, running water, restrooms, tall trees, and great swimming holes in the Eel River. A grocery store is located 0.2 mile south at the small town of Weott. Showers for the camp are located 1.7 miles south at Burlington Campground.

Marine Garden Club Grove to Standish-Hickey State Park Recreation Area (48 Miles)

South of Marine Garden Club Grove, the route continues south on the Avenue of the Giants, passing through beautiful stands of redwood, such as the Garden Club of America Grove, where you may quietly enjoy some of nature's most regal handiwork. Along with the natural wonders are man-made "attractions" such as a drive-through tree and one-log house.

At the end of the Avenue of the Giants you must return to US 101 and follow it through the narrow South Fork Eel River valley. Redwood groves are soon replaced by dry, open hillsides. Temperatures soar, rising as much as 15 degrees away from the protective shade of the redwoods. Be sure water bottles are full and sunglasses handy.

The Avenue of the Giants is not the end of the redwoods. Just 14 miles south lies Richardson Grove State Park. This narrow band of redwoods grows in an area otherwise bare of tall trees. Trails in the park climb from cool redwood groves to sun-dried ridgetops and open viewpoints. For a quick introduction to the park, a short nature trail provides insight to the life cycle of the redwoods and their ability to survive infestation, fire, and flood.

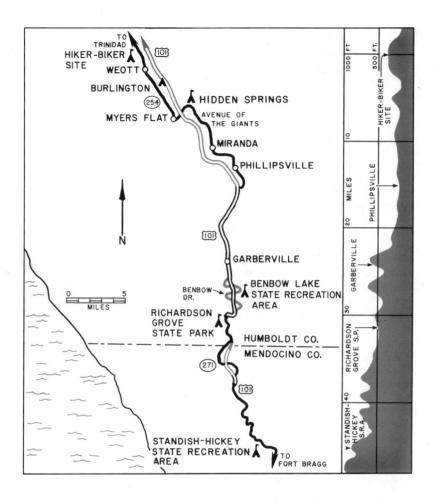

Beyond Richardson Grove, the South Fork Eel River valley widens, then narrows again. The road twists and rolls, passing right over Confusion Hill, an area of unexplained mysteries that can be viewed for a small fee.

This short day ends at Standish-Hickey State Park Recreation Area, a delightful place to spend an afternoon swimming, hiking, or exploring redwood groves.

Two alternate routes offer relief from the noise and dirt of US 101. The first follows a winding road through a portion of Benbow Lake State Recreation Area, rejoining US 101 in 3.9 miles. The second follows Percey Cook Valley Rd. (Highway 271) for 5.7 miles, paralleling the hot and dry US 101 under the partial shade of deciduous trees.

Throughout this section, US 101 is very busy, with a seemingly endless stream of trucks, cars, and oversized tourist vehicles. For most of the

Avenue of the Giants

distance, the highway is wide—almost a freeway—with broad shoulders. Unfortunately, the road narrows in several sections, and 4 lanes of traffic squeeze onto an appallingly narrow, shoulderless, 2-lane road that twists and bends with the narrow valley. Trucks and cars rarely slow down when the road narrows, and cyclists are forced to fend for themselves. To be on the safe side, start this ride early in the morning and ride defensively. When you have to share the road with large vehicles, take the coward's way out and live to tell about it.

Mileage Log

0.0 From the hiker-biker camp at the Marine Garden Club Grove of Humboldt State Park, cycle south on the Avenue of the Giants.

1.7 Pass Burlington Campground on the left (east): water, showers, and a small visitor center.

3.5 Garden Club of America Grove: restrooms and running water. A short path and bridge lead across the South Fork Eel River to a large redwood grove.

4.7 Williams Grove, a day-use area: picnic tables, restrooms, running water, giant trees, and river access. Open summer only. Williams Grove has free admission for cyclists (but not for cars). Overnight camping is allowed for self-contained motorhomes only.

5.4 Myers Flat. Like all towns along the Avenue of the Giants, this one has a touch of tinsel in its rustic setting. Myers Flat's main attraction, besides grocery stores, cafes, and Laundromats, is a drive- or ride-through tree. Admission is charged.

6.7 Turnoff to Hidden Springs Campground: hiker-biker area, hot showers, and trails through the redwoods. Open summer only.

11.4 Leave Humboldt Redwoods State Park.

11.7 Miranda: groceries and fast food.

15.4 Franklin K. Lane Grove: a picnic area under cool, shady trees, running water, and restrooms.

15.6 Phillipsville: grocery store and restaurants. If intrigued, visit a house made from a single log.

18.5 Avenue of the Giants (Highway 254) ends. Return to US 101, a wide 4-laner. Shoulders vary from several feet wide to nonexistent for the next 10 miles as the highway climbs two distinct hills. Northbound cyclists exit US 101 here (mp 17.5) to follow the Avenue of the Giants.

23.8 (mp 13.30) First Garberville exit.

24.7 (mp 11.29) Second Garberville exit; grocery stores.

26.7 (mp 8.58) Benbow Lake *Alternate Route.* Turn off US 101 at Benbow Lake State Recreation Area exit. Go left under the freeway and follow the river south on Benbow Dr. At 1.1 miles, pass Benbow Lake Campground: hiker-biker campsite, running water, swimming, hiking trails, boat rentals, and ranger-led "hikes" in canoes. No hot showers.

28.6 (mp 5.22) Benbow Lake Alternate Route rejoins US 101. Southbound cyclists must cross the freeway without the aid of a traffic light, but gaps in traffic are common. US 101 narrows from a 4- to a 2-lane highway here and shoulders disappear.

32.5 (mp 2.03) Enter Richardson Grove State Park, a welcome refuge from the hot, dry surrounding countryside. US 101 narrows more.

32.8 (mp 1.73) Richardson Grove State Park campground entrance: hiker-biker area, hot showers, hiking trails, nature loop, small store, and swimming holes in the South Fork Eel River. A small grocery store is located 1 mile south.

33.4 (mp 1.18) Leave Richardson Grove State Park and the shaded coolness of the redwoods as US 101 returns to a wide, fast-moving 4-lane highway. Shoulders return to a comfortable size, but not for long.

33.9 (mp 0.68) Pass a private campground and small grocery store.

34.3 (mp 0.35) Percey Cook Valley *Alternate Route.* Exit US 101 on Highway 271 and pedal south for the next 3.4 miles along the South Fork of the Eel River. When the road divides, go left under the freeway, then right for another 2.3 miles before returning to US 101.

34.7 (mp 0.0 and 104.2) Leave Humboldt County and enter Mendocino County.

37.7 (mp 101.47) Highway 271 passes under US 101, providing a second access to the alternate route.

40.1 (mp 99.1) Highway 271 returns to US 101 as the road enters a narrow section of the valley. The steep hillsides slide frequently. Most of the shoulders have been carried off downhill somewhere. Shoulders come and go until approximately 0.5 mile before Standish-Hickey State Park Recreation Area.

42.5 (mp 99.45) Confusion Hill. Strange magnetic forces cause unexplained mysteries. For a small fee you can view these phenomena. (The forces may have affected the mileposts in this area.)

42.9 (mp 99.1) Tree house and small cafe. Last chance to see a hollowed-out, but still living, redwood tree.

45.3 (mp 96.42) Frankland and Bess Smith Redwood Grove: running water and restrooms. A small oasis of cool shade in an otherwise hot river valley.

47.1 (mp 94.51) Eel River Redwoods Hostel: sauna, river access, laundry, free use of swim tubes, bike rentals, and rooms for couples.

48.0 (mp 94.00) Standish-Hickey State Park Recreation Area has everything for the cyclist: hiker-biker campsite, hot showers, a lake for swimming, and trails for hiking. Groceries are available at the small store and deli across US 101, or 1 mile south in Leggett.

Standish-Hickey State Park Recreation Area to MacKerricher Beach State Park (39.4 Miles)

Just south of Standish-Hickey State Park Recreation Area, the bicycle route leaves US 101 and heads back to the coast on California's famous Highway 1. The highway starts out by climbing over the much maligned Leggett Hill, which, at nearly 2,000 feet, is the highest point on the Pacific Coast Bike Route. Cyclists talk about Leggett Hill up and down the coast, increasing its proportions as they go. Contrary to popular rumor, abandoned touring bags do not line the road, nor are there graves of cyclists who did not make it.

From the summit of Leggett Hill, gaze out over the miles of forested hills and deep valleys, where US 101 can be seen rushing south toward San Francisco. To the west lies the Pacific Ocean, sometimes shimmering in the sun, but more often shrouded in a thick cover of fog.

The descent from Leggett Hill is exhilarating and much too short. The road almost reaches sea level before beginning another steep climb over 690-foot Rockport Hill. The descent of this second hill leads to the ocean and stunning viewpoints of a sea stack-studded coastline, which look more like giant fangs than the friendly, offshore bird rookeries they are.

A narrow section of Highway 1

The day ends at MacKerricher Beach State Park. This is a wonderful place to explore, with fascinating tide pools, harbor seals sunbathing on offshore rocks, a small lake for swimming, and an abandoned log-haul road for riding or walking right on the shore.

Standish-Hickey State Park Recreation Area to MacKerricher Beach State Park is a section of changes. When the Coast Bike Route leaves US 101, it also leaves behind the drier inland climate, where summer temperatures average from 80 to 100 degrees. (On the coast, summer temperatures average between 50 and 60 degrees.) Vegetation changes from forest to windswept grasslands. Much of the commercial traffic is left behind, and the road quality changes from quasi-freeway to a uniformly narrow 2 lanes, with little or no shoulder.

Riding on narrow, winding roads is hazardous. It's important to ride in single file and to always stay on the correct (right) side of the road. Never climb by switchbacking. Never cut corners when descending. Wear bright clothing and be conscious of the motorists coming up from behind.

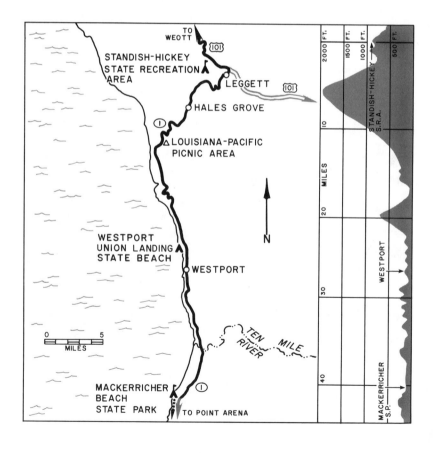

Between Standish-Hickey State Park Recreation Area and MacKerricher Beach State Park, stores and restaurants are few, so plan food stops ahead. Small grocery stores may be found in Leggett, Westport, and just before MacKerricher Beach State Park.

Mileage Log

0.0 (mp 93.87) Leaving Standish-Hickey State Park Recreation Area, follow US 101 south. The 2-lane highway is narrow with a variable shoulder of up to 2 feet. Terrain is rolling, mountainous, and dry.

1.5 (mp 91.20 and mp 105.21) Exit US 101 onto Highway 1.

1.6 (mp 105.11) Leggett. The grocery store is located 0.1 mile left (south) on Drive Through Tree Rd.; 0.2 mile south on the same road is the Drive Through Tree. Admission is charged. After Leggett, Highway 1 descends rapidly 0.3 mile to cross the South Fork Eel River. Expect some logging truck traffic.

2.1 (mp 104.61) The ascent of Leggett Hill begins at 1,100 feet. You see, it is not so hard.

5.6 (mp 101.10) Leggett Hill summit, elevation 1,950 feet. The road traverses the ridge crest for 0.8 mile, then drops steeply through heavy forest. This is a great descent, but don't get too enthusiastic. Large potholes are often hidden in deep shade at the corners.

9.4 (mp 97.32) Hales Grove. The road levels for a mile, then resumes its descent.

15.2 (mp 90.87) Highway 1 takes the name of the Shoreline Highway as it heads south.

15.4 (mp 90.60) Cottoneva Creek marks the end of Leggett Hill.

17.0 (mp 88.95) Louisiana-Pacific picnic area: tables, restrooms, and a small demonstration forest with a short nature walk.

18.2 (mp 87.85) Recross Cottoneva Creek and pass the abandoned community of Rockport, tucked around the base of Rockport Hill. Beyond the creek, the road climbs steeply. The highway is narrow, the hillsides clearcut.

19.7 (mp 86.38) Rockport Hill summit, elevation 690 feet. No views or turnouts, just a wonderful descent.

21.5 (mp 84.59) The crossing of Hardy Creek marks the end of Rockport Hill.

21.7 (mp 84.39) A small gravel turnout is the first of many spectacular vantage points overlooking the Pacific Ocean. Sea stacks, arch rocks, nesting birds, and barking seals may be seen and heard. Shortly after returning to the coast, the road broadens to include a 2- to 3-foot shoulder.

23.5 (mp 82.59) Vista point.

23.9 (mp 82.10) Westport Union Landing State Beach and vista point: restrooms, ocean views, camping, and water (not potable). Beach

Coastal viewpoint south of Leggett

access and picnic tables are located at the south end of the park. The highway parallels the state beach for the next mile.

25.4 (mp 80.70) Dehaven Creek day-use parking area: picnic tables and pit toilets.

25.7 (mp 80.40) Shoulder ends, marking the start of a 16-mile section of narrow, winding road. On foggy or rainy days, wear bright clothing and use blinking lights to increase your visibility.

26.2 (mp 79.90) Wages Beach Creek Camp (private).

27.3 (mp 77.71) Westport, a small town with grocery store and restaurant. Beyond town, Highway 1 traverses grassy hillsides overlooking the ocean. The hills give way to steep cliffs, and the road clings to the scenic coastline, exposed to the wind and elements. Watch for sudden changes in wind direction when dipping into small coves and then climbing steeply back to the open cliffs.

30.1 (mp 74.01) Vista point: a parking lot.

35.1 (mp 68.85) Ten Mile River Bridge ushers in a 0.5-mile section of good shoulder.

39.1 (mp 64.87) Two small grocery stores, the last before MacKerricher Beach State Park and Fort Bragg.

39.4 (mp 64.67) MacKerricher Beach State Park: hiker-biker site, running water, and hot showers. From December through April, this is an excellent place to watch migrating gray whales. Large grocery stores are located 2.7 miles south in Fort Bragg, which is reached by a scenic ride along the beach on the old logging haul road.

MacKerricher Beach State Park to Manchester State Beach (42.1 Miles)

Although short, this very scenic ride is strenuous. Highway 1 hugs the rugged coastline, dropping in then climbing out of the many narrow canyons that cut into the steep cliffs. Some sections of the road are without shoulders. Traffic is generally light, except on midsummer weekends.

Although this is a short ride, you can easily devote an entire day to exploring this section of the coast. The day starts with a ride through Fort Bragg, a lumber town whose main attraction is the Skunk Railroad. The not-so-charming name was derived from the smell of the original engines, which have been replaced with a less pungent variety. The Skunk Train travels east through farmlands and redwood country to end at the town of Willits. Also in Fort Bragg is a large logging museum, tree nursery, and Noyo Harbor, which is the largest working harbor between Eureka and San Francisco. During the Fourth of July weekend, the harbor is home of the world's largest salmon barbecue.

A few miles south, at Jughandle State Reserve, you can see a half-million years of the earth's history by walking a nature trail up an ecological staircase with five distinct terraces, each about 100 feet higher and 100,000 years older than the last. From the ocean's edge, the nature trail heads inland through changing vegetation, starting with north coastal prairie, moving into coast redwood and Douglas fir forests, and ending near a pygmy forest. The entire 500,000 years is covered in a 5-mile round trip. A shorter ½-mile loop covers the most recent history, about 100,000 years' worth.

Continuing south, the route passes Mendocino, a quaint New England–style village perched on a cliff overlooking the Pacific Ocean. The village, founded in 1852, has been beautifully maintained ever since.

Russian Gulch and Van Damme State Parks north and south of Mendocino offer camping with hiker-biker sites, trails to a couple of waterfalls at Russian Gulch, and a pygmy forest at Van Damme. The pygmy forest, in which 70-year-old trees are barely knee-high, can also be reached by a side trip off Highway 1.

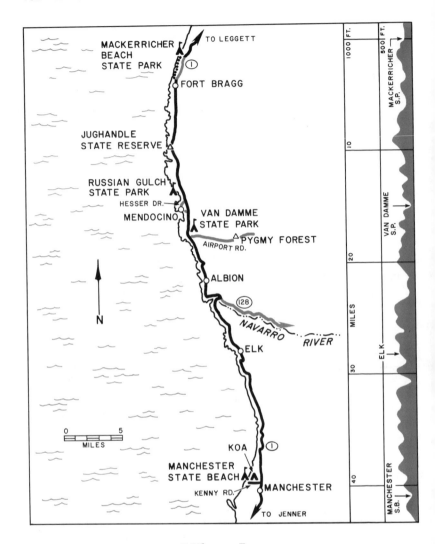

Mileage Log

0.0 Leaving MacKerricher Beach State Park, do not return to Highway 1. Instead, descend toward the beach, passing a small lake. Cycle under an overpass, then immediately turn left and head up the gravel access to the old logging haul road. Head south on the haul road, passing two gates. The road is rough, but the views are excellent as you parallel the coast for the next 2 miles.

2.2 Bridge ahead is closed. Return to Highway 1 by riding through a public parking lot located next to a band of tall, windswept trees. Back on Highway 1, head right on the busy road that descends to

Rugged coast north of Elk

cross Pudding Creek, then climbs to enter Fort Bragg. The large lumber mill in town explains the thundering truck traffic. The largest attraction in Fort Bragg is the Skunk Railroad. For rates and schedules, turn right (west) on Laurel St. to the station. The redwood museum (free) is adjacent to the Skunk Railroad. A large supermarket and well-stocked bike shop are located at the southern end of town on the east side of Highway 1.

4.4 (mp 60.48) Noyo Harbor is to the left (east) of Highway 1.

5.8 (mp 59.08) Mendocino Coast Botanical Gardens. For a fee, you may walk down paths lined with rhododendrons and through a fern canyon.

7.9 (mp 56.00) Jughandle State Reserve: restrooms, picnic tables, water, beach access, and nature trail through the ecological staircase.

8.8 (mp 55.10) Vista point with view of coast and the Casper Creek bridge. This bridge, like most others on Highway 1, has no shoulder.

10.8 (mp 53.2) Russian Gulch State Park: hiker-biker sites and hot showers. A 2.5-mile bicycle path up a narrow gulch leads to a 1½-mile loop hiking trail to the Russian Gulch Falls. On the beach is a spectacular "Punch Bowl."

12.5 (mp 51.5) Mendocino Headlands State Park exit and start of a scenic *Alternate Route* along the ocean's edge through Mendocino. Exit Highway 1. After 0.5 mile turn right on Hesser Dr. for a quiet ride along the rocky cliffs. The wide-open state park makes a

Spur road to Manchester State Beach

nice lunch stop; watch for seals bobbing in the surf. Continue to follow the coastline through the quaint New England-style town of Mendocino with its grocery stores, delis, bakeries, craft shops, art galleries, and bookstores. The road will return you to Highway 1.

13.0 (mp 50.50) Mendocino Headlands State Park Scenic Alternate Route rejoins Highway 1.

13.2 (mp 50.37) Big River State Beach: beach access only.

13.5 (mp 50.00) Commercial campground on left.

13.7 (mp 49.84) Vista point. The best way to savor the New England flavor of Mendocino is to look at it from a distance.

15.2 (mp 48.34) Town of Little River: grocery stores.

15.5 (mp 48.03) Van Damme Beach State Park: hiker-biker sites, water, beach access, and hiking and biking trails to a fern canyon and pygmy forest. The forest may also be reached by road as described below. Park entrance is located on the east side of Highway 1.

16.0 (mp 48.55) Highway 1 becomes narrow and winding with a minimal shoulder that occasionally disappears altogether. *Side Trip* to pygmy forest. Exit left (east) off Highway 1 on Airport Rd. A moderately steep climb of 2.7 miles leads to a nature loop, located on the left (north) side of the road.

19.3 (mp 44.07) Albion: last grocery stores for 10 miles. Highway 1 heads through open coastal grasslands. At about the 22-mile point, the road descends steeply, with some tight corners, along the canyon walls of the Navarro River.

23.1 (mp 40.28) Intersection of Highway 1 and Highway 128. Turn right on Highway 1 and cross the Navarro River (Highway 128 heads east to Cloverdale and US 101). Shift to your lowest gear and wish for a lower one. The mile-long ascent out of the river valley is steep and hot. A sign along the road reading NARROW WINDING ROAD FOR THE NEXT 21 MILES indicates that road conditions will remain the same for some time to come.

28.7 (mp 34.05) Enter the town of Elk, the last chance to pick up groceries before Manchester State Beach. Beyond Elk, the road descends to cross a small creek, then climbs back up with a series of tight, steep switchbacks. Take heart; this short climb is probably the steepest on the entire Pacific Coast.

37.5 (mp 25.27) Vista point with ocean views.

41.4 (mp 21.4) Manchester State Beach turnoff. Follow Kenny Rd. right (west) past a private KOA campground with hot tub, swimming pool, camping cabins, and hot showers.

42.1 Manchester State Beach: hiker-biker camp, water, 4½ miles of beach, and views from a windswept bluff of the ocean and Point Arena Lighthouse. No showers. Nearest grocery store is in Manchester, 1 mile south on Highway 1.

🚲

Manchester State Beach to Bodega Dunes State Beach
(65.4 Miles)

Grass-covered hills, miles of traditional wooden fences, surf-battered cliffs, sheltered coves, and a wide array of weathered sea stacks provide an awe-inspiring backdrop for the ride from Manchester State Beach to Bodega Dunes State Beach.

And, as if the scenery weren't enough of a distraction, Salt Point State Park has numerous trails to lure you off your bike for quiet walks to sheltered coves, fern canyons, tall timber, and large rhododendron trees. Farther south, bikes will again be set aside for a tour of Fort Ross Historical Park. The fort was built by a group of Russians and Eskimos who were sent south in the early 1800s to grow grain for the Alaskan settlements. The fort has been reconstructed and is open to visitors. A visitor center offers a slide show and historical notes describing the fate of these little-known pioneers.

The day ends at Bodega Dunes State Beach. This is a large park set on

---

Cattle guard near Fort Ross

Bodega Bay, at the edge of the sand dunes. Hours can be spent wandering over these hills of sand.

The ride from Manchester State Beach to Bodega Dunes State Beach is long and demanding. The road is narrow, winding, and steep. Traffic is light, except on summer weekends. Wandering sheep and cattle, and the cattle guards that are supposed to keep the livestock from straying too far, add an extra challenge to the 5-mile section south of Fort Ross. It is best to approach the guards straight on, at a moderate pace.

As there are numerous campgrounds along this section of coast, it is easy to stop and linger if you desire. Beyond Bodega Dunes, campgrounds are few and far between, and the pace becomes hectic as the route heads into the Bay Area.

Mileage Log

0.0 From Manchester State Beach, go left on Kenny Rd., and return to Highway 1.

0.7 (mp 21.40) Head right (south) on Highway 1, passing numerous coastal access points.

1.1 (mp 20.90) Manchester city limits: two grocery stores. Beyond Manchester, the road continues to be steep and narrow. Sheep and cows graze on the open hillsides and, in search of greener grass, occasionally wander out onto the road.

4.9 (mp 17.00) Pass a commercial campground. *Side Trip* to Point Arena Lighthouse and museum. The lighthouse, located 2.3 miles off Highway 1, has a distinctive, tall, slender tower visible for many miles along the coast. It is now a museum and open to the public from 11:00 A.M. to 2:30 P.M. on weekdays and 10:00 A.M. to 3:30 P.M. on weekends. Admission is charged. Even if you don't go inside, the ride is rewardingly scenic. Once at the lighthouse, you are standing at the closest point on the West Coast to Hawaii.

5.7 (mp 16.20) Point Arena: complete tourist facilities, including grocery stores. Highway 1 parallels the coast with occasional views.

16.4 (mp 4.71) Anchor Bay, a minute-sized town with a small grocery, private campground, and restaurant.

19.5 (mp 1.31) Gualala has many amenities dear to the heart of a touring cyclist: grocery stores, delis, restaurants, ice creameries, and motels. Watch out, you may ride completely through this small town before you figure out how to pronounce its name.

20.9 (mp 0.00 and 58.68) Leave Mendocino County, enter Sonoma County at Gualala River bridge.

21.3 (mp 58.20) Gualala Point Regional Park. The campground, on the east side of Highway 1, has a hiker-biker area and running water, but no showers. The day-use area, on the west side of Highway 1, has a visitor center with restrooms, running water, and beach access.

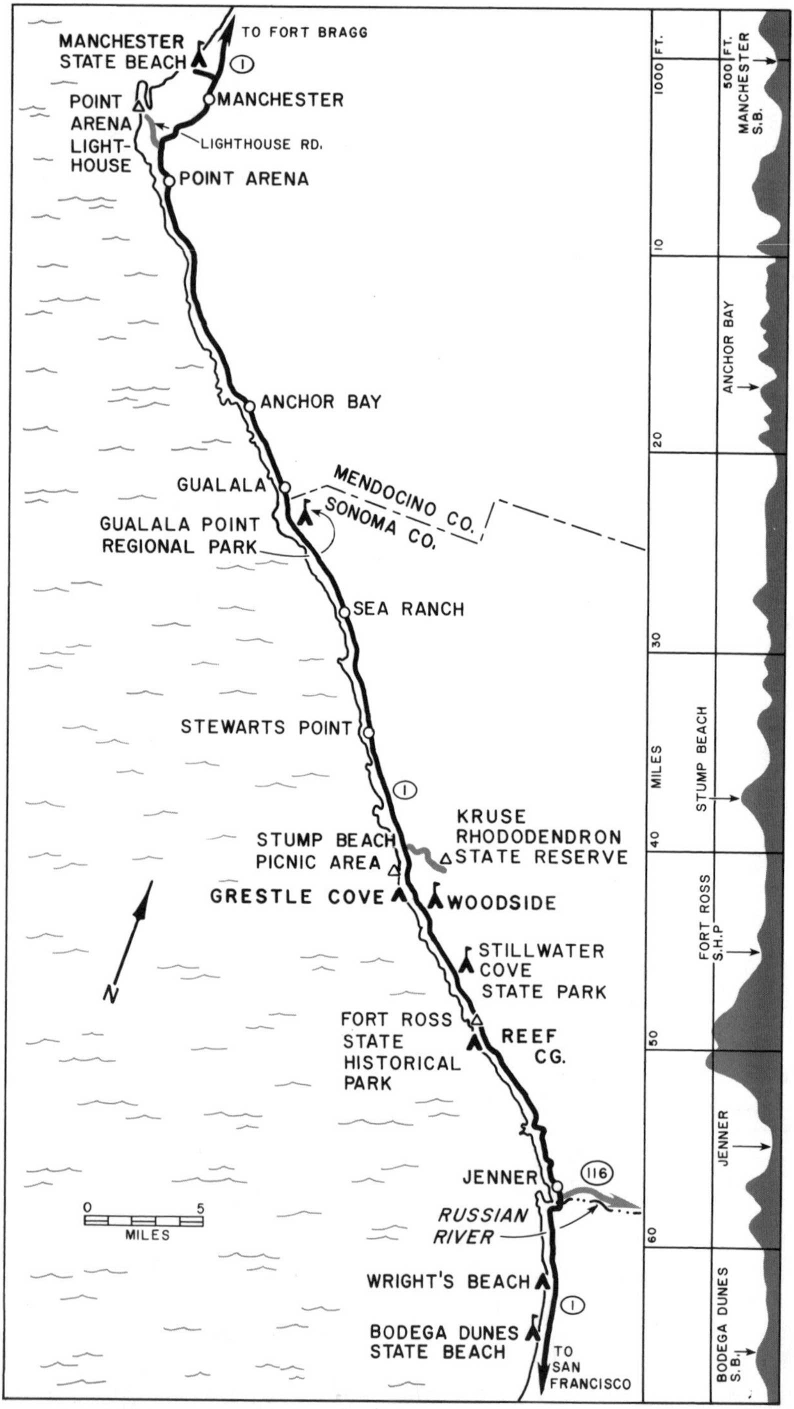

MANCHESTER
STATE BEACH

TO FORT BRAGG

MANCHESTER

POINT
ARENA
LIGHT-
HOUSE

LIGHTHOUSE RD.

POINT ARENA

ANCHOR BAY

GUALALA

MENDOCINO CO.

SONOMA CO.

GUALALA POINT
REGIONAL PARK

SEA RANCH

STEWARTS POINT

KRUSE
RHODODENDRON
STATE RESERVE

STUMP BEACH
PICNIC AREA

GRESTLE COVE

WOODSIDE

STILLWATER
COVE
STATE PARK

FORT ROSS
STATE
HISTORICAL
PARK

REEF
CG.

N

JENNER

RUSSIAN
RIVER

0   5
MILES

WRIGHT'S BEACH

BODEGA DUNES
STATE BEACH

TO
SAN
FRANCISCO

1000 FT.

10

20

30

MILES

40

50

60

500 FT.

MANCHESTER S.B.

ANCHOR BAY

STUMP BEACH

FORT ROSS S.H.P.

JENNER

BODEGA DUNES S.B.

Beyond the park, Highway 1 enters Sea Ranch, a long, rambling community of expensive beach houses. The area is generally quiet during the week until Friday afternoon, when there is a mass migration up from the San Francisco Bay Area. On Sunday afternoon, the process is reversed as everyone dashes south. All side roads through Sea Ranch are private. The state park system has set up four coastal access points where you can leave your bike and walk to the beach; they have restrooms but no water.

29.6 (mp 49.64) Leave Sea Ranch and return to the cow- and sheep-dotted landscapes.

31.3 (mp 48.1) Stewarts Point, a small, tourist-oriented community. The grocery store is open daily from 8:00 A.M. to 6:00 P.M. Beyond Stewarts Point, the road remains narrow, winding, and steep, with several short, tantalizing sections of shoulder.

34.7 (mp 44.48) Enter Salt Water State Park.

36.3 (mp 42.75) *Side Trip* to Kruse Rhododendron State Reserve. Turn

Point Arena Lighthouse

left (east) off Highway 1 and cycle up Kruse Ranch Rd. to the end of the pavement and an intersection. Walk or ride the right fork 0.4 mile to the reserve. Trails vary from ¼ to 5 miles in length. This area is at its best from late April through mid-June when the rhododendrons are in bloom.

36.4 (mp 42.63) Fisk Cove: restrooms, beach access, and picnic tables.

37.8 (mp 41.22) Stump Beach picnic area: restrooms and access to a sandy cove. No running water.

38.9 (mp 39.90) Grestle Cove Campground: campsites, beach access, and running water. Hiker-biker site is located 50 feet south on the left side of the road at Woodside Campground.

39.0 (mp 39.89) Woodside Campground: hiker-biker site, water, and many miles of trails to the beach, along the bluffs, up the hills to vista points, and to a pygmy forest behind the park. No showers.

40.7 (mp 38.2) Ocean Cove: a tourist community with a very small grocery store and a commercial campground.

41.6 (mp 37.02) Stillwater Cove State Park: hiker-biker site, running water, showers, and beach access. This small park is popular with skin divers.

44.8 (mp 33.83) Fort Ross store: limited groceries.

45.4 (mp 33.00) Fort Ross State Historical Park: fort, visitor center, slide show, historical displays, restrooms, water, picnic facilities, and a grassy bluff for strolling. Fort Ross marks the start of 10 strenuous and scenic miles as Highway 1 climbs over headlands and drops into deep coves. The highway becomes a bare etching across the steep, unstable cliffs ahead. Caltrans has installed a gate that is closed when the road or hillsides ahead are deemed unsafe.

46.5 (mp 31.90) The first of seven cattle guards to be crossed in the next 5 miles.

46.1 (mp 31.37) Reef Campground. This primitive facility, located in a sheltered fold of the hill, has pit toilets and beach access.

51.6 (mp 26.50) Long, moderate ascent leads to the top of a 520-foot hill and the end of the cattle guards. A steep road on the right climbs to the Vista Trail and a scenic view along the hillcrest. Highway 1 sweeps back to sea level with an exhilarating switchback.

53.1 (mp 24.40) Russian Gulch bridge marks the end of the descent and the start of another steep, though lesser, climb.

55.6 (mp 21.5) Jenner, a small town perched on a steep hillside overlooking the Russian River and a long sandspit. A small gas station–convenience store on the left side of the road is your last chance to purchase groceries before Bodega Dunes.

57.3 (mp 20.28) Junction of Highway 1 and Highway 116. Highway 1 continues south, while Highway 116 heads east to California's famous wine country.

Replica of the old buildings at Fort Ross State Historical Park

57.4 (mp 20.00) Cross the Russian River. A restaurant is located on the left at the south end of the bridge. A commercial campground is located on the right.

58.3 (mp 18.6) Turnoff to Goat Rock State Beach, the first of a series of Sonoma Coast State Beaches. Goat Rock State Beach has two access roads. The first access descends 0.8 mile, the second is a steep 2-mile descent. Restrooms and water at both access points.

59.2 (mp 18.2) Shell Beach: tide pool exploration and surf fishing. No facilities.

60.6 (mp 16.77) Wright's Beach, a small campground: restrooms and running water. No showers or hiker-biker sites.

61.1 (mp 16.35) Duncan's Landing Beach, an historical loading area for coastal trading ships. The rocky headland next to the beach earned the name of Death Rock among sailors.

62.7 (mp 14.68) Portuguese Beach, a popular day-use area. No facilities.

63.0 (mp 14.33) Schoolhouse Beach: restrooms and tide pools to explore.

64.4 (mp 12.90) North Salmon Beach: sandy beaches, surf fishing, and restrooms. Highway 1 is lined with ice plants.

65.4 (mp 11.67) Bodega Dunes State Beach campground: hot showers, restrooms, and a sandy hiker-biker area. A hiking trail through the dunes leads to a sandy beach. The nearest grocery store is 1.2 miles south in Bodega Bay.

Bodega Dunes State Beach to Samuel P. Taylor State Park (40.6 Miles)

Three large bays, Estro Americano, Tomales Bay, and San Francisco Bay, cut deep into the coastline between Bodega Bay and San Francisco. Highway 1 turns inland to bypass Estro Americano, then skirts along the edge of Tomales Bay before heading east around the Marin Headlands to cross San Francisco Bay at the Golden Gate Bridge.

The main point of interest on this ride is Point Reyes National Seashore, a beautiful 64,000-acre park with over 70 miles of coastline. This unique area, geologically isolated from the mainland by the San Andreas Fault, is habitat for several hundred species of birds and seventy kinds of mammals. Trails are the only access to many of the park's beaches, sand dunes, and lakes, making it a difficult area to explore on a bicycle. The best place to begin is at the visitor center which has displays, movies, a nature trail along the San Andreas Fault, and an authentic replica of a Native American village. To fully explore the park requires several days—or weeks—to hike or mountain bike the trails and ride the paved road to the lighthouse. Camping is permitted at a hiker-biker site in Tomales State Park (adjoining the national seashore). There is also a youth hostel in the park. If touring

Tomales Bay

on a mountain bike, you can take advantage of the park's backcountry campsite system, accessed by well-maintained, double-track trails.

Beyond Tomales Bay, the route leaves Highway 1 and heads inland to the San Francisco Bay Area. Although Highway 1 appears tempting on the map, it's considered extremely hazardous south of Olema—narrow, winding, shoulderless, and busy.

Inland, away from coastal breezes, the temperatures rise—quite a surprise, especially to those with empty water bottles. But that is not the end of the surprises: once past the first set of hot, dry hills, the route abandons the road in favor of a well-shaded bicycle path through the redwoods, ending at Samuel P. Taylor State Park.

Samuel P. Taylor State Park was one of the first areas in the United States where outdoor camping was promoted as a recreational pursuit. The park has numerous trails and, time and energy permitting, you can explore a fire lookout or the foundations of a paper mill, where the first square-bottomed paper bags were made in the late 1800s.

If you are lucky enough to secure a campsite, you may opt to pass up Samuel P. Taylor State Park in favor of a fantastic site 30 miles south at Marin Headlands National Recreation Area. This extraordinary hiker-biker site has a stunning view overlooking San Francisco and the Golden Gate Bridge. Space is limited and advance reservations are required, so call ahead—if possible, by several days—to the visitor center, (415)331-1540.

To reach Marin Headlands National Recreation Area, it is necessary to negotiate a fair amount of city traffic—a very slow process. See the next section for details.

Mileage Log

0.0 (mp 11.67) From Bodega Dunes State Beach, head south on Highway 1.

0.5 (mp 11.17) Fast-food haven, an excellent spot to fill those empty stomachs.

1.2 (mp 10.47) Town of Bodega Bay has adequate facilities to feed the hungriest cyclist, as well as motels, restaurants, grocery store, and a Laundromat. From the center of town, look across Bodega Harbor to the large fishing fleet. Keep an eye out for brown pelicans and other aquatic life. Beyond Bodega Bay, the shoulders are excellent as Highway 1 heads inland, climbing over grass-covered hills.

9.5 (mp 2.10) Valley Ford: grocery stores and restaurants. Shoulders end here.

11.3 (mp 0.18) Junction of Highway 1 and Valley Ford Rd. Turn right (south) on Highway 1. Valley Ford Rd. heads inland to Petaluma and US 101.

11.5 (mp 0.0 and 50.5) Leave Sonoma County and enter Marin County. The terrain is open as the highway rolls over short, steep hills.

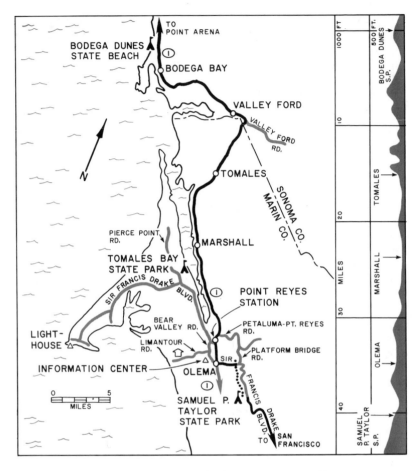

Shoulders are infrequent and when present, usually very narrow. Traffic is moderate. Cattle ranches appear. Redwood groves give way to eucalyptus trees.

16.0 (mp 46.00) Tomales: limited groceries, and a few bed-and-breakfast houses. Leaving town, Highway 1 descends, twisting with little shoulder, to parallel Tomales Bay for the next 19 miles.

21.7 (mp 40.11) Popular wind surfing area.

23.1 (mp 38.41) Marshall: restaurants and a grocery store.

28.2 (mp 33.65) Coastal access: parking lot, restrooms, and bay access.

31.5 (mp 30.65) Tomales Bay Trail access.

32.4 (mp 29.28) Sharp corner and intersection. Go right and follow Highway 1 toward Point Reyes Station and two grocery stores.

32.8 (mp 28.94) First turnoff to Point Reyes National Seashore; do not turn here.

32.9 (mp 28.77) Point Reyes Station. Purchase groceries for the night here. This small town has numerous restaurants and coffee shops.

34.3 (mp 27.37) Turnoff for Point Reyes National Seashore. (For side trip details, see end of this mileage log.) Just before the turnoff is Olema Ranch Campground, a commercial facility with a grocery store, restaurant, showers, water, and laundry facilities. This campground can be used as an alternate when Samuel P. Taylor runs out of water and closes, as happens occasionally in the late summer and fall.

34.6 (mp 26.76) Olema: limited groceries. The route leaves Highway 1 and heads left (east) up Sir Francis Drake Blvd. Climb a steep hill then descend into a narrow valley.

37.1 (mp 20.54) Just before crossing a short bridge over Lagunitas Creek, go right and descend a gravel trail to the paved Marin Bicycle Trail. Head left and parallel Sir Francis Drake Blvd. as it heads along Lagunitas Creek.

38.5 Jewell Trail branches off to the right. Continue straight, paralleling the creek into the state park.

40.6 Cycle through the camp area to an intersection. Turn right, crossing the creek to reach the entrance booth for Samuel P. Taylor State Park, and register. The park offers a hiker-biker site and hot showers under the deep shade of the redwood forest.

Point Reyes Lighthouse

Point Reyes National Seashore Side Trip

Turn right (west) on Bear Valley Rd. At 0.5 mile, go left to the Information Center for a park map, movie, slide show, restrooms, water, picnic tables, San Andreas Fault Trail, Native American village, beach trails, and backcountry campsite reservations. To reach the hostel, it is necessary to ride up Limantour Rd. (2.1 miles north of the Information Center), gaining 1,400 feet before descending back to sea level. The hiker-biker campsite at Tomales State Park is a pleasant place to stay, and very easy to reach. Cycle north from the Information Center on Bear Valley Rd., which merges with Sir Francis Drake Blvd. At 8.2 miles, go right (north) on Pierce Point Rd. for 1 mile to the park. Follow the signs to the hiker-biker site (the only camping allowed in the park). If you ride the entire 21.1 miles to the end of Sir Francis Drake Blvd., you'll reach the famous Point Reyes Lighthouse. Visitors descend 300 steps to the light and an impressive view of the surrounding coast, including sea lions on the offshore rocks.

Samuel P. Taylor State Park to Half Moon Bay State Beach (58.1 Miles)

Between Samuel P. Taylor State Park and Half Moon Bay State Beach sprawls the Bay Area megalopolis, which includes San Francisco and a dozen satellite cities. If you are having any mechanical problems with your bike or equipment, this is the time to take care of them.

The Bay Area is excellent for cycling, if taken at a leisurely pace. Bike paths crisscross the cities, connecting parks, viewpoints, and beaches. However, if you are planning to traverse this large metropolitan area in a single day, even an early start will not leave much time for exploration. Winding through residential streets and stopping for lights and stop signs makes for slow going, requiring any number of extra hours.

Much of the route through the Bay Area is delineated by green and white city bike route signs and an occasional Bicentennial or Pacific Coast bike route marker. Some riders find it helpful to trace the route on a city street map before starting. You may also find it useful to make a copy of the mileage log and keep it handy.

The route through the Bay Area is very scenic, with views of San Francisco Bay, Alcatraz, the Golden Gate Bridge, classic residential areas, sandy beaches, and Devil's Slide. Close to, but not on the route are the famous Marin Headlands, Fort Point, and Golden Gate Park. Marin Headlands is a national recreation area with a magnificent view of San Francisco and the Golden Gate Bridge. Fort Point is a classic brick fortress that was outdated almost before it was completed in 1861, and Golden Gate Park is a beautiful island of green in the middle of San Francisco with lakes,

Residential San Francisco near Golden Gate Park

botanical and Japanese gardens, a buffalo paddock, museums, the Academy of Science, and quiet groves of trees.

Cyclists spending time in San Francisco can stay at any number of places in or near the city—on the Marin Headlands (hiker-biker campsites and a 300-person hostel); in San Francisco at the International Hostel (east of the Golden Gate Bridge); or at the Montara Lighthouse Hostel (20 miles south of San Francisco but on a main bus route to town). Advance reservations are necessary for all these facilities during the summer.

If planning to end your ride at San Francisco, check at the end of the mileage log for routes to the airport and railroad station.

South of San Francisco, the route returns to Highway 1 just in time to tackle the slide prone Devil's Headland. The road is very narrow. Try to reach this area as early as possible to avoid the afternoon traffic. Detours are common, especially in the spring. If your budget cannot handle an emergency stop-over at a motel, you should check road conditions ahead of time by calling the San Francisco branch of Caltrans (California Transit) before you reach the Bay Area.

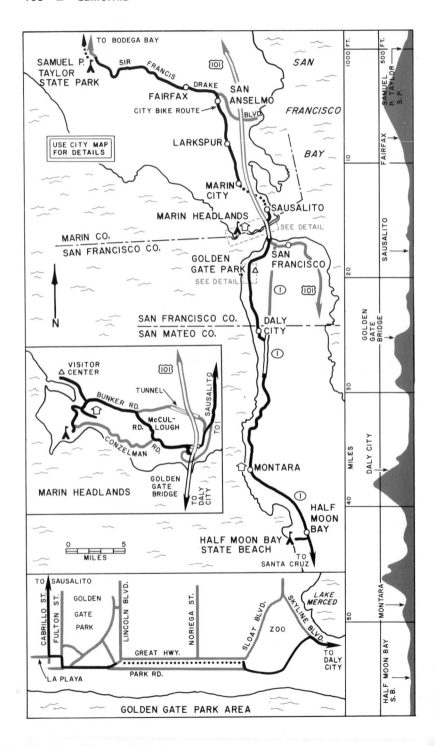

Mileage Log

0.0 Leaving Samuel P. Taylor State Park Campground, head southeast on Sir Francis Drake Blvd. The shoulderless road is narrow and winding, shaded by dense foliage, and full of potholes.

1.7 Leave Samuel P. Taylor State Park.

2.4 Lagunita, a small town with a grocery store. The road widens as it leaves the redwoods to include a shoulder.

3.0 Forest Knolls, a sprawling residential community with a small store. Head out into the open countryside for 5 miles of straightforward riding. Use caution as you descend the steep hill into Fairfax; large water drains make riding on the shoulder hazardous.

8.4 At the entrance to Fairfax, go right on Olema Road and follow city bike route signs through town. The next 3.5 miles are on city streets.

8.9 Pass a second sign announcing Fairfax city limits.

9.2 Go right on Manor Rd. When Manor Rd. divides, stay left.

9.4 Take a left on Scenic Rd.

9.6 Turn left on Azala and almost immediately after go right on Broadway. Ride through the town center passing numerous small businesses and eating establishments.

10.0 Broadway becomes Center Blvd.

10.2 Jog right on Lansdale, a narrow, alley-type road which parallels Center Blvd.

10.4 Enter San Anselmo.

10.6 Jog to the right again on San Anselmo Ave. and continue following bike route signs through quiet residential streets.

10.9 Arrive at a T intersection and go left.

11.2 Go left again on Hazel Ave., once again paralleling Center Blvd.

11.3 Intersection. A jog to the left puts you back on San Anselmo Ave.

11.5 Go right, still on San Anselmo Ave., and head through the town center.

12.1 Go left on Bolinas Ave.

12.2 A right turn returns you to Sir Francis Drake Blvd., which is now a busy road with a very minor shoulder. Before long you will pass the Kendall city limits.

13.4 Go right on College Ave. Follow it as it turns into Magnolia Ave. at the Larkspur city limits. Note Mount Tamalpais, the birthplace of mountain biking, on the right.

15.5 Pass Oliver Park on the right: restrooms.

16.1 Turn left on Redwood Ave. and descend 1 block, then go right on Tamalpais Dr. Continue straight for 0.5 mile.

16.7 At the second-to-last stoplight before the US 101 freeway entrance, turn right on Casa Buena Dr. Climb a steep hill while paralleling US 101.

17.6 At the top of the second of two steep rises, the road bends sharply uphill. Go straight ahead on an unmarked bike path, paralleling the freeway.

18.1 The bike path ends. Follow Lomita Dr. as it bends to the right and stay with it until reaching an old elementary school-turned-business center.

18.6 When Lomita Dr. bends left, go straight ahead on a narrow, gravel-surfaced bike path. After a short 0.1 mile, go left again on a paved path that heads up the hill to a wide bikeway.

19.1 The bikeway crosses Blithedale Ave. Continue straight, following the bikeway over a marsh, pass a small lagoon, under US 101, and then along the boat harbor.

21.5 Bikeway ends. (This is a very confusing area. If you suddenly find yourself riding on a sidewalk, turn around and go back to the last intersection.) Cross Bridgeway, a busy 4-laner, at the intersection, then go left. Ride on Bridgeway until it ends.

23.9 Bridgeway ends. Turn right and pedal up Richardson St. At the first intersection turn left on 2nd St. and follow it through a congested area of small shops, then up a steep hill.

24.1 As 2nd St. ends, turn left on South St.

24.2 South St. bends right and becomes S. Alexander Ave.

25.2 Continue straight, ignoring a city bike route sign pointing to the left, and ride through an underpass of US 101.

25.4 Go right at the freeway interchange and head uphill following, briefly, signs to Marin Headlands National Recreation Area. Take the first left, which leads to a parking lot. Ride across the parking lot to find an entrance to the westside Golden Gate Bridge Pedestrian Way. For details of the Headlands side trip, see the end of this mileage log.

25.6 Head across this classical bridge, beautiful in sun, fog, or smog.

26.0 Leave Marin County; enter San Francisco County.

27.6 Follow the bike path as it loops around then under US 101 to the east side of the bridge. Unless shrouded in fog, take the time to visit the vista point for a long look over San Francisco Bay.

27.7 Ride as straight as possible through the busy parking area to reach Lincoln Blvd.

27.8 Turn right on Lincoln Blvd. *Side Trip* to Fort Point National Historic Site. Go left (east) on Lincoln Blvd. for 0.5 mile to the fort's access road.

28.5 Pass an unsigned turnoff to Bakers State Beach: restrooms, picnic tables, water, and a sandy beach.

28.9 Lincoln Blvd. becomes Camino Del Mar. Continue straight for 3 more blocks.

29.1 Turn left on 28th Ave. and ride up and over a hill through the tightly packed and beautifully maintained residential district of San Francisco.

Golden Gate Bridge

30.1 At Cabrillo St., go right. (If you are heading for the Amtrak Station, check directions at the end of this mileage log.)

31.4 Cabrillo St. ends. Go left on a bike path paralleling the busy Great Highway (also called Park Rd.).

31.5 Intersection. Southbound travelers should cross Park Rd. here, then go left either on the wide shoulder or on the beachside bike path. The tops of two windmills can be seen over the crest of the trees, marking the famous Golden Gate Park to the left. The park makes an excellent side trip or a lunch stop.

34.3 Bike path ends. All riders must now return to the shoulder of the highway.

35.1 Skyline Blvd. joins Park Rd. from the left. The combined road, now called Highway 35, continues south with a broad bicycle lane on the shoulder.

36.1 Pass two accesses to Fort Funston on the right: beach access.

36.4 Leave San Francisco County and enter San Mateo County.

36.8 (mp 31.00) Daly City: fast food and supermarkets.

38.2 (mp 29.80) Begin Daly City bypass route. At the false summit of a steep hill, leave Highway 35 and go right on Westmoor Ave. After 1 block, bear left on Skyline Dr. Pedal up a rather steep hill through a residential area. Once up, go very steeply down; do not allow the excellent view south over the coast to distract you. (If heading to the San Francisco International Airport (SFO), leave the bike route here. See the end of this mileage log for details.)

40.0 While still descending steeply, pass a school on the right, then take the first left on Crenshaw Dr. In 1 block, go right on Palmetto Ave. and stay with it as it parallels Highway 1 past freeway entrances and a shopping center.

42.5 At the end of Palmetto Ave., go left on Clarendon, then immediately right on Lakeside Ave.

42.7 Lakeside Ave. exits onto Francisco Blvd. Continue south, passing along the right side of Sharp Park: picnic tables, restrooms, and water.

43.3 Francisco Blvd. turns into Bradford Way; continue straight. Circumnavigate around to the south side of Moose Lodge. When the road divides, stay left. Just before reaching Highway 1, go right up an unusually steep bike path that parallels the freeway. (Ignore bike path signs pointing away from the road.)

43.8 (mp 42.50) Bike path ends; continue on the shoulder of Highway 1.

45.3 (mp 40.00) Lind Mar Rest Area: a parking lot with restrooms and beach access but no water. No easy access for northbound cyclists.

45.7 (mp 39.63) Highway narrows as it begins its steep climb over Devil's Slide. The shoulder narrows then disappears entirely. Note the THINK TUNNEL bumper stickers on cars. If you reach this area during rush hour, you will soon be ready to grab a shovel and help them start digging.

46.6 (mp 38.40) Pass the first of two old military installations precipitously perched on the headlands. Find a turnout if you wish to stop and look at this spectacular area.

49.9 (mp 36.00) Enter Montara, a coastal tourist town with grocery stores and fast food. The route is now on level terrain, and the shoulders are good and remain so for the rest of the day.

50.1 (mp 35.8) Beach access, restrooms, but no water.

50.8 (mp 35.4) Montara Lighthouse Hostel.

Highway 1 in the Devil's Slide area, a very unstable region

51.0 (mp 35.42) Enter the small coastal town of Moss Beach: no grocery stores near Highway 1. Pass the turnoff to James Fitzgerald Marin Reserve, where you can explore the marine habitat on a large band of coast rocks. Sea lions are often seen sunbathing on the outer rocks.

53.2 (mp 33.4) El Granada. A small grocery store is 1 block left from Highway 1.

53.8 (mp 32.8) Half Moon Bay city limits.

55.8 (mp 30.6) Access to Dunes Beach, a park designed to accommodate equestrians and their mounts.

57.5 (mp 28.80) Junction of Highway 1 and Highway 92: bike shop and major shopping center are located on the east side of the road.

57.8 (mp 28.50) Turnoff to Half Moon Bay State Beach and campground. Turn right on Kelly Rd., opposite a small but adequate convenience store.

58.1 Half Moon Bay State Beach: beach access, restrooms, cold outdoor showers, and a hiker-biker site at the far end of the camping area.

Marin Headlands National Recreation Area Side Trip

At the northern entrance to the Golden Gate Bridge, pass the parking area turnoff and continue up the steep grade of Conzelman Rd. Viewpoints are numerous and, in good weather, so are the automobiles. At 1.2

miles the road divides. Cyclists looking for views should stay left and continue up the final mile to the summit. To reach the hiker-biker camp or hostel, follow the right fork on a 1-mile descent to Bunker Rd., then go left. Follow Bunker Rd. 1.2 miles to a Y intersection. If the hostel is your destination, stay left on Field Rd. for 500 feet, then turn uphill, following the signs. If the hiker-biker camp is your destination, continue on Bunker Rd. for another 0.8 mile, register at the visitor center, and receive directions to the camp area. Be prepared to put up with some inconveniences (no showers, no running water, although water is available nearby) and enjoy the tremendous view. You must call ahead to the Marin Headlands National Recreation Center Visitor Center for reservations: (415)331-1540.

Amtrak and the Oakland Airport

San Francisco does not have an Amtrak Station. The nearest station is located across the bay in Oakland, and the best way to get there is by BART (Bay Area Rapid Transit). Follow the bike route through San Francisco for 30.1 miles to Cabrillo St. Go right on Cabrillo St. to 43rd Ave., then turn left and ride through Golden Gate Park on 37th Ave. At Yorba St. go left, then right on Sunset Blvd., which will turn into Lake Merced Blvd. At John Daly Blvd., go left and follow this major street until it crosses a freeway. Exit and go left (north) to BART Station No. 1. Bicycles are allowed on BART from 9:30 A.M. to 3:30 P.M. Monday through Friday and all day on weekends and holidays. Once at the station take the elevator down then look for a station agent to let you through the gate. If you cannot find an agent, buy your ticket, go through the gate, then lift your bike over the four-foot barrier.

San Francisco International Airport

Follow the mileage log for the first 38.2 miles. Stay on Highway 35 after the bike route exits in Daly City and follow it to Bruno Ave. Head east. Near the airport you will cross over US 101. Continue straight until Bruno Ave. ends, then go right and follow the busy frontage road to the terminal.

Half Moon Bay State Beach to New Brighton State Beach (56.5 Miles)

The coast south of San Francisco is a popular vacation getaway. During the summer, this area overflows with tourists from around the world. On weekends fishermen, surfers, sunbathers, and beachcombers from the Bay Area mob the beaches. Despite its popularity, the coast is remarkably unspoiled, with only a few towns marring the open grasslands and

Bean Hollow State Beach

sandy beaches. Where the highway parallels the ocean, an observant cyclist may spot sea lions basking in the sun or otters playing in the surf.

A stop at Ano Nuevo State Reserve is highly recommended. From December through April, elephant seals breed and raise their young here. During the summer, they can be spotted sunning themselves on the offshore rocks.

Tide pools are excellent in this area. Some of the richest pools are at Bean Hollow and Natural Bridges State Beaches. If you have never explored a tide pool, take this opportunity to do so. The variety of life that survives

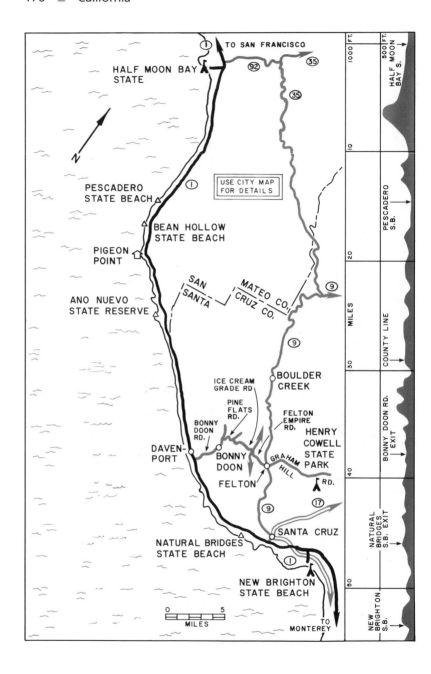

in the precarious and ever-changing environment of these small pools is amazing.

In Santa Cruz, Highway 1 turns into a busy, congested freeway. The bike route wisely heads west for a spectacular tour along the coast, passing Natural Bridges State Beach, overlooks, surfing beaches, and a surf museum. The route then follows city streets through town to New Brighton State Beach.

Highway 1 has a good shoulder throughout most of this section, and riding is generally very enjoyable—a marked contrast to the trek through San Francisco. One note of caution: Before leaving Half Moon Bay, be sure to check your food and water supplies. The first water stop is at 27.7 miles, and the first grocery store is 37 miles south.

Mileage Log

0.0 From Half Moon Bay State Beach, follow Kelly Rd. back to Highway 1.

0.2 (mp 29.10) Kelly Rd. ends at Highway 1. The Pacific Coast Bike Route heads south toward Santa Cruz.

2.9 (mp 26.30) Cowell Ranch beach access: pit toilet, trail to beach, and historical information.

10.7 (mp 18.15) San Gregorio State Beach: beach access, toilets, no running water.

12.3 (mp 16.59) Pomponio State Beach: beach access, toilets, no running water.

14.1 (mp 14.65) Pescadero State Beach: beach access, chemical toilets, no running water. Translated from Spanish, Pescadero means "the fishing place," and this one is well known for surf fishing. In the next mile, two more Pescadero State Beach accesses are passed.

15.0 (mp 13.54) Turnoff to Butano State Park campground, located several miles inland from the coast. The park has some nice redwood groves and mountain biking trails but no hiker-biker sites or showers.

16.6 (mp 12.00) Bean Hollow State Beach, also known as Pebble Beach: beach access, tide pools, and a mile-long, self-guiding nature trail along the bluff. Pebble Beach gets its name from the thousands of tiny, multicolored pebbles. Don't mine the beach; leave it for others to enjoy.

17.6 (mp 11.20) A second Bean Hollow State Beach access: restroom, southern end of the nature trail, and beach access.

20.7 (mp 8.00) Turnoff to Pigeon Point Light Station and hostel. This beacon, the second tallest in the nation, is visible from great distances, by land or sea. If spending the night at the hostel, take a walk along the beach to look for whale bones, common here, or watch for live whales on their annual migration.

22.8 (mp 5.89) Gazos State Beach: beach access, chemical toilets, no water.

27.2 (mp 1.41) Turnoff to Ano Nuevo State Reserve, the first watering hole since Half Moon Bay. In winter, this is a very popular area for viewing gray whales and elephant seals. From December through March you may enter the reserve only if accompanied by a park naturalist. For reservations call (800)444-7475. For the remainder of the year, you are free to explore the tide pools, while watching for sea otters and harbor seals in the surf.

28.6 (mp 0.0 and 37.5) Leave San Mateo County and enter Santa Cruz County.

29.5 (mp 36.45) Walden Beach: toilets but no running water. On the left, a short dirt road heads into the western tip of Big Basin Redwoods State Park. (No state park facilities here. The main entrance and the redwood giants are accessed from Highway 9.) The shoulder remains good as you head south past miles of artichoke and Brussels sprout farms.

31.0 (mp 35.0) Greyhound Rock: public fishing and toilets.

36.9 (mp 29.13) Davenport. At long last, food. The solitary store in this tiny community is very popular among bicyclists. From here to Santa Cruz are numerous beach access points.

44.3 (mp 21.73) Wilder Ranch State Park: water, toilets, visitor center, beach access, mountain bike trails, guided tours to historic buildings.

45.6 (mp 20.42) Santa Cruz: supermarkets, bike shops, beaches, fishing piers, tide pools, and lots of people. Some tricky navigation is needed to ride through this small metropolis. However, Santa Cruz is a college town, and bicycles are an accepted mode of transport.

46.1 (mp 19.92) Turn right off Highway 1 on Western Dr., following Pacific Coast Bicycle Route signs. Go 1 block to the Wrigleys factory then take a right on Mission St. and head north for 1 block.

46.2 Turn left on Natural Bridges Dr. and ride west toward the coast.

46.6 Go left again at Delaware Ave.

46.7 At Swanton Blvd., turn right and ride along the south side of Natural Bridges State Beach.

47.1 Before taking a left on West Cliff Dr., go right to Natural Bridges State Beach Overlook and descend to the 20-minute parking lot for a cliff's edge view over the rocky beach. (The most spectacular natural bridge eroded away several decades ago.) You have already passed several park entrances; this is yet another chance to visit this interesting day-use area, which features a sandy beach, tide pools, butterfly trees (wintering spot for monarch butterflies), restrooms, picnic tables, running water, and guided walks. After visiting the beach, head southwest along W. Cliff Dr.

49.0 At Lighthouse Field State Beach, check out the Santa Cruz Surfing

Museum, located in the old lighthouse on the point. W. Cliff Dr. now heads east around Santa Cruz Harbor. The waters here are popular with long-board surfers because of the small, slow waves.

49.9 Stay with W. Cliff Dr. as it leaves the harbor, just before reaching the pier, casino, boardwalk, and amusement park.

50.1 West Cliff Dr. ends. Ride straight across Washington St. to Pacific Ave. Before long, Pacific Ave. will become Front St.

50.2 Go right on Laurel St. and ride across an overpass.

50.3 Route divides. Pacific Coast Bicycle Route signs indicate that the route should go straight on a very confusing tour through Capitola. We suggest staying left on Laurel St.

50.5 Laurel St. becomes Broadway.

51.7 Broadway ends. Turn left on Frederick St.

52.0 Frederick St. ends. Turn right on Soquel Dr. and follow it for the next 4 miles to the New Brighton State Beach turnoff. Purchase food for the night along this section.

56.0 Turnoff to New Brighton State Beach. Go right on Park Ave.

56.5 New Brighton State Beach: hiker-biker site (a one-night limit), hot showers, and beach access. *Side Trip.* After you set up camp, cycle west on Park Ave. to the town of Capitola for a walk on the beach, then follow East Cliff Dr. back to Santa Cruz and the famous Boardwalk Amusement Park. If leaving your bicycle for even a moment, be sure it is locked.

Comfortable shoulders south of Half Moon Bay are a pleasant reward after a hectic day of riding through the San Francisco Bay area

🚲

New Brighton State Beach to Vet's Memorial Park, Monterey (40.8 Miles)

Between New Brighton State Beach and Monterey, 32.4 miles are spent touring through farmlands on back roads and bike paths. Unless you find Brussels sprouts, strawberries, artichokes, and chicken farms to be incredibly interesting, start your day's ride early and sprint all the way to Monterey, which is a fascinating place to explore.

Although completely lacking in scenic interest, this is a great area for riding. Terrain varies from gently rolling to level. The greatest hazard to cyclists, especially in the Monterey area, is dense fog.

The day's ride ends at Vet's Memorial Park, a small city park with a small hiker-biker area. Cyclists are turned away only when the site actually overflows. Arrive early to claim a space for your tent. Monterey attracts visitors from around the world, so expect an international crowd at the campsite.

The Monterey area more than makes up for the uneventful ride, and you can spend the remaining hours of the day enjoying this vibrant town. At the end of the mileage log is a special tour of Monterey, including stops at Fisherman's Wharf, Cannery Row ("restored" to an elegance it never had in Steinbeck's famous novel), Point Lobos Light Station (beautifully situated at the edge of the Point Lobos Refuge), the wintering spot for monarch butterflies (these fragile insects fly all the way down from Alaska), and the beautiful 17-Mile Drive (possibly the most famous stretch of road on the California Coast). An afternoon is the absolute minimum amount of time required to see to this area. To see it all, an extra day is needed.

The newest addition to this area, an aquarium located at the southern end of Cannery Row, is a masterpiece. Visitors are taken on a visual journey from the estuary at Elkhorn Slough to the tidelands, then down below the wharf through the kelp beds to the ocean floor. If you enjoy the ocean or just like to space out looking at glowing jellyfish, a trip to the aquarium is a must. Plan to spend 3 or more hours there.

Mileage Log

0.0 From New Brighton State Beach, pedal back up Park Ave.

0.6 Turn right at Soquel Dr., rejoining the Santa Cruz city bike route. Stay on Soquel Dr. for the next 4.8 miles.

2.5 *Side Trip* to Sea Cliffs State Beach. Turn right (west) on State Park Dr. for 0.6 mile to the long, sandy beach, a favorite with sunbathers. Amenities include picnic tables and restrooms. An old shipwreck has been converted into a pier for fishermen.

4.6 Confusing intersection. After passing Rio Del Mar Blvd., follow Soquel Dr. as it makes a sharp turn to the right.

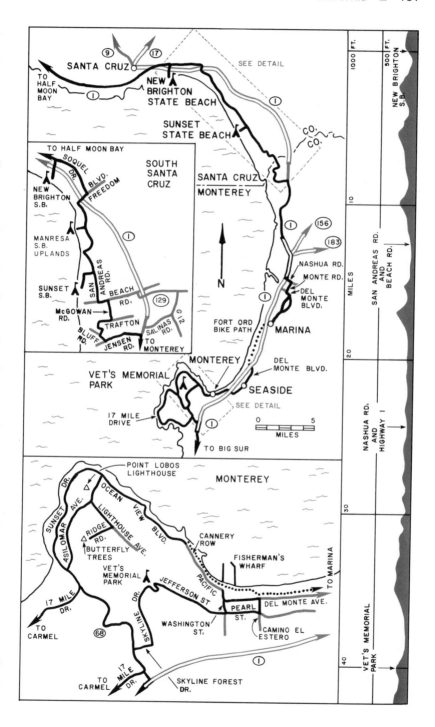

5.4 Soquel Dr. ends. Turn right on Freedom Blvd.

5.7 Cross Highway 1, then turn left on Bonita Dr. The Santa Cruz city bike route ends here.

6.8 Bonita Dr. ends. Go right on San Andreas Rd. and follow it for the next 6.1 miles.

8.7 La Selva Beach, a popular surfing area. Beyond La Selva Beach, San Andreas Rd. heads inland through farmlands. Traffic varies from light to extremely busy during harvest season.

9.2 Manresa State Beach Uplands Campground, a tents-only area with water, restrooms, hot showers, and a hiker-biker area. The campground is located off Sanddollar Road.

11.0 Sunset State Beach turnoff. Follow Sunset Beach Rd. 2.2 miles past fields of Brussels sprouts and artichokes to this isolated park. The campground offers hiker-biker sites, hot showers, and beach access. Cyclists spending the night at the park should buy food in Santa Cruz; no food is available near the park. This intersection marks the halfway point of your California Coast tour.

12.9 San Andreas Rd. ends. Go left (east) on Beach Rd., then take the first right on McGowan Rd. (not signed). Go straight on McGowen Rd. Cross the Pajaro River bike path (to Watsonville), cycle over a narrow bridge, then cross the Santa Cruz–Monterey County line.

14.1 At the end of McGowan Rd., take a right on Trafton Rd.

15.6 Trafton Rd. ends. Turn left on Bluff Rd., cycling through a small residential community, then pass chicken and mushroom farms.

16.4 Bluff Rd. ends at Jensen Rd. Go left (east).

17.1 (mp 100.00) Return to Highway 1, opposite a fruit stand. This busy highway has good shoulders.

17.9 (mp 99.10) Moss Landing: a long, narrow town.

18.7 (mp 98.30) Turnoff to Zmudowski State Beach. The beach lies 2 miles west and has no facilities.

20.0 (mp 97.00) Moss Landing State Beach turnoff. The beach is located 0.5 mile to the southwest on Jetty Rd.: beach access, views of Moss Landing harbor, and restrooms, but no water.

20.5 (mp 96.60) Cross Elkhorn Slough.

20.9 (mp 96.10) Pass Moss Landing power plant, whose twin towers dominate the skyline. Highway 1 enters the business section of Moss Landing and passes the access to Elkhorn Slough Reserve.

21.7 (mp 95.30) Pass Salinas River State Beach access.

23.0 (mp 94.00) Enter Castroville, Artichoke Capital of the World.

23.5 (mp 93.60) Junction with Highway 156 (heading east) and Highway 183 (heading south). Stay on Highway 1, now a divided freeway.

25.5 (mp 90.20) Nashua Rd.; cyclists must exit Highway 1. Turn right. At the end of the off ramp, turn right, crossing over the freeway.

25.8 Bicycle path from Castroville joins Nashua Rd. Continue straight.

Pelicans drying their wings after plunging into the ocean on a fishing expedition

25.9 Turn right on Monte Rd., paralleling Highway 1. No shoulders, but traffic is light (except during harvest season) as you pass large artichoke fields.

27.8 Turn left on Del Monte Blvd. for 100 feet to a Y intersection. Stay right on Lapis Rd., which rejoins Del Monte Blvd. in 1.3 miles.

29.3 Enter Marina on Del Monte Blvd.: several small grocery stores in this section.

29.7 Start of a two-way bike path paralleling Del Monte Blvd.

31.4 The bike way passes under Highway 1 then turns left, becoming the Fort Ord Bike Path as it parallels the freeway south through the Fort Ord area.

33.2 Seaside city limits. The bike path continues to parallel the freeway.

35.8 Bike path passes under Highway 1 and ends. The bike route returns to Del Monte Blvd., then heads through a busy business district. Watch for cars parked on the shoulder.

37.3 Busy intersection. Go straight, crossing Cyn Del Rey, then take a right onto a bike path.

37.4 Monterey: supermarkets, restaurants, hotels, and several bike shops.

39.1 Follow the bike path until you are riding along the edge of the beach. Just before the path makes a sharp left turn, leave it and cross Del Monte Ave. Ride up Camino El Estero for 2 blocks.

39.3 Turn right on Pearl St.

39.5 Go straight, following Pearl St. through a confusing intersection with Abrego St. (Even the street signs are confusing; Abrego St. changes names here, becoming Washington St.)

39.7 Pearl St. becomes Jefferson St. as it heads steeply up.

40.8 Vet's Memorial Park: picnic area and campground, hot showers, and hiker-biker camp. No beach access; however, the incessant barking of the sea lions can be heard day and night, keeping campers in tune with the ocean.

Monterey Tour

As mentioned in the introduction, a trip around Monterey is a must. Although you can ride from one attraction to the next, a lot of places cannot truly be explored from the seat of your bicycle. Carry a bike lock and be prepared to walk a little. You can also enjoy the luxury of free bus service (summer only) from Fisherman's Wharf to Cannery Row and the aquarium.

From the intersection of Pearl St. and Washington St., ride down Washington St. to its end at the hotel/convention center. Walk your bike through the plaza to the waterfront and lock it. Start your tour by exploring the wharf.

0.0 Fisherman's Wharf is divided into two parts, tourist and commercial. On the commercial wharf, join the pelicans in watching the fishermen unload their catch; on the tourist wharf, purchase a seafood meal from outdoor vendors.

0.4 Leaving Fisherman's Wharf, ride along the waterfront on a wide bike path, watching for harbor seals and otters.

0.9 *Side Trip* to the Coast Guard jetty. Descend from the bike path to the large parking area, then walk out to the end of the jetty where sea lions nap on the breakwater.

1.1 The bicycle path crosses through the upper portion of Cannery Row, past shops and restaurants located in old buildings made famous by John Steinbeck.

1.6 At the end of Cannery Row, descend 1 block to the Monterey Aquarium, built in an old cannery building. Admission is expensive, but worth the price. Plan to spend several hours. Continuing south, the path parallels the beautifully sculptured coastline. Watch for sea otters floating on their backs (and hundreds of skin divers floating on their stomachs) through the kelp beds.

2.7 Bike path ends. Go right on Ocean View Blvd. and continue along the coast.

3.9 Go straight through an intersection, entering Point Lobos Refuge.

4.6 Exit Point Lobos Refuge to meet Sunset Dr. Ride along the waterfront past Asilomar State Beach (no facilities) to 17-Mile Drive. *Side Trip* to lighthouse (open from 1:00 P.M. to 4:00 P.M. Saturdays and Sundays). Turn left on Sunset Dr. for 0.2 mile, then go left again on Asilomar Ave. to the lighthouse entrance. Deer often graze near the lighthouse. *Side Trip* to butterfly trees. Follow the directions to

Monterey Aquarium

the lighthouse, except turn right on Lighthouse Ave. immediately after turning onto Asilomar Ave. Cycle 0.5 mile to the Butterfly Grove Inn. Walk through the Inn's parking area to the trees.

6.2 Turn right on 17-Mile Drive.

6.3 Entrance station to 17-Mile Drive. This is a private road, and you must stop here and sign a form waiving your rights to sue, should you be run over. You will receive a guide and map of the scenic highlights along the drive. Bike route signs located along the drive make routefinding easy.

16.4 Pass Carmel gate and follow 17-Mile Drive as it climbs steeply through a tree-lined canyon.

17.0 Exit 17-Mile Drive at the Highway 1 gate. Follow Highway 68 back toward Monterey.

17.8 Turn right onto Skyline Forest Dr.

18.0 Turn left on Skyline Dr.

19.1 Vet's Memorial Park.

🚲

Vet's Memorial Park, Monterey, to Kirk Creek Campground (60.2 Miles)

South of Monterey, Highway 1 heads over a wild, undeveloped section of the coast. Rugged cliffs descend at near-vertical angles from the mountains to the pounding surf, leaving little room for man or his roads. As a consequence, Highway 1 is narrow and winding, as if etched along the hillsides with a shaky hand.

Riding the steeply rolling terrain is strenuous, both physically and mentally. The road is narrow, with little to no shoulder when you need it. Traffic is moderate to heavy, consisting mainly of tourists and tour buses. If you can get yourself moving at dawn, you will have several relatively peaceful hours before the rush of vacationers hits the road at around 9:00 or 10:00 A.M. Stores, restaurants, and water stops are few and far between, so plan ahead to avoid shortages.

Between Monterey and Kirk Creek Campground are only three "must" stops. The first is Point Lobos State Reserve, a Registered National Landmark. Small groves of the nearly extinct Monterey cypress thrive in the harsh environment of the point. The wind has sculptured these trees into graceful shapes that can be enjoyed by riding the 3 miles of park roads or walking one of the short trails over the headlands and through the groves.

The second stop for the day is Pfeiffer–Big Sur State Park. This park has two distinct parts, an ocean area with a walk-in campground and back-to-nature atmosphere, and the redwoods area with every amenity to pamper the camper. Little of the area's mystique is visible to the passing cyclist. From the highway, the commercial rather than the natural aspects stand out. To get a better feel for Big Sur, leave the bikes and spend a day hiking one of the park trails to high viewpoints, narrow canyons, or ocean beaches, or walk all the way to the very popular hot spring.

The third stop of special interest is Julia Pfeiffer Burns State Park, where a short trail leads to a spectacular vantage point of a waterfall streaming over the cliffs to the beach.

If a long and difficult ride and three "must" stops are more than you wish to tackle in one day, this section divides into perfect halves, creating two leisurely days with plenty of time to explore and relax.

Mileage Log

0.0 Heading south from Vet's Memorial Park, follow Skyline Dr. steeply uphill.

1.1 Turn right on Skyline Forest Dr.

1.4 Take a left on busy Highway 68.

2.3 Pass a 17-Mile Drive entrance, then descend the freeway ramp onto southbound Highway 1. Freeway ends in 0.1 mile. Shoulders are nasty with dangerous drains.

3.7 Exit right off hectic Highway 1 on Ocean Ave. Descend through Carmel, a tourist-oriented town with small shops, restaurants, and art galleries, including the Weston Gallery featuring photographs by Edward Weston and Ansel Adams. (If you are short on time you may stay on Highway 1 rather than tour through Carmel.)

4.7 Turn left on San Antonio St. Straight ahead is the large Carmel Beach parking area.

5.4 San Antonio St. ends. Go left on Santa Lucia St.

5.9 Take a right on Rio Rd.

6.0 Pass the grandly restored San Carlos Mission on the right. Visitors are welcome from 9:30 A.M. to 5:00 P.M. for a small entrance fee.

6.6 (mp 72.65) Return to Highway 1 and head south. On the east side of the intersection are the last grocery stores before Big Sur. Stock up on food as well as pastries from the bakery.

7.1 (mp 72.30) Cross the shoulderless Carmel River Bridge on Highway 1. The shoulder reappears on the opposite side and remains good, except at slide areas.

8.2 (mp 71.20) Carmel River State Beach: restrooms and beach access. The beach is a popular skin-diving area.

9.0 (mp 70.40) Point Lobos State Reserve: restrooms, running water, picnic tables, and trails.

Highway 1, south of Carmel

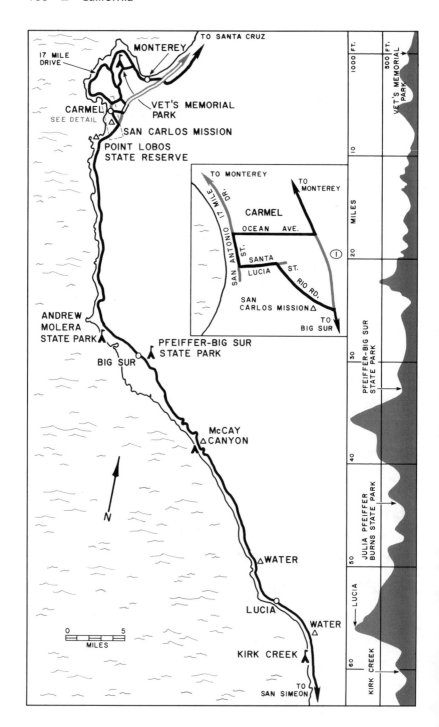

9.5 (mp 69.9) Carmel Highlands, a residential area that lasts for several miles. No grocery stores. Highway 1 travels near the coast, climbing over headlands, and passing over several slide areas where the shoulder disappears.

19.2 (mp 60.1) Rocky Creek Bridge.

19.7 (mp 59.6) Bixby Creek Bridge.

24.6 (mp 53.7) Pass Point Sur Lighthouse; not open to the public.

28.2 (mp 51.1) Andrew Molera State Park: camping, beach access, and hiking trails. The walk-in campground is located 0.3 mile from the road on a trail suitable for mountain bikes (bikes with narrow tires should be pushed). The camping is in an open field with pit toilets and water brought in by a tank trailer. No wood for fires may be gathered or purchased. The camp area is ¼ mile inland from a sandy beach.

30.1 (mp 49.3) Highway 1 heads inland, under the shade of the redwoods.

30.6 (mp 48.8) Enter Big Sur: private campgrounds, grocery stores, motels, and restaurants.

32.1 (mp 47.3) Pfeiffer–Big Sur State Park: a large campground with hiker-biker site, hot showers, wading in the Big Sur River, hiking trails, a lodge, restaurant, and grocery store.

33.0 (mp 46.4) Big Sur Station, a Forest Service Information Center and a large trailhead parking area with toilets and water on the left side of the road. Beyond Big Sur Station, Highway 1 climbs a long hill and then drops back to the coast. Shoulders on the southbound side remain good; views are spectacular.

34.0 (mp 45.2) Last grocery/convenience store for the next 22 miles.

42.3 (mp 36.7) Julia Pfeiffer Burns State Park vista point. An information sign discusses the park as well as the migration of monarch butterflies and whales.

43.2 (mp 35.8) McCay Canyon day-use area: restrooms, picnic tables, environmental camping (walk-in campsites located 0.2 mile from the road), and a short ¼-mile hiking trail to a scenic vantage point overlooking the beach and a waterfall.

51.7 (mp 27.80) Vista point over the rugged coast.

52.7 (mp 26.80) Picnic table on east side of the highway.

56.1 (mp 23.20) Lucia. This is the last chance to purchase food before Kirk Creek Campground.

58.2 (mp 21.10) Limekiln State Park, a privately operated facility that has been incorporated into the state park system. As of 1998, no hiker-biker sites. The campground does have hot showers and a trail to some old limekilns.

60.2 (mp 19.20) Kirk Creek Campground, operated by the Los Padres National Forest: hiker-biker site, running water, and beach access, but no electric lights, showers, or hot water.

Kirk Creek Campground to San Simeon State Beach
(40 Miles)

From huge hills to almost flat coastal grasslands, the terrain is the key interest along these 40 miles. Leaving Kirk Creek Campground, the route continues to climb and dive its way along the rugged coast for another 22 miles. Then, as if by magic, the hilly countryside is transformed into gentle, low rolling hills.

Once the terrain levels, the miles fly by. While speeding over the lowlands, keep an eye on the tumbling surf; sea otters are often spotted playing just a few yards offshore. Sea lions gather by the hundreds in this area to sunbathe and roll in the sand.

Near San Simeon, a casual glance east is all that is needed to spot

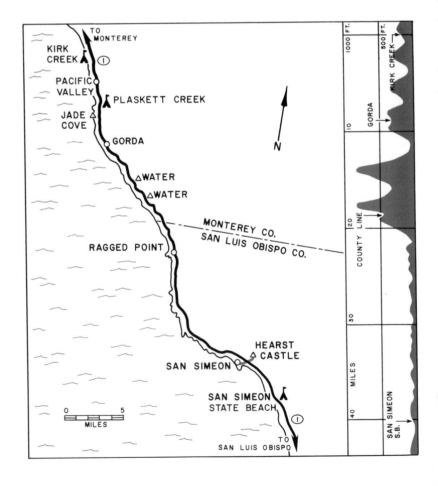

Sunbathing seals

Hearst Castle perched high on a hill above Highway 1. The massive castle, built by William Randolph Hearst, houses one of the world's largest private collections of art treasures. These treasures may only be viewed by taking one or more of the four organized tours offered by the California State Parks. Each tour lasts approximately 1 hour and 45 minutes and must be booked in advance by calling (800)444-4445. Of course, you can always check at the visitor center for unreserved tickets when you arrive.

For the cyclist without extra time or money for a tour, the stop at Hearst Castle Visitor Center allows you a free visit to the museum for insights into the life and times of William Randolph Hearst, as well as information on the design and construction of this massive structure.

Mileage Log

0.0 (mp 19.10) Leaving Kirk Creek Campground, head south along Highway 1. The shoulder is whimsical at best.

0.4 (mp 18.70) Mill Creek Picnic Area: beach access and restrooms.

5.0 (mp 13.9) Sand Dollar picnic area: picnic tables, running water, and restrooms.

5.3 (mp 13.6) Plaskett Creek Campground on the east (left) side of Highway 1: hiker-biker site and running water, but no showers.

5.4 (mp 13.5) First of two access trails to Jade Cove: a stroll along this beach may turn up bits of jade. Bicycles may be left at Plaskett Creek Campground or at the trailhead.

7.1 (mp 11.90) Willow Creek picnic area and vista point: no facilities.

7.2 (mp 11.80) Picnic table on the left.

8.4 (mp 10.30) Gorda. A very small store and restaurant mark the center of this community.

18.9 (mp 0.0 and 74.32) Leave Monterey County and enter San Luis Obispo County.

20.2 (mp 73.02) Enter Ragged Point. If planning to stop for a bite to eat, start slowing down. When you are flying down the hill, it's easy to miss this small community of fast-food outlets and cliff-hanging houses.

22.2 (mp 70.70) The hill bottoms out and the road heads across a grassy prairie.

29.5 (mp 63.30) Piedras Blancas Lighthouse. No visitors allowed.

29.7 (mp 63.03) The road narrows as it skirts the edge of the coast.

30.0 (mp 62.70) A section of blocked-off shoulder signals the next point of interest. Stop and check out the beach below. If it appears to be covered with driftwood, take a closer look. This is a favorite sunning location for the sea lion.

31.7 (mp 62.1) Vista point: view of Hearst Castle, beach access, and tide pools. Beyond the vista point, the shoulder returns and remains good for the rest of the day.

34.8 (mp 58.5) San Simeon city limits.

35.4 (mp 57.9) Turn left (east) for an easy 0.3-mile climb to the Hearst Castle Visitor Center: restrooms, water, tours, museum, gift shop, bike rack, lockers, and snack bar. To the right (west) is the town of San Simeon, which has a small grocery store, and William Randolph Hearst Memorial State Beach, with a picnic area, fishing pier, restrooms, running water, and beach access.

38.4 (mp 54.9) San Simeon's motel and restaurant row, which also has several small grocery stores.

40.0 (mp 53.2) San Simeon State Beach Campground. Turn left (east) off Highway 1 to reach the campground access. The campground has two parts. The first, San Simeon State Beach, has a small hiker-biker site located next to the freeway, with water, hot showers, and beach access. The second part is Washburn Campground, situated on a hill overlooking the beach area. This primitive area has neither hiker-biker sites nor showers; however, it is clean, quiet, and scenic.

San Simeon State Beach to Oceano Campground
(52.6 Miles)

The ride from San Simeon State Beach to Pismo State Beach marks the beginning of the transition from Central to Southern California. The isolation and spectacular scenery of the Northern and Central Coast is replaced by freeways and large urban areas with a Spanish flavor. The very

Mission San Luis Obispo de Tolosa

distinctive smell of eucalyptus trees fills the air, palm trees line the beaches, and oaks dot the hillsides. Ants are everywhere, so keep the tent door closed and don't leave food out. The ocean is warmer and swimming is a refreshing, rather than a heart-stopping, way to end the day's ride.

Between San Simeon and Pismo Beach is open riding country. You can cover many miles and still have time to relax at the end of the day. With the exception of a brief excursion along the coast at Cambria, the first 23.6 miles are spent following Highway 1 (a quasi-freeway) south to Morro Bay. The second part of the ride is entirely on back roads through well-developed farmlands. Temperatures in this section may be quite warm, especially in the San Luis Obispo area.

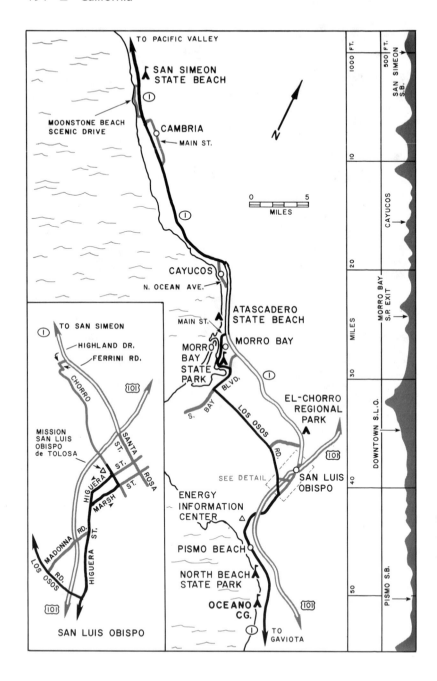

Chief attractions are Morro Bay, a popular beach resort and fishing area known for its distinctive rock, and the sand dunes at Pismo Beach. An optional side trip takes you to Mission San Luis Obispo, founded in 1772.

The day ends at Oceano Campground in Pismo State Beach. The beach is a popular place, and people drive jeeps and cars to favorite surf-fishing or sunset-watching spots. Inland from the beach is the Sand Dunes Reserve, a natural area closed to motorized vehicles. It's a great place for exploring, sitting, sliding, or just looking.

Mileage Log

0.0 (mp 53.20) Leave San Simeon State Beach on Highway 1. Shoulder width is ample, up to 8 feet wide, except at bridges.

0.4 (mp 52.80) Picnic area and vista point on the right.

0.9 (mp 52.30) At Moonstone Beach Scenic Dr., exit right (west) off Highway 1 for a scenic ride along the coastline. The picnic area at the turnoff has tables and beach access.

1.1 Leffingwell Landing State Beach is a whale-watching area in the winter: picnic tables, water, and restrooms. Continue south, passing long, sandy beaches.

2.3 (mp 50.80) Return to Highway 1. *Alternate Route.* Cross to the east side of Highway 1 and follow Main St. south through the center of Cambria past shops and grocery stores. Main St. loops back to Highway 1 in 2.4 miles.

5.0 (mp 48.20) Alternate route through Cambria returns to Highway 1. Continue inland, traversing sun-baked pastures for the next 10 miles.

16.1 (mp 37.10) Cayucos, a small tourist-oriented town: grocery stores.

16.3 (mp 36.90) *Alternate Route* through Cayucos. Cyclists wishing to shop in Cayucos should exit Highway 1 on N. Ocean Ave. The road parallels the waterfront, passes through town, then returns to Highway 1 in 1.7 miles. Past the Cayucos exit, Highway 1 becomes freeway.

18.3 (mp 34.90) Cayucos Alternate Route returns to Highway 1.

20.5 (mp 32.70) Morro Bay city limits. Markets and shopping centers are visible from the freeway. The town has several state parks, long, sandy beaches, and a wildlife refuge.

21.5 (mp 32.20) Morro Strand State Beach campground: running water, restrooms, many trailer hookups, and cold outdoor showers, but no hiker-biker site.

24.6 (mp 28.60) Exit Highway 1 at Main St. Go right on Main St. and follow the signs through town to Morro Bay State Park. The road parallels Morro Bay, winding through a residential district before entering the park, where it turns into State Park Rd. Follow the park road past the golf course, museum, and marina. *Side Trip* to Morro

Rock. Go right off Main St. on Beach St. and ride to its end. Turn left on Embarcadero for 1 mile to Morro Rock and the state park: restrooms, picnic tables, and water.

26.4 Morro Bay State Park campground entrance: hot showers. The hiker-biker site is located in the picnic area. Tents may not be set up until 5:00 P.M. during the summer and 4:00 P.M. during the winter. Tents must be down by 9:00 A.M. If camping at the park, no entrance fee is charged to visit the natural history museum or to enjoy its excellent view of Morro Rock. The rock is a National Preserve and nesting ground for the rare and endangered peregrine falcon. Continue beyond the campground to S. Bay Blvd.

27.0 Turn right (south) on S. Bay Blvd. and continue around Morro Bay. The road starts out narrow, then gradually widens to include a comfortable shoulder.

31.0 Turn left on Los Osos Valley Rd., which heads east away from the ocean. Temperatures soar as the road rolls through open farmlands. (Expect to see numerous cyclists on this road; this is part of a popular training ride.)

31.8 Los Osos Oaks State Reserve: hiking trails through groves of 700-year-old oaks.

37.9 Pass Foothills Blvd., access to Cuesta College. The route continues straight on Los Osos Valley Rd., entering the residential outskirts of San Luis Obispo.

40.1 Cross over a freeway (US 101 and Highway 1 combined).

40.3 Los Osos Valley Rd. ends. Go right on S. Higuera St. **Side Trip** to Mission San Luis Obispo de Tolosa. Go left (north) on S. Higuera St. until the road divides in 2.4 miles. Continue north on Marsh St. (one-way) for 0.3 mile, then turn left on Chorro St. for a final 0.2 mile to the mission. Tour the mission, then stroll down to San Luis Obispo Creek. Restaurants, grocery stores, bakeries, and a bike shop are close by. The park has a restroom and water. To return to the route, take Higuera St. (one-way) back to S. Higuera St.

42.1 Cross under US 101, staying on S. Higuera St.

42.2 Turn right on Ontario Rd. and parallel the freeway for the next 3 miles. Note the sirens located along the road. If trouble occurs at the nuclear power plant in Diablo Canyon, a warning signal will be blasted, lasting from 3 to 5 minutes. The sirens are just one of the those little nuisances that must be endured when a nuclear power plant is located on a fault line.

44.3 PG&E (Pacific Gas and Electric) Community Center: picnic tables and running water. Before the nuclear reactor was built, the center housed elaborate and expensive displays on energy and conservation.

45.2 Turn left on Avila Rd., passing a private campground and pool heated by a hot springs.

Sand dunes at Pismo Beach

45.5 Turn right on Palisades Rd.

45.7 Pismo Beach. Stay on Palisades Rd., sandwiched between the freeway and beach. The road becomes Shell Beach Rd., then turns into Price St.

49.5 (mp 16.05) When the road divides, descend right on Dolliver St. (you are now back on Highway 1). Ride through the center of Pismo Beach on a wide bike lane.

50.7 (mp 14.70) North Beach Campground: hiker-biker site, water, and beach access. No showers in this open-field park.

51.0 (mp 14.40) Grover Beach access.

52.1 (mp 13.24) Oceano city limits.

52.4 (mp 13.00) Turn right off Highway 1 at Pier Ave. The small grocery store on the far side of the intersection is the closest store to the campground.

52.6 Oceano Campground: hiker-biker site complete with bike rack, hot showers, and a trail to the beach. Keep valuables, touring bags, and food stored well out of reach of the flock of marauding ducks and thieving raccoons. ***Side Trip*** to Pismo Dune Preserve. The sand dunes are located 0.2 mile beyond the campground. Due to the large amount of loose sand, it is best to leave bikes at the campground and walk on Pier Ave. or one of the campground trails to the beach. Head south on the beach for another ¼ mile, cross a creek, then go inland, passing through a low fence designed to keep motor vehicles out of the dunes. Walk beyond the reach of the dune grass to enjoy the sand. This is a great place to watch the sunset.

The roads and houses near the Dunes Beach have special problems. In winter, sand tries to engulf the surrounding area. The roads are marked with tall poles—the same as those used in snowbound mountain passes—to define the roads for the sandplows.

Oceano Campground to Gaviota State Beach
(61.5 Miles)

For the next 61 miles, the huge Vandenburg Air Force Base lies between Highway 1 and the coast. Consequently, the day is spent riding through inland valleys and over rolling hills. Scenery in the valleys ranges from fragrant groves of eucalyptus trees to massive farm fields. Two major hills, each over 900 feet in elevation, save the ride from becoming tedious. Both hills have elegant scenery to look at on the long grinds up followed by short but thrilling descents.

Food and water stops are limited to three towns: Guadalupe, Orcutt, and Lompoc. Temperatures along the route frequently reach 90 degrees during the summer, so start early and carry plenty of water. However, the greatest discomfort comes when the northern trade winds whip across the plowed fields, filling the air with dust.

A highly recommended alternative to the standard Pacific Coast Bike Route (and California Bicentennial Route) is the Santa Ynez Valley Route, starting at Lompoc. The route heads inland to Solvang, then through the Santa Ynez Valley, before returning to the coast at Santa Barbara. Solvang was founded and settled by Danes, who have kept its heritage alive through customs, architecture, and a friendly spirit. One facet of Danish life—cooking—is tastefully represented here. The slightest breeze is filled with tempting aromas from bakeries and fudge factories.

Santa Ynez Valley is scenic country and a superior cycling area, with rolling grass hills dotted with California oak trees. The bright blue sky here is a prime soaring area for hawks and ravens. In the heart of the Santa Ynez Valley is Lake Cachuma County Park, a complete recreation area with everything from camping and swimming to miniature golf and horseback riding. The alternate route makes a long, difficult climb over San Marcos Pass then descends to Santa Barbara. Views of the coast are outstanding.

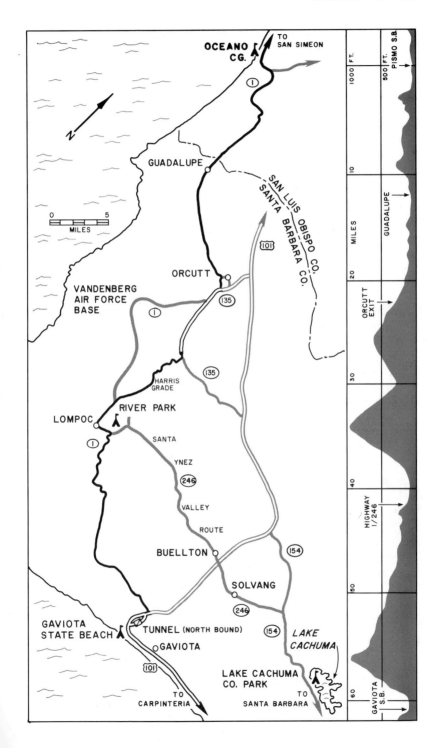

In short, the Santa Ynez Valley Alternate Route is a scenic, tasty, and downright enjoyable ride that bypasses a long stretch of freeway riding. This alternate route is not recommended in July or August, when temperatures soar into the 100s.

Mileage Log

0.0 From Oceano Campground, cycle back to Highway 1. Head south through peaceful countryside. Shoulders are narrow and traffic moderate.

2.7 (mp 10.41) Intersection. Turn right (south) following Highway 1 toward Guadalupe. After the turn, ascend a short, steep hill.

12.8 (mp 0.0 and 50.6) Leave San Luis Obispo County and enter Santa Barbara County at the city limits of Guadalupe. Le Roy County Park, with restrooms, picnic tables, and water, is located just 1 block off the route. As you ride through town, you'll notice the signs on grocery stores, restaurants, and bakeries are all in Spanish.

15.1 (mp 48.3) Solomon Canyon Creek. Shoulder narrows.

23.7 (mp 36.05) Intersection; Highway 135 Business branches off to the left, heading into Santa Maria.

24.1 (mp 35.0) Highway 1 merges with Highway 135 and becomes a busy 4-lane freeway with a wide shoulder.

28.0 (mp R31.50) Highway 1 bears right and heads up a steep hill,

Highway 1 near Guadalupe

climbing into the Vandenburg Air Force Base. Ignore bike signs and leave Highway 1 here. Continue straight ahead on Highway 135. Use caution crossing the Highway 1 exit; most traffic turns off here. *Alternate Route.* Highway 1 may be followed to Lompoc. It has steep hills and a lot of traffic.

30.3 Freeway ends. The highway returns to 2 lanes and a narrow shoulder.

30.8 Turn right (south) on Harris Grade and follow signs to Lompoc. Over 600 feet of elevation are gained in the next 3 miles as the narrow, twisting road climbs over a small band of hills, reaching an elevation of 950 feet. Traffic is light.

34.0 Top of the hill. Enjoy the views across the open farmlands before starting the brisk trip down.

35.9 Historical marker commemorating the La Purisima Mission State Historical Park.

38.4 (mp 21.80) Bike route rejoins Highway 1; continue straight ahead. Truck traffic increases as the road widens to 4 lanes with shoulder.

38.5 (mp 21.70) Lompoc: food, Laundromats, bike shops, cafes, hotel, a campground, and the last grocery store before Gaviota State Park.

41.1 (mp 19.1) Following Highway 1, turn left (south) on Ocean Ave.

42.4 (mp 20.3) Stay with Highway 1 as it makes a 90-degree turn to the right (south) and begins a 13.5-mile rolling climb to an elevation of over 900 feet. The shoulder is good, except at bridges. Santa Ynez Valley Alternate Route to Santa Barbara starts from this intersection (see details below). *Side Trip* to River Park Campground: primitive site, picnic area, and water, but no hot showers. When Highway 1 turns right, continue straight on Highway 246 for 0.5 mile. The park entrance is located on the left (north) side of the road.

56.0 (mp 2.6) Summit of hill and start of a fast, 2.5-mile descent to US 101.

58.6 Intersection of Highway 1 and US 101. Take a left turn to head up the US 101 on ramp. US 101 is a freeway with wide shoulders and lots of noisy traffic. (Northbound travelers, just before the Highway 1 turnoff, must ride through a short tunnel with a very narrow shoulder and, frequently, a very strong headwind. It is like trying to cycle out of a high-suction vacuum hose.) *Side Trip* to Gaviota State Beach Hot Springs. At the junction of Highway 1 and US 101, cross the freeway, then go left on the frontage road to a parking area. A brisk ½-mile hike leads to springs and swimming area.

60.5 (mp 46.1) Rest area: tourist information, water, restrooms, and cool shade. For southbound travelers only.

61.0 (mp 45.6) Turnoff to Gaviota State Beach.

61.5 Gaviota State Beach: hiker-biker campsite, beach access, surfing, swimming, pier fishing, hiking trails, and a very limited grocery store. No hot showers.

If time, energy, and the desire are there, continue south on US 101 for 9.1 miles to Refugio State Beach, which has a hiker-bike site located on the edge of a palm-lined beach, a small store, and hot showers.

Santa Ynez Alternate Route

0.0 The junction of Highway 1 and Highway 246 marks the start of the alternate route through Santa Ynez Valley to Santa Barbara. Follow Highway 246 east over rolling terrain. Shoulders vary from 1 to 8 feet wide, traffic from light to heavy.

16.0 Enter Buellton, home of Anderson's split pea soup (which, if you like pea soup, is supposed to be the best). Leaving Buellton, continue southeast on Highway 246, crossing US 101 to reach Solvang.

19.5 Solvang. The main road through town is Mission St. (Highway 246). However, bakeries, fudge factories, wine-tasting rooms, and tourist shops are on Copenhagen St., 1 block west. Continue south from Solvang on Highway 246. Hills get steeper and traffic volume increases.

24.5 Turn right (south) on Highway 154. The shoulders will gradually disappear.

30.5 Lake Cachuma County Park, the recommended overnight stop. The campground has excellent facilities, including a hiker-biker site, hot showers, fishing, boat rentals, horseback riding, complete grocery store, swimming and wading pools, game room, miniature golf, and inline skating.

36.5 Start of 4-mile climb to San Marcos Pass.

40.5 San Marcos Pass, elevation 2,225 feet. From the summit, it is a rapid 7-mile descent on a narrow, twisting road with heavy traffic.

47.5 Cyclists take the Foothill Rd. exit (State 192). At the base of the exit, turn left on Foothill Rd. and follow it for 2 miles through the outskirts of Santa Barbara.

50.0 At Alamar Ave., turn right and descend to State St.

50.2 Turn left on State St. and ride to the beach to rejoin the Coast Bike Route.

Gaviota State Beach to Carpinteria State Beach
(44.4 Miles)

The mix of freeways, back roads, farmlands, and cities serves to remind you that you are now well into that unique area called Southern California. Riding conditions are good, the freeway has a wide shoulder, city streets have wide bike lanes, and only one short, steep hill breaks the harmony of gently rolling terrain.

Santa Barbara is the center of interest along this portion of the coast. The day's ride is short, leaving plenty of time to savor the city's strong Spanish flavor in an optional city tour, and to visit the Santa Barbara Mission, founded in 1786; the county courthouse, which was modeled after a Spanish-Moorish palace with hand-painted ceilings, giant murals, and a sweeping view from the clock tower; the El Paseo, known as "a street in Spain," with sidewalk cafes and art galleries; El Presidio, a fort built by the Spanish in 1782; and the Historical Society Museum depicting four eras of settlement: Indian, Spanish, Mexican, and American. The tour ends at Stearns Wharf, where the sight of sunbathers, inline skaters, and wind surfers make for a strictly modern view.

Cyclists passing through Santa Barbara in mid-August have a chance to catch the Fiesta Days celebration, which features a parade, street dancing, and every kind of Mexican food imaginable.

Mission Santa Barbara

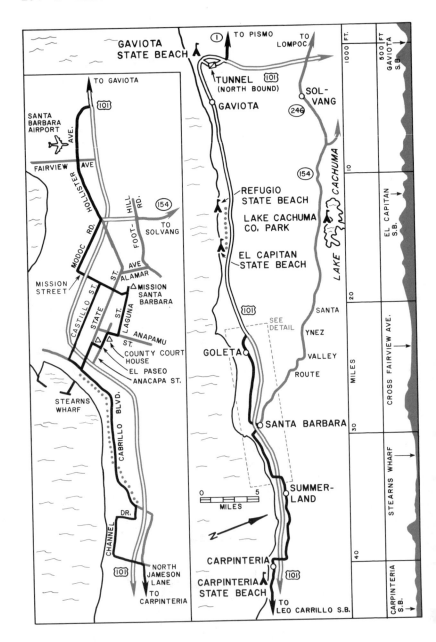

Carpinteria State Beach, at the end of the day's ride, claims to have the world's safest swimming beach—long and sandy with no undertow. On the beach are several tarpits, where natural tar seeps out onto the sand, so watch where you sit and step.

Mileage Log

0.0 Day's ride starts from the Gaviota State Beach hiker-biker site.

0.5 (mp 46.3) Head south on US 101. Shoulder is broad along the freeway, averaging 4 to 8 feet except at bridges, where it completely disappears. Timing is very important when you cross these narrow bridges in the company of thundering 18-wheel trucks; use lots of caution.

1.8 (mp 44.5) Vista Del Mer, first of two beach accesses.

5.1 (mp 41.00) Vista point, a chance to get off your bike and stroll over an old highway bridge.

10.0 (mp 36.1) Turnoff to Refugio State Beach: scenic hiker-biker camp, hot showers, and small store. ***Alternate Route.*** A 2-mile bike path connects Refugio State Beach with El Capitan State Beach to the south, providing a scenic escape from the noise and dirt of the freeway. From the freeway, ride down the campground access road, then go left. The bike path skims along the edge of a bluff, overlooking the ocean. The path is subject to slides; check with the park personnel before starting out.

11.8 (mp 34.30) El Capitan State Beach: large hiker-biker campsite located at the north end of the park in sight and sound of the freeway, hot showers, nature trail, small visitor center, camp store, sandy beach with lifeguards in the summer, and a 2-mile bike path to Refugio State Beach.

18.9 (mp 27.16) Hollister Ave. exit. Bicycles must leave US 101.

19.2 At the top of the freeway exit ramp, turn right on Hollister Ave. Numerous grocery stores, bike shops, restaurants, and motels will be passed in the next 20 miles. Traffic is often heavy; however, most roads have a wide lane for bikes.

21.3 Cross Storke Rd., access to UCSB (University of California at Santa Barbara).

23.8 Cross Fairview Ave. at a busy intersection in the center of the town of Goleta. Two large bicycle shops are located within 4 blocks (west). Continue south on Hollister Ave.

27.1 Bear right on Modoc Rd. just before Hollister Ave. passes under a railroad bridge. Modoc Rd. changes to Catania Way after the first mile, which then becomes Parks Rd.

30.2 Turn left on Mission St. at the end of Parks Rd. Cycle under an overpass.

30.4 One block after riding under the freeway, turn right on Castillo St. and follow it for the next 2 miles. (Santa Barbara Tour starts here.)

Cycling palm-lined coastal bike path in Santa Barbara

31.9 Castillo St. passes under US 101. (Do not attempt this after a rainstorm.)

32.4 Go left on Cabrillo Blvd. Plaza Del Mar is passed on the right: restrooms. A city bike path is located between the road and the beach for those who wish to brave a perpetual rush-hour traffic of joggers, inline skaters, and walkers.

32.8 Pass State St. on the left. Santa Ynez Valley Alternate Route rejoins the Coast Route here.

34.2 Pass entrance to Santa Barbara City Zoo on the left.

35.0 Opposite the Andree Clark Bird Refuge (just before the road passes under US 101), turn right on Channel Dr.

35.2 Channel Dr. becomes a bike path as it heads to the beach. The bike path soon turns back into a road. Channel Dr. heads inland, becoming Olive Mill Rd. when it crosses US 101.

36.0 Take the first right after crossing the freeway on N. Jameson Lane. The road is shoulderless and moderately busy.

36.4 Pacific Coast Bicycle Route signs indicate that you should return to the freeway at San Ysidro Rd. Unless you have developed an addiction to freeway riding, or are simply allergic to hills, continue on N. Jameson Lane.

37.6 Go right and ride up Ortega Hill Rd. From the top of this short, steep hill, descend to the small community of Summerland, which has restaurants and a small grocery store. Paralleling the freeway, Ortega Hill Rd. becomes Little Ave., then Via Real.

42.9 Via Real ends. Turn right on Santa Ynez Ave. and cross to the west side of US 101.

43.1 Take a sharp left on Carpinteria Ave. and follow the bike lane through town.

43.8 Turn right on Palm Ave. and glide to the campground. (No signs point to the state park.)

44.4 Carpinteria State Beach: hiker-biker site, hot showers, beach access, a small store, and a visitor center featuring the history of the Chumash people who used to camp here. Several large grocery stores and numerous restaurants are located nearby. Excellent bus service to Santa Barbara. From Carpinteria south, hiker-biker sites have become hang-outs for transients. If a regular site is available, you may find it a better bargain than the cheaper sites. When you leave camp, lock your bike and carry all your valuables with you.

Santa Barbara Tour

At the intersection of Mission and Castillo, continue straight on Mission St. After 0.8 mile Mission St. ends. Turn left for 0.2 mile and ride up Laguna St. to the Santa Barbara Mission, known as the Queen of Missions because of its graceful architecture. Mission and museum may be toured for a fee.

From the mission, ride down Laguna St. for 1.1 miles to Anapamu St., then go right 0.2 mile to Anacapa St. and turn left. The county courthouse, on the left, is the next stop. Walk through the halls, then climb to the top of the clock tower for a view of the whole city. Just 2.5 blocks farther down Anacapa St., stop for a tour of the El Paseo, a shopping mall containing the Casa de la Guerra, the original adobe home of Jose de la Guerra, Commandante of the Presidio. Across the street, tour El Cuartel (the site of the original fortress founded by Spain in 1782) and the Presidio Gardens, located behind the post office. The Historical Society Museum is located 1 block south. After exploring the museum, take the first right and go west 2 blocks to State St. Follow State St. to the beach and go left on Cabrillo Blvd. to rejoin the bike route. The tour may be continued from the end of State St. by heading out on Stearns Wharf or by cycling right, around the boat harbor and out on the breakwater, a scenic place to watch boats and eat lunch.

🚴

Carpinteria State Beach to Leo Carrillo State Beach
(47.8 Miles)

A generous mix of Spanish architecture, palm trees, famous surfing beaches, a national monument, and an historic mission combine to create that famous Southern California ambiance as you ride south from Carpinteria State Beach. Of course, people play a large role in creating ambiance. Many Californians spend a great deal of time outdoors—swimming, sunbathing, sailing, walking, and bicycling. Take this opportunity to check out some of the extremes in cycling attire. (Some of these fashions will work their way to the conservative north in the next few years.)

Terrain is nearly level, except near Leo Carrillo State Beach, and miles go quickly. One short section of the ride is on the freeway, where broad shoulders give you some protection from the traffic. The most hazardous section is the shoulderless thoroughfares in the Oxnard–Port Hueneme area. Avoid riding through town during rush-hour traffic.

Two side trips are recommended. The first is to visit the restored San Buenaventura Mission and Ventura County Historical Museum in the Historical District of Ventura. The historical museum has indoor and outdoor exhibits depicting local history from the lives of the Native Americans to oil exploration. The mission also has a museum (admission charged).

Farther south, a second side trip leads to the Channel Islands National Monument and Wildlife Refuge Visitor Center, which features displays of the natural history on and around the islands. Charter boats take visitors for half- or whole-day trips to observe the islands. Reservations for these trips should be made up to 2 weeks in advance. For cyclists who do not have an entire day to devote to the islands, the 30-minute movie at the visitor center is an excellent way to experience them vicariously.

Mileage Log

0.0 Leave Carpinteria State Beach and follow Palm Ave. back to Carpinteria Ave.

0.2 Turn right on Carpinteria Ave. and head south, paralleling US 101.

2.2 At the end of Carpinteria Ave., turn left, then take an immediate right to descend the on ramp to US 101 (mp 00.43). For the next 4.8 miles you will be riding around the edge of a broad bay on a wide shoulder of the busy freeway. At the north end of this bay is Rincon Point, an area which attracts surfers from around the world.

2.9 **(mp 00.00 and mp 43.80)** Leave Santa Barbara County and enter Ventura County.

7.0 **(mp 39.30)** Exit freeway at the small community of Sea Cliff: county parks, state beaches, homes, but no stores.

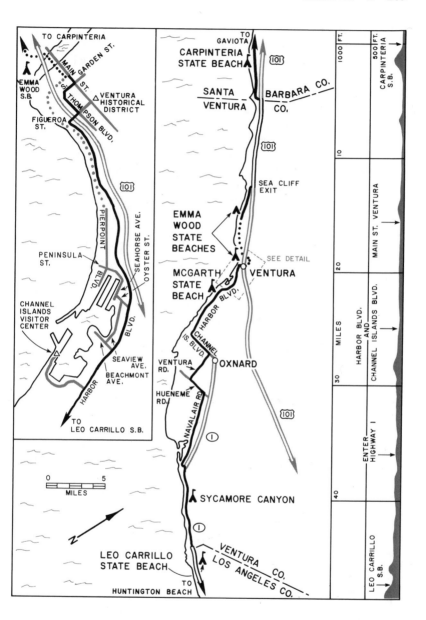

7.2 At the base of the US 101 exit ramp, turn right on Old Highway, passing the entrance to Hobson County Park: camping. The road heads south passing the community of Faria Beach.

9.8 Faria County Park: camping, water, a small store, but no hiker-biker site.

13.3 Ride up the freeway entrance ramp. To the right is the access to Emma Wood State Beach self-contained camping area.

13.7 At the top of the ramp, turn right on a narrow bike path that parallels the coast.

14.6 Ventura city limits.

15.1 Bicycle path enters the south section of Emma Wood State Beach: picnic area, water, hiker-biker site, group campsites, cold outdoor showers, and beach access. Stay on the bicycle path as it passes under US 101 and winds around a commercial campground.

15.6 Cross the Ventura River, then turn left (east) off the bike path to Main St. *Alternate Route.* The bike path turns west, offering a scenic route around downtown Ventura. The route heads out to the beach, where it skirts the Ventura County Fairgrounds before passing Surfers Point. The path heads through Promenade Park then enters San Buenaventura State Beach, where it returns to city streets and continues south on Pierpoint Blvd. for 1 mile. Go left on Peninsula St., then right on Seahorse Ave. Turn left on Oyster St., right on Seaview Ave., and left on Beachmont Ave. to return to the bike route at Harbor Blvd.

15.7 Pass Ortega Adobe Historical Site on the left (east) side of Main St.

15.8 Turn right on S. Garden St. *Side Trip* to Ventura Historical District. Continue straight on Main St. 0.3 mile.

15.9 Follow S. Garden St. as it bends left (south) at the base of the freeway, becoming Thompson Blvd.

16.2 Turn right on Figueroa St. and cross under US 101.

16.3 Take a left on Harbor Blvd. immediately after the railroad tracks.

16.7 Beach Park, a small picnic area with tables but no water.

17.8 Cross San Pedro St., passing the turnoff to Buenaventura State Beach, a day-use area with restrooms, water, picnic tables, and beach access.

18.2 Harbor Blvd. heads through a congested commercial area with grocery stores. Continuing south, ride through a residential district, then around the Ventura Harbor.

20.2 *Side Trip* to Channel Islands National Monument and Wildlife Refuge Visitor Center. Turn right into the harbor area and ride west for 1.3 miles to the end of the spit: restrooms, beach access, and running water.

20.7 The road crosses a corner of McGarth State Beach.

21.2 Enter Oxnard.

21.4 McGarth State Beach campground: hiker-biker area, hot showers, beach access, lake, bird-watching, sand dunes, and nature trail. Beyond the park entrance, Harbor Blvd. passes the Mandalay Steam Plant electric generating station, then heads by an exclusive residential area.

San Buenaventura Mission

24.6 Oxnard State Beach: a picnic area with restrooms, tables, water, and beach access.

25.0 Harbor Blvd. divides. Go left, heading east over Channel Islands Harbor into Oxnard, where Harbor Blvd. becomes Channel Islands Blvd. This is the start of a very congested area. Much of the road is narrow without a shoulder. Shops and grocery stores, located on the left (north) side of the road, are the last before Leo Carrillo State Beach.

27.1 At the eastern end of a large golf course, turn right on Ventura Rd. and ride the bike path for the next 1.5 miles. Watch out for the narrowly spaced posts at the intersections.

28.8 Go left on Port Hueneme Rd. (pronounced "wye-nee-mee") and enter the town of Port Hueneme. This is a navy area and many side roads are gated. The road is very busy as it leaves the city and heads into farm country; however, the shoulder is good.

33.7 Turn right on Navalair Rd. just before reaching Highway 1, and ride past naval installations and the airport.

34.3 Intersection. Continue straight past a display of rockets and jets, or stop and inspect them. Picnic tables are located in the shade of the fighter planes.

36.7 (mp 10.30) Turn onto Highway 1 and head back toward the coast.

39.2 (mp 7.80) Leave the military reservation and enter a public access area. Before long the road enters Point Mugu State Park, which is spread out along the coast. Use caution—the wide shoulder is used as a parking lot for those who do not wish to pay at the state beaches. This nifty system may alleviate congestion in the parking lots but it forces cyclists onto the highway.

41.2 (mp 6.10) La Jolla Canyon on left: trailhead and group camp area.

41.3 (mp 6.00) Thornhill Beach Campground is located on a sandy area between the highway and the beach. The campground has cold outdoor showers and chemical toilets, but no hiker-biker area.

42.6 (mp 4.47) Sycamore Cove and Canyon has picnicking at the cove on the west side of the highway and camping in the canyon on the east side. This campground, with its hiker-biker site, running water, and several trails, is preferable to Leo Carrillo. If you can manage the longer ride through Los Angeles tomorrow, spend the night here.

47.0 (mp 00.00 and mp 62.87) Leave Ventura County and enter Los Angeles County.

47.8 (mp 62.10) Leo Carrillo State Beach, the last public campground north of Los Angeles: hiker-biker site, hot showers, beach access, and a very small camp store (open in summer only). No stores or restaurants nearby. This campground is at the end of the bus line from Los Angeles, providing easy access to and from the city. (If you have the energy, continue on another 12.5 miles to Malibu Beach RV Park. Call ahead. See the next section for details.)

Leo Carrillo State Beach to Newport Dunes Aquatic Park (78.2 Miles)

If you are touring on a tight budget, arrange for your night's lodging or campsite before you start your ride, otherwise you may be disappointed when you arrive at your chosen destination!

Riding through the Los Angeles area is more than just physically demanding, it is mentally exhausting. This long ride requires you use every riding skill you have. You must remain constantly alert and concentrate on the directions to avoid missing crucial turns and intersections. Riders who have big-city commuting practice will have a definite advantage.

Heading south from Leo Carrillo State Beach, Highway 1 has a moderate shoulder and low traffic volume (except on weekends) for the first 7 miles. Near Malibu, the traffic increases and the shoulder virtually disappears. While cycling through Malibu, you will notice that this is one of

Sunny day at the beach

the few places in the country where hilltop property annually becomes beach-front property: The effects of sliding are visible everywhere.

South of Malibu, Highway 1 (now called Pacific Coast Hwy., or PCH) enters the gigantic urban sprawl that is loosely called Los Angeles by non-residents. Cyclists must leave the PCH and make their way along a series of hectic bike paths and crowded city streets.

Travel through any large city is demanding. Riding through the nine cities that make up the Los Angeles coastal area forces the word "demanding" into a whole new dimension. Do not expect to make good time, no matter how strong a rider you are. City streets are shoulderless and busy, and progress is constantly interrupted by stoplights. Wildcat growth combined with rolling hills causes the streets to constantly change directions or simply dead-end. The easy-to-follow bike path that weaves along the beaches for part of the way is often jammed with people, causing travel to be slow and frustrating.

South of Redondo Beach the route leaves the coast and returns to the Pacific Coast Hwy. for a 20-mile stretch on the rough, often shoulderless, and frequently busy roadways. The smell of car exhaust and the stench of oil refineries dominate until the route returns to the refreshing ocean air at Seal Beach.

On a rare smog-free day, the Los Angeles area is beautiful. From the bike path, views extend up and down the coast, and east to the San Bernardino Mountains. Start the day at first light to reach the bike path before the midday haze sets in and the crowds arrive. Take your time, enjoy the beaches, then head back to the city streets by noon to ensure you make it to the coast before rush hour.

There are no public campgrounds between Leo Carrillo State Beach and Dana Point, 94.4 miles south. Newport Dunes Aquatic Park is the first area south of Malibu to accept tents. This is a very upscale park with numerous restrictions. Tents must be set up without stakes. You must pay for two nights on weekends in July and August. Holiday weekends require that you pay for three nights. Reservations are a necessity during the summer. Call ahead to (800)288-0770.

As an alternative to camping, you may stop at one of the three hostels along the route. The Westchester YMCA hostel is located near the Los Angeles International Airport at 8015 S. Sepulveda Blvd. Call for reservations and directions, (213)642-8277. The Los Angeles International Hostel is scenically located in Angels Gate Park, near Long Beach, at 3601 S. Gaffey St., Bldg. 613, San Pedro. Call ahead for reservations and cycling directions: (213)831-8109. Colonial Inn Hostel in Huntington Beach is the easiest of the three to reach from the bike route. This hostel is near the beaches, within riding distance of Disneyland, and on bus routes to Hollywood. It is essential to call ahead for reservations, (714)536-9184.

If you have extra time at the end of the day or are taking a well deserved rest day at the campground, take a trip to Balboa Island. The island specialty is frozen bananas dipped in chocolate, with the topping of your choice—a real taste treat. The island can be reached by a short side trip from the campground or by following an alternate route that takes you to The Wedge (a famous body-surfing area), before crossing to the island on a ferry.

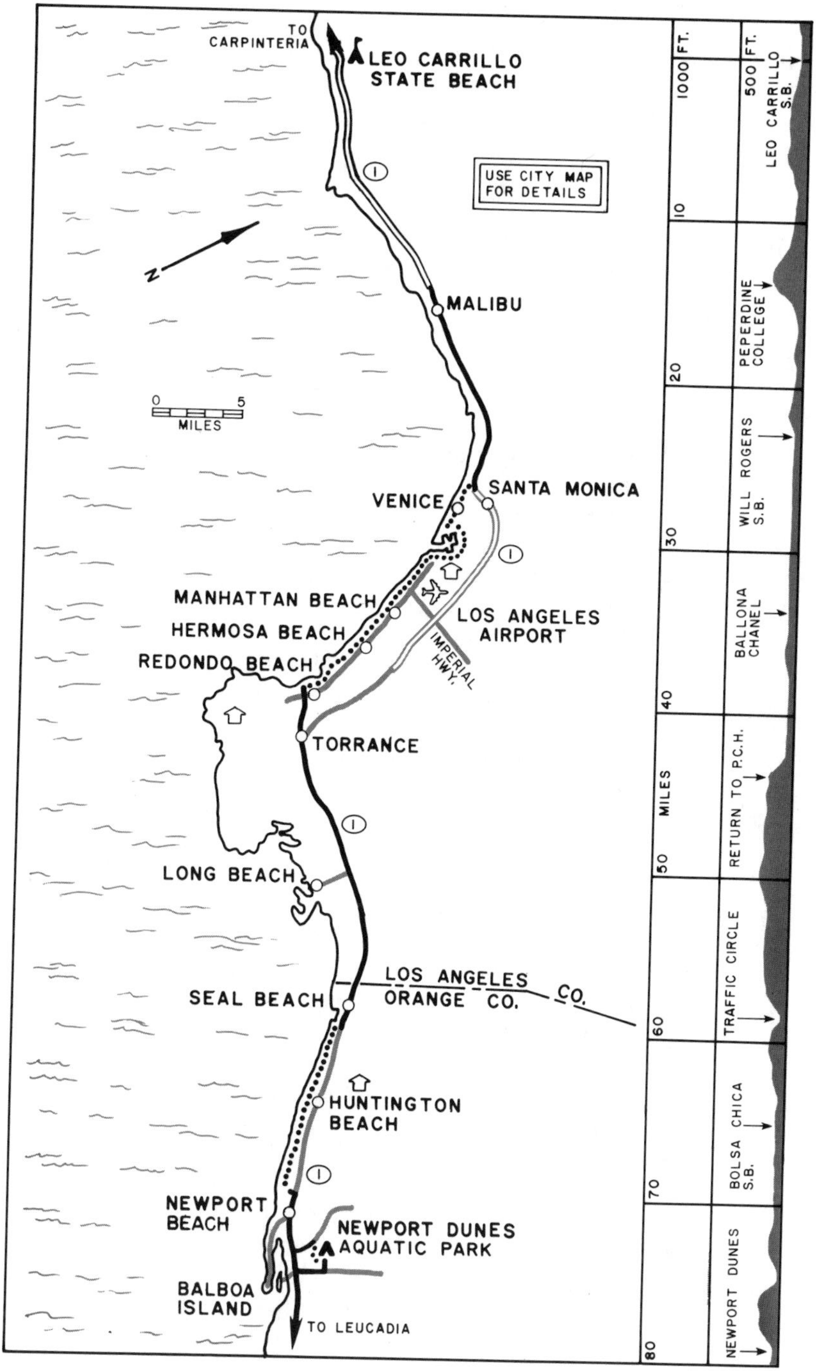
TO CARPINTERIA
LEO CARRILLO STATE BEACH
1
USE CITY MAP FOR DETAILS
N
MALIBU
0 5
MILES
VENICE
SANTA MONICA
MANHATTAN BEACH
HERMOSA BEACH
REDONDO BEACH
LOS ANGELES AIRPORT
IMPERIAL HWY.
TORRANCE
LONG BEACH
LOS ANGELES CO.
ORANGE CO.
SEAL BEACH
HUNTINGTON BEACH
NEWPORT BEACH
NEWPORT DUNES AQUATIC PARK
BALBOA ISLAND
TO LEUCADIA
1000 FT.
500 FT.
LEO CARRILLO S.B.
PEPERDINE COLLEGE
WILL ROGERS S.B.
BALLONA CHANEL
RETURN TO P.C.H.
TRAFFIC CIRCLE
BOLSA CHICA S.B.
NEWPORT DUNES
MILES
10
20
30
40
50
60
70
80

Mileage Log

0.0 (mp 62.10) Head south from Leo Carrillo State Beach on the Pacific Coast Hwy.

1.1 (mp 61.00) Nichilas County Beach: chemical toilet.

2.5 (mp 59.70) El Pescador State Beach, the first of three beach accesses.

5.0 (mp 57.10) Malibu. General urban clutter increases as you ride by expensive houses teetering over endless beaches.

5.4 (mp 56.70) Zuma Beach County Park, one of many popular Los Angeles County swimming beaches.

12.5 (mp 50.30) Malibu Beach RV Park is located on the left. The park has tent spaces; call ahead for reservations, (213)456-6052.

14.4 (mp 48.40) Pepperdine College on the left and community park on the right: restrooms. Official shoulder ends.

15.9 (mp 46.90) Beach access.

16.2 (mp 46.60) Malibu Lagoon State Beach and museum.

16.4 (mp 46.40) Pass Malibu Pier. This is a favorite hangout for sunbathers and surfers who flock to the rocky point west of the pier nearly every day of the year.

22.2 (mp 40.60) Topanga State Beach: restrooms.

23.5 (mp 39.30) Will Rogers State Beach (Sunset Blvd. section).

25.2 (mp 37.60) Start Los Angeles Bike Path at the second section of Will Rogers State Beach; restrooms and food available in several locations along the path.

28.4 Ride past a pier and a ferris wheel.

30.7 Venice Beach, where the people of Los Angeles come to look and be looked at. The large pavilion for rollerbladers, dancers, weight lifters, as well as masses of people distinguishes this beach from the others. Check out Muscle Beach, the open-air gym where body builders come to tan their biceps.

31.4 At the end of the Venice Beach area is a pier. Leave the beach path here. Turn left and head northeast on Washington St., following the green bike route signs.

31.9 Ride past a pond. Then, at Milred Ave., go right on the well-signed Marina Del Rey Bike Path.

32.2 Cross Bali Way and follow the bike path through the alleyways and parking lots of the Marina Del Rey boat basin.

32.7 Bike path ends. Turn right on Fiji Way.

33.4 A traffic circle marks the end of Fiji Way. Ride about three-quarters of the circle, then take a sharp right on a bike path. Go straight up the path for 200 feet, then turn right and ride along a strip of land between Ballona Channel and the entrance to the boat basin.

34.1 Cross Ballona Channel on a wide bridge, then take an immediate right back onto the beach-front bike path for 8 miles of moderately easy riding. If the traffic lights at Hermosa Beach indicate that you must walk, leave the path and go inland 1 block to Beach St. for 0.3 mile. If heading to Los Angeles International Airport (LAX), leave the bike path after crossing Ballona Channel and continue straight onto Pacific Ave. At Vista Del Mar, put in your earplugs, turn right, and ride 1.6 miles along the end of the runway. At Imperial, go left and follow it to the airport entrance.

42.8 Beach path ends at Redondo Beach. Go left, then take the first right on Harbor Dr. following the city bike route.

43.5 At Redondo Beach Municipal Pier, the bike path winds through a parking garage. On the far side you will exit onto the pier. After looking around, go left and leave the bike path in favor of the pier access road. Pass the tour bus loading area and ride up a steep hill.

44.0 Turn right on Catalina Ave.

44.1 Go right on Esplanade and follow the coast.

45.3 Ignore the Pacific Coast Bicycle Route at Avenue H and continue on to make your left turn at Avenue I.

45.5 Turn right on Pacific Coast Hwy. and enter the city of Torrance. Following the PCH for the next 27 miles is not easy on the nerves. Traffic is very heavy, shoulders irregular, pavement full of potholes and broken glass, and the air is truly foul. Don't delay. Get busy and get it over with; the beaches ahead are wonderful. If you have lingered until rush hour, linger some more and complete this section as an after-dinner treat.

49.6 Enter Lomalita.

51.7 Pass a regional park on the right: restrooms. Soon after, you will enter Wilmington.

56.5 Ride past an entrance to the Long Beach Freeway. This is a dangerous interchange, with drivers vying for position to get on or off the freeway. Ride with brain engaged and use your hand signals aggressively.

59.0 Drop down a short hill, then head around a traffic circle. Stay to the right in the well-marked PCH lane. About halfway around the PCH veers to the right, heading toward Newport Beach. The riding relaxes a bit here and the streets become wider. However, the traffic is often heavy.

62.6 Leave Los Angeles County and enter Orange County and the town of Seal Beach.

63.6 A bike lane begins at the outskirts of Seal Beach.

65.1 Enter Sunset Beach.

66.5 As you leave Sunset Beach and enter Huntington Beach, go right, ride partway around a traffic circle, then head to the right on a beachside bicycle path. Restrooms and water are found at the start of the path. (Or, you may stay on the PCH which has a wide shoulder for the next 8 miles.)

Surfer at Huntington Beach pier

71.5 Pass 8th St. To reach the Colonial Inn Hostel, go left on 8th St. 4 blocks to Pecan St. The hostel is located on the corner at 421 8th St. It has twenty-eight beds, showers, a full kitchen, and bicycle storage. Check-in is from 4:30 P.M. to 10:30 P.M.

71.7 Huntington Beach Pier, the best vantage point along the coast to watch surfers. Surfing was first introduced in California here and the tradition is still going strong. Continue south on the shoulder of the highway or on the beach path.

72.7 Huntington State Beach entrance: restrooms, water, and beach access.

74.4 Newport Beach city limits. The Huntington Beach bike path ends; return to the PCH, which has a wide shoulder.

75.6 Cross Balboa Blvd. This is the start of the Balboa Island Alternate Route (for details, see the end of the mileage log). Continuing on, the shoulder disappears as you head through Newport Beach. The highway descends, then crosses a wide bridge over Newport Bay.

77.2 After the bridge, continue on a few feet to the first intersection and prepare for a left turn on Bayside Rd. When traffic is heavy, go to the south side of the intersection and use the pedestrian signal. (If you are not spending the night at Newport Dunes, continue straight on PCH.)

77.7 Turn right and follow a bike path along the edge of Newport Dunes Aquatic Park.

78.2 Bike path ends. Go left to campground entrance booths. Congratulations—you made it through L.A.! *Side Trip* to Balboa Island. From the campground entrance go right and ride 0.2 mile south on Black Bay Rd. Go right again on Jamboree Rd. and head uphill 0.3 mile to a major intersection. Go straight across the PCH and descend 0.3 mile to the island and frozen bananas. The Balboa Island Alternate Route ends here.

Balboa Island Alternate Route

Turn right (southwest) on Balboa Blvd. for a shoulderless 3.5 miles down the long sandspit that protects Newport Bay and Balboa Island. Most of the spit is covered with stores and private homes. The west side has a pier, fish market, and state park which ends at The Wedge, a famous and very dangerous body-surfing area. On the east side are Newport Bay Harbor and Balboa Island. To return to the main route, ride 2.7 miles down the spit and catch the Balboa Island ferry. You will return to the PCH via a bridge on the east side of the island.

Newport Dunes Aquatic Park to San Elijo State Beach
(59.7 Miles)

The coast south of Newport Beach is a popular escape from the heat and smog of the interior. Throughout the summer, the four major state park campgrounds and numerous state beaches along this 59.7 mile section are full to overflowing. The coastal towns attempt to accommodate the vast influx of tourists by lining the streets with restaurants, motels, fast-food outlets, and surf shops.

Roads traveled in this section vary from busy thoroughfares to quiet residential streets. Shoulders are nonexistent in towns and are frequently used for beach parking in the country. The best feature of this area is the gently rolling terrain—perfect for riding.

The route follows the busy Coast Hwy. (Pacific seems to have been dropped at Newport Beach) until it merges with Interstate 5 at Dana Point. The route then heads through a maze of city streets at San Clemente before reaching open country on the nearly deserted roads of Camp Pendleton—deserted unless the army is on maneuvers. Beyond the camp, the route winds its way through Oceanside, Carlsbad, Leucadia, and Encinitas on city streets and highways. The advantage of all this urbanism is that grocery stores and bike shops are readily available when needed.

Take time for one important side trip to Mission San Juan Capistrano, a short 4 miles off the route. Every year, on March 19, the swallows return

San Elijo State Beach Campground

to Capistrano, heralding the beginning of spring. The swallows stay at the mission and a nearby shopping center through the second week of October. Even if you are not on hand when the swallows return, the mission is worth a visit. It was founded in 1776 and destroyed by an earthquake in 1812. A new mission was built behind the ruins of the old church, creating an elegant setting for the gardens.

The day's ride ends at San Elijo State Beach, the last public campground north of the Mexican border. Although the hiker-biker site has been closed to discourage transients, a space will be found for anyone arriving on a bicycle. You may have to pay full price for your site. A large grocery store and bike shop are located directly across the road from the campground.

Mileage Log

0.0 Leaving Newport Dunes Aquatic Park, ignore the bike path and go right (heading south) on Black Bay Rd.

0.2 Go right again on Jamboree Rd. and head uphill.

0.5 Take a left turn on Pacific Coast Hwy. and head south.

2.3 Marguerite Ave. is passed on the right. South Corona Del Mar Beach Park is located 0.3 mile west: restrooms, water, and views north to Newport Harbor, The Wedge, and Balboa Island.

3.1 Start a brief spell through open country.

3.3 Pass a bike path on the right that descends into Crystal Cove State Beach and returns to the highway 2 miles to the south. The bike path is scenic and passes several restrooms. If you choose the path you will have opportunities to return to the highway at the three auto entrance points.

6.4 Laguna Beach: grocery stores. In 1.3 miles the route will leave the highway and follow side streets in an attempt to avoid some of the congestion.

7.5 At Cliff Dr. take a right turn off the Coast Hwy. and head into a residential area. Cliff Dr. bends left, then twists and turns along the top of a bluff overlooking the coast.

8.0 Pass Diver's Cove Park: restrooms, water, benches, picnic tables, and views, as well as access to the beach's ecological reserve area.

8.6 Return to the highway, busy and shoulderless.

9.0 At the crest of a steep hill take a left turn on Legion St. (When traffic is heavy you may find the pedestrian signal on the south side of the intersection to be helpful.)

9.1 Go right (south) on Catalina St.

9.5 Catalina St. ends temporarily. Turn right on Thalia St., then take the first left back on Catalina St.

9.9 Catalina St. becomes Calliope St. Take the first left on Glenneyre St.

10.2 At Diamond St., turn right and return to S. Coast Hwy. (Coast Hwy. has officially changed names again). The highway soon broadens to include a shoulder, which serves as a parking lot. In general, riding is less than perfect in this area.

11.9 Aliso Beach County Park entrance: restrooms, water, and a pier.

14.1 S. Coast Hwy. leaves the urban sprawl for another short stint through open country. A large supermarket is located on the left side of the highway.

14.9 Salt Beach County Park, a picturesque day-use area with restrooms, water, pavilion, fountain, and beach access.

16.0 Dana Point. This long, narrow town spread along the highway has grocery stores and restaurants.

16.2 The road divides. Stay right on Del Padra Ave. and follow the city bike route signs.

16.6 Go right on Golden Lantern and descend. (Not far ahead, Highway 1 joins Interstate 5 and ends.)

16.9 At the base of the hill make a left turn on Dana Point Harbor Rd.

17.2 Go right on Park Lantern Rd. and ride into Doheny State Beach: hiker-biker sites, showers, and beach access. If you plan to stay at the park, check in at the entrance station. If continuing on, ride by the booth and follow the park road as it parallels the S. Coast Hwy. When the road forks, stay left on the Old Coast Hwy. Cross a short

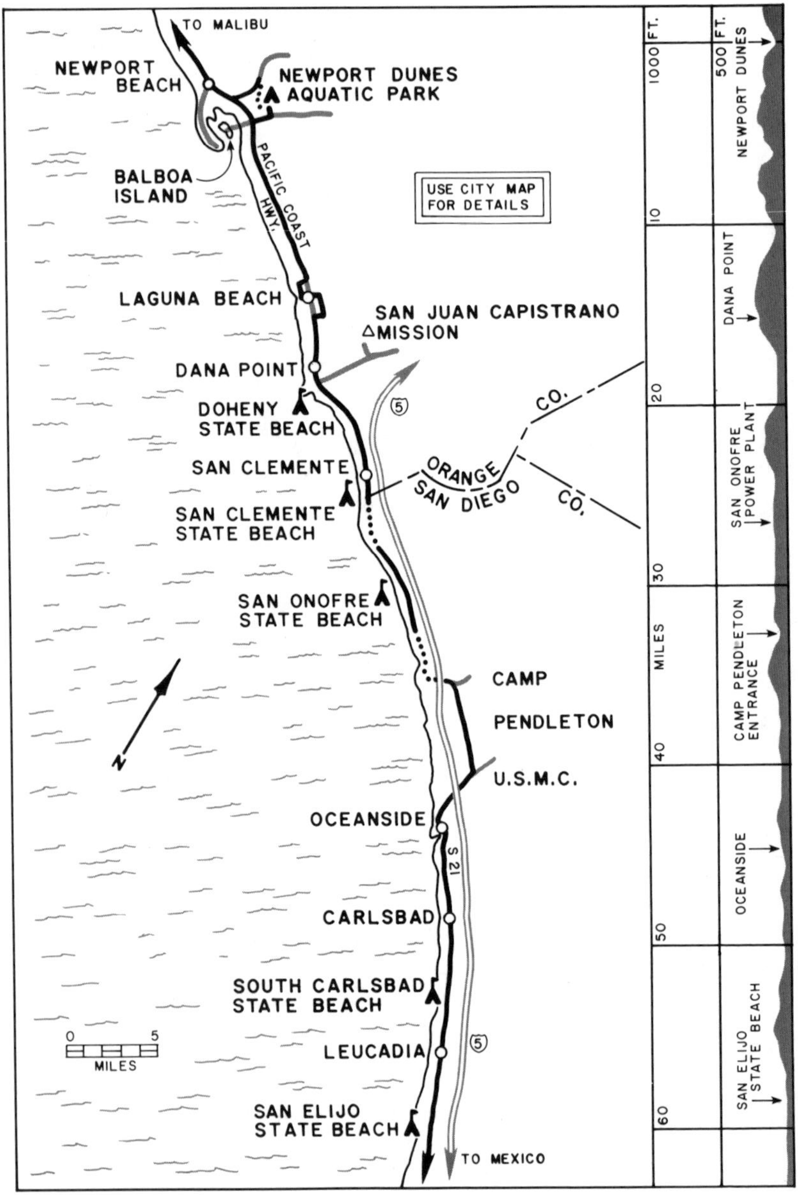

TO MALIBU

NEWPORT
BEACH

NEWPORT DUNES
AQUATIC PARK

BALBOA
ISLAND

PACIFIC COAST HWY.

USE CITY MAP
FOR DETAILS

LAGUNA BEACH

SAN JUAN CAPISTRANO
△MISSION

DANA POINT

⑤

DOHENY
STATE BEACH

SAN CLEMENTE

ORANGE CO.
SAN DIEGO CO.

SAN CLEMENTE
STATE BEACH

SAN ONOFRE
STATE BEACH

CAMP

PENDLETON

U.S.M.C.

OCEANSIDE

S 21

CARLSBAD

SOUTH CARLSBAD
STATE BEACH

0   5
MILES

LEUCADIA   ⑤

SAN ELIJO
STATE BEACH

TO MEXICO

N

1000 FT.

10

20

30

MILES

40

50

60

500 FT.

NEWPORT DUNES

DANA POINT

SAN ONOFRE
POWER PLANT

CAMP PENDLETON
ENTRANCE

OCEANSIDE

SAN ELIJO STATE BEACH

bridge, then ride through the day-use parking area. **Side Trip** to Mission San Juan Capistrano. Continue on Dana Point Harbor Dr. for 0.3 mile. Cross S. Coast Highway and continue straight inland on Del Obispo St. After 3.2 miles go left on Camino Capistrano for a final 0.2 mile to the mission.

18.7 At the end of the day-use parking area, continue south on a bicycle path along the edge of the sandy beach.

18.9 Bicycle path ends at the entrance to Capistrano State Beach. Go left to Old Coast Hwy. and continue south on a wide bicycle lane. (Northbound bicycle lane varies from good to nonexistent, depending on recent slide activity.)

20.5 San Clemente, a city whose narrow main roads are avoided by a well-marked bike route starting at the city limits. Take the first right after the city sign on Ave. Estagon and ride to the entrance of the Metro Link (commuter train) parking area.

20.6 Following the city bike route signs, turn left on Calle Deschecha.

20.7 Take a right on Pico St.

20.8 Go left on Boca de la Playa.

20.9 Turn left again on Calle las Bolas and soon after take a right on Ave. Florencia.

21.3 Go left on Ave. Pelayo.

31.4 Turn right at Calle Puente, which takes you past a city park with restrooms.

31.9 Bear right on Ave. Palizada.

22.0 At Calle Seville, steer left.

22.3 Go straight on Ave. Santa Barbara.

22.4 Swing right on S. Ola Vista and relax for a bit.

23.8 Ola Vista ends. Go left and ride uphill. To the right are San Clemente State Beach and Califia Beach Park. San Clemente State Beach has picnicking, camping, hiker-biker site, showers, impressive views of the ocean, and a nearby store. Califia Beach Park offers picnicking, restrooms, and access to an impressive beach at the base of sandstone cliffs.

23.9 Take a right on Avenue del Presidente and ride south on a wide bicycle lane, sandwiched between Interstate 5 and San Clemente State Beach.

24.9 Leave Orange County and enter San Diego County.

25.1 Avenue del Presidente ends. Continue straight on a bike path starting just before the freeway entrance. The bike path parallels Interstate 5 on the Old Coast Hwy., passing an access to Trestles Beach, one of the most crowded surfing areas on the southern coast.

26.6 Bike path ends. Go left, around the gate, then continue south on a wide bike lane along the San Onofre State Beach access road.

28.1 Pass the San Onofre nuclear plant. Expect considerable traffic when the work shifts change.

29.3 Ride past the entrance booth for San Onofre State Beach campground. The bike path heads straight through the 3-mile-long campground that is located between the freeway and the ocean. Hiker-biker camp, cold outdoor showers, a small store (rarely open), beach access, and no electricity.

32.4 At the southern end of San Onofre State Beach, the bike path heads into the Camp Pendleton restricted area. Allow enough time to ride the next 12 miles before the camp closes at dusk. Entrance into Camp Pendleton requires negotiating the narrowly spaced bars on the left-hand side of the gate. Beyond the barrier the road belongs to bicycles and army tanks.

34.1 The bike route turns inland, passing under Interstate 5.

34.3 After the freeway, the road branches. Stay to the right.

35.7 The road you have been following ends. Go left and head east on an unnamed road that takes you through the Santa Fe Railroad underpass.

35.9 Camp entrance checkpoint. Sign in and receive an official camp map. Continue, bearing right when the road splits.

36.4 Intersection and first stop sign; go right. (Routefinding through the camp is easy; at every major intersection, go right.)

San Elijo State Beach

43.2 Cycle around a small pond to arrive at a major intersection. Turn right on Vandegrift Blvd.

44.6 Exit Camp Pendleton and follow Harbor Dr. south.

45.0 After passing under Interstate 5 take the first left on Coast Hwy. and enter Oceanside.

45.9 Turn right (west) on Surfrider Way. (If you are looking for restaurants or groceries, stay on the Coast Hwy., which is busy but rideable if you are hungry enough.)

46.1 Cross railroad tracks, then take a left on Pacific St. ***Alternate Route***, for southbound riders only. Continue down Surfrider 1 more block to palm-lined beaches. Go left on The Strand and follow it to its end. Go left for 1 block, then turn right on Pacific St.

48.0 At Cassidy St., go left under a bridge and head inland.

48.2 Following the city bike route signs, go right on Broadway.

48.5 Broadway ends. Take a left on Easton for 1 block.

48.6 Turn right and head south on Coast Hwy. (also known as State 21).

48.8 Coast Hwy. dips across Buena Vista Lagoon, a bird sanctuary, then enters the town of Carlsbad.

49.8 Carlsbad State Beach: no facilities.

53.9 South Carlsbad State Beach campground: small store, Laundromat, showers, and beach access. No hiker-biker site due to transient problem. No bikers will be turned away; however, you may be asked to pay full price.

55.5 Leucadia, a congested town with small shops and grocery stores.

57.0 Encinitas, another congested town with small shops and grocery stores.

57.7 Pass access to Moonlight State Beach: beaches, restrooms, and water.

58.7 Swamis City Park: restrooms and water.

59.7 San Elijo State Beach: campsites, small store, hot showers, and access to beaches and tide pools. Groceries may be purchased across the street.

San Elijo State Beach to the Mexican Border
(45.3 Miles)

The final leg of California, and of the Pacific Coast Bike Route, consists of 45.3 challenging miles. The challenge is not the terrain—there are only two hills of notable size—but comes from riding yet another entire day through cities.

The first 6 miles to Torrey Pines State Reserve are the easiest; the towns are small and somewhat spread apart. Beyond the state reserve, it's uphill to La Jolla Mesa and the start of the San Diego urban sprawl. The remainder of the ride is spent weaving through the maze of La Jolla, San

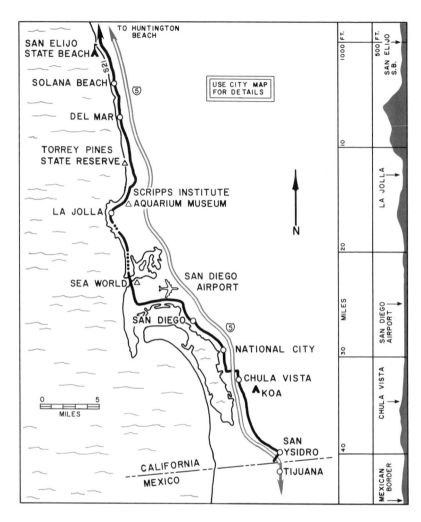

Diego, National City, Chula Vista, and, finally, San Ysidro on exceptionally well-marked bike routes.

San Diego is a friendly city with fascinating places to explore. Make your first stop the Torrey Pines Reserve, one of the last places on earth where these trees grow. A little farther south, hours can be spent at the Scripps Institute Stephen Birch Aquarium-Museum. This aquarium is a little less theatrical and not as pricey as the one in Monterey, but overall is an excellent place to spend 3 or more hours. Open daily from 9:00 A.M. to 5:00 P.M. except on Christmas and Thanksgiving.

Continuing south, performing sea animals tickle the fancy of the young and old at Sea World. Open daily.

The San Diego area beaches are excellent; surfing is passable, body surfing is popular, sunbathing is outstanding, and the people-watching is as good as it gets. Try Mission Beach if you are staying in the central San Diego area, and Imperial Beach if you are in the south. Rental surfboards, boogie boards, or skateboards are available near the beaches.

If spending a few days in San Diego, visit Balboa Park, home of a fascinating collection of museums, a velodrome, and the famous San Diego Zoo. San Diego Wildlife Park, located 30 miles north of downtown, is an extension of the zoo and well worth the hassle of getting there. The wildlife park may be reached by bicycle—if you don't mind the desert heat—or by bus. Check for information at your hotel or the KOA office. The Coronado Peninsula makes an excellent, easy day ride. To get there, take a passenger ferry from downtown San Diego or follow the signed bike route from Imperial Beach.

Reaching the California–Mexico border is a thrill. It is also a good place to turn around and head back north. If planning to visit Mexico for a day, it is best to leave your bike in a secure place and ride the Red Commuter Train to the border. Unless you are comfortable with riding in downtown Manhattan, the streets and the traffic south of the border are not for gringos on bikes.

The closest campground to the border is the San Diego Metro KOA in Chula Vista, 7 miles south of the train and bus stations and 9 miles south of the airport. San Diego also has three hostels and numerous hotels.

As noted above, San Diego is a bicycle-friendly city, and it is only fitting that the Pacific Coast Bicycle Route should, on its final leg, pass right by the entrance to the airport and within 2 blocks of the Amtrak and Greyhound stations.

Mileage Log

0.0 From San Elijo State Beach, continue south on County Highway S21, enjoying the wide bicycle lane.

0.5 Cardiff by the Sea, a sunning and swimming beach with chemical toilets and no running water.

2.1 Pass Solana Beach County Park turnoff on the right: picnic tables, restrooms, running water, and ocean views.

3.5 Del Mar, a town with a Danish theme. Beyond Del Mar the highway rambles along the coast; watch for cars making abrupt turns, attempting to squeeze into parking spaces.

5.9 Pass Torrey Pines State Beach on the right.

6.8 The highway begins a long climb to La Jolla Mesa. *Side Trip* to Torrey Pines State Reserve. At the end of the state beach, go left up a steep, mile-long hill to scenic views and the rarest pine trees native to the United States: trails, restrooms, water, and a visitor center.

8.8 County Highway S21 becomes Torrey Pines Blvd.

9.6 The road divides. Go right, following N. Torrey Pines Blvd., and ride around the western edge of the University of California at San Diego.

11.1 Following signs to the Stephen Birch Aquarium, go right on Expedition Way and begin a steady and often steep descent off La Jolla Mesa.

11.6 Sign for SCRIPPS INSTITUTE'S STEPHEN BIRCH AQUARIUM is located to the left. You can't miss it. If not stopping for a visit, stay to the right and continue the descent on Downwind Way.

11.8 Go left on La Jolla Shores Dr.

13.0 Bear right, following Torrey Pines Rd., and enter La Jolla. The route through the town is marked by green bike-route signs.

13.8 Near the crest of a hill, go left on Prospect Pl. for 1 block.

13.9 Turn right on Virginia.

14.3 Go left on High St.

14.4 At Pearl St., go right.

14.5 Take a left on Girand Ave.

Whale sculpture outside Scripps Institute's Stephen Birch Aquarium

14.8 Turn left on Fay Ave.

15.1 Fay Ave. ends at the T intersection. Cross to the sidewalk on the opposite side, then descend 100 feet to find a bicycle path on the left. This path is 0.7 mile long and easy to follow. (Northbound riders will have one intersection at 0.4 mile; keep right.)

15.8 At the end of the bike path, go left for half a block, then turn right on Beaumont Ave.

16.2 Turn right and go for 1 block on Camino de la Costa.

16.3 Turn left on La Jolla Hermosa Ave., still following the city bike route signs.

16.9 Pass Bird Rock Elementary School, then turn left and ride up a narrow alley.

17.1 Pass the school playfield and turn right into another unnamed alley.

17.2 Take a left on Agate St., the second normal-looking street off the alley.

17.3 Turn right at Jolla Mesa Rd. and follow it as it merges with La Jolla Blvd. which, in turn, becomes Mission Blvd.

17.7 *Alternate Route* along the beach. The main route stays on Mission Blvd.; however, if you want a view of San Diego beach life and don't mind cycling through crowds, turn right at Law St. for 0.1 mile, then head left on a bicycle path overlooking the coast. Follow the bike path south for 2.2 miles.

19.9 Turn left onto Mission Bay Dr. just before passing an amusement park. Mission Bay Dr. passes a large park (restrooms and running water), then heads across Mission Bay Channel on a wide bridge.

20.8 After crossing the bridge, exit to the right on Quivira Rd., then go left (south), paralleling Mission Bay Dr. *Side Trip* to San Diego Sea World. Turn left after crossing Mission Bay Channel Bridge on Dana Landing Rd. (opposite the Quivira Rd. exit), and follow it to the right for 0.5 mile. Cross a major 4-lane road then ride Perez Cove Way 0.2 mile to the entrance of Sea World. Plan to spend at least 3 hours; admission is charged.

21.3 Following the bike route signs, go left on a bike path that takes you to Sunset Cliffs Blvd. and ride over the San Diego River.

21.8 At the south end of the bridge, merge left in preparation for a left turn on Nimitz Blvd. This is a tricky intersection in heavy traffic, and from this point on traffic is always heavy. You are nearing the heart of San Diego's downtown and business district so there will be lots of stoplights and numerous bumpy railroad tracks.

24.1 Nimitz Blvd. ends in the heart of the naval training center. Turn left on North Harbor Dr. and ride over a large bridge either on the road or on the wide sidewalk that doubles as a bicycle path. The road now heads around the West Basin of San Diego Bay.

24.5 Spanish Marine Bayside Park: restrooms, water, and picnic tables.

Leave the road here and ride the meandering bicycle path for the next 6 miles.

25.8 San Diego International Airport exit.

26.6 *Side Trip* to Balboa Park and San Diego Zoo. Turn left on Laurel St. for a very steep 1.7 miles to the entrance of Balboa Park. Continue straight into the park on El Prado to reach the information center, museums, and zoo.

27.8 Intersection of Harbor Dr. and Broadway. The Amtrak station is located 2 blocks left up Broadway at the Santa Fe Train Depot. The Red Train to the Mexican border is located just beyond and the Greyhound bus station is a couple of blocks farther at the corner of Broadway and First Ave. The passenger ferry to the Coronado Peninsula departs just to the right of this intersection. If not looking for immediate transport to somewhere else, continue straight ahead on Harbor Dr.

28.7 Pass the massive San Diego Convention Center.

32.1 Enter National City.

32.9 Turn right on 13th St. and follow it for 1 short block then go left on Cleveland Ave.

33.6 Go left on W. 24th St. and ride under Interstate 5.

33.9 Make a right turn on Hoover Ave.

34.6 Hoover Ave. ends. Go left on W. 33 St.

34.8 Go right (south) on National City Blvd. and cross the Sweetwater River.

35.2 At the south end of the bridge, take an immediate left on C St., leaving National City and entering Chula Vista.

35.4 Turn right on 5th Ave. entering a residential area. Intersections have shallow culverts across them to drain rain water; ride carefully.

35.6 If planning to spend the night at the San Diego Metropolitan KOA campground, go left on D St. for 0.7 mile to 2nd Ave. Go left again for 0.7 mile to the campground. To be on the safe side, call ahead to (619)427-3601 for reservations.

36.9 Farther progress down 5th Ave. is blocked by a shopping center. Go left on H St. for 1 block.

37.0 Turn right on Fig Ave. and follow it to I St.

37.1 Take a right on I St., then go left, back onto 5th Ave.

38.9 Turn right (west) on Palomar St. and descend to the second major intersection.

39.2 Go left on Broadway, which soon becomes Beyer Blvd.

42.0 Directly after passing under the Highway 117 freeway, go right on Dairy Mart Rd.

42.6 Turn left (east) on San Ysidro Blvd., just before crossing Interstate 5. Before long the road enters San Ysidro. Streets are jammed with traffic and the main enterprise seems to be money changing. Everyone

¡AJÚA!

speaks Spanish; very few will admit to understanding English. (English is much more commonly spoken across the boarder in Tijuana.)

44.0 Pass under the US 805 freeway and head into the most congested section of town.

44.7 Turn right on Camino de la Plaza. Cross over Interstate 5. Take the first left, following signs for bus and taxi parking.

45.3 ¡AJÚA! La Frontera Mexicana, 2,906.4 kilometers al sur de Vancouver, British Columbia. (YAH HOO! The Mexican Border, 1,816.5 miles south of Vancouver, British Columbia.)

■ RECOMMENDED READING ■

Bicycle Touring

Lovett, Richard A. *The Essential Touring Cyclist*. Camben: Ragged Mountain Press, 1994.

Sloane, Eugene A. *The Complete Book of Bicycling*. 5th ed. New York: Simon & Schuster, 1995.

Bicycle Maintenance

Bicycling Magazine's *Basic Maintenance and Repair*. Emmaus: Rodale Press, 1995.

Cuthbertson, Tom, and Rick Morrall. *The Bag Book*. Berkeley, CA: Ten Speed Press, 1981.

Henderson, Bob. *The Haynes Bicycle Book*. Newbury Park: Haynes North America, Inc., 1995.

Van Der Plas, Rob. *Roadside Bicycle Repair*, 3d ed. San Francisco: Bicycle Books, 1995.

Area Bicycle Tour Guides

British Columbia

Perrin, Tirn, and Janet Wilson. *Exploring by Bicycle: Southwest British Columbia and the San Juan Islands*. Vancouver, B.C.: Douglas and McIntyre, 1979.

California

Adventure Cycling Association, The. *Adventure Cycling in Northern California*. Seattle: The Mountaineers, 1996.

Brown, Ann Marie. *Easy Biking in Northern California*. San Francisco: Foghorn Press, 1996.

Oregon and Washington

Henderson, Jean. *Biking the Great Northwest*. Seattle: The Mountaineers, 1995.

Washington

Woods, Erin and Bill. *Bicycling the Backroads around Puget Sound*, 4th ed. Seattle: The Mountaineers, 1995.

—— *Bicycling the Backroads of Northwest Washington*, 2d ed. Seattle: The Mountaineers, 1984.

—— *Bicycling the Backroads of Southwest Washington*, 3d ed. Seattle: The Mountaineers, 1994.

▪ INDEX ▪

▪ ABOUT THE AUTHORS ▪

Tom Kirkendall and Vicky Spring are avid cyclists and all around out-door people. They have crafted their successful photography business to require them to spend long hours biking, hiking, climbing, skiing, and paddling to get just the right photograph. The couple keeps their permanent base camp in Western Washington where they live with their two children.

THE MOUNTAINEERS, founded in 1906, is a nonprofit outdoor activity and conservation club, whose mission is "to explore, study, preserve, and enjoy the natural beauty of the outdoors . . . ." Based in Seattle, Washington, the club is now the third-largest such organization in the United States, with 15,000 members and five branches throughout Washington State.

The Mountaineers sponsors both classes and year-round outdoor activities in the Pacific Northwest, which include hiking, mountain climbing, ski-touring, snowshoeing, bicycling, camping, kayaking and canoeing, nature study, sailing, and adventure travel. The club's conservation division supports environmental causes through educational activities, sponsoring legislation, and presenting informational programs. All club activities are led by skilled, experienced volunteers, who are dedicated to promoting safe and responsible enjoyment and preservation of the outdoors.

If you would like to participate in these organized outdoor activities or the club's programs, consider a membership in The Mountaineers. For information and an application, write or call The Mountaineers, Club Headquarters, 300 Third Avenue West, Seattle, Washington 98119; (206) 284-6310.

The Mountaineers Books, an active, nonprofit publishing program of the club, produces guidebooks, instructional texts, historical works, natural history guides, and works on environmental conservation. All books produced by The Mountaineers are aimed at fulfilling the club's mission.

Send or call for our catalog of more than 300 outdoor titles:
The Mountaineers Books
1001 SW Klickitat Way, Suite 201
Seattle, WA 98134
1-800-553-4453
e-mail: mbooks@mountaineers.org
website: www.mountaineers.org

Other titles you may enjoy from The Mountaineers:

ADVENTURE CYCLING IN™ NORTHERN CALIFORNIA:
Selected On- and Off-Road Rides, *The Adventure Cycling Association*
A guide to 44 classic on- and off-road bike routes for single and multi-day trips, with expert advice on safety, equipment, weather, road and trail rules, and more.

BICYCLING COAST TO COAST: **A Complete Route Guide,**
Virginia to Oregon, *Donna Ikenberry*
The definitive coast-to-coast biking guide. The route covers ten states and more than 4,000 miles, divided into 77 daily segments for a complete route or shorter rides.

MAKING CAMP: **A Complete Guide for Hikers, Mountain Bikers,**
Paddlers & Skiers, *Steve Howe, Alan Kesselheim, Dennis Coello, John Harlin*
A comprehensive, detailed camping how-to compiled by *Backpacker* magazine field experts for anyone traveling by foot, boat, bicycle, or skis, through all kinds of terrain, year-round.

BIKING THE GREAT NORTHWEST: **20 Tours in Washington, Oregon,**
Idaho, and Montana, *Jean Henderson*
A collection of multi-day tours, many of them loops, for great Northwest cycling vacations, including mileage logs and notes on terrain, history, scenic highlights, and cycling smarts.

BICYCLE GEARING, *Dick Marr*
A complete guide to gearing and shifting strategies.

EXPLORING THE WILD OREGON COAST, *Bonnie Henderson*
A comprehensive guide to the best hiking, canoeing, bicycling, horseback riding and wildlife watching spots along the Oregon coast.

EXPLORING WASHINGTON'S WILD OLYMPIC COAST, *David Hooper*
The most detailed guide available to hiking the beaches of Olympic National Park, including camping, safety, and information on wildlife, human history, shipwrecks and environmental concerns.

BICYCLING THE BACROADS™ AROUND PUGET SOUND, Fourth
Edition, *Bill & Erin Woods*
BICYCLING THE BACKROADS™ OF NORTHWEST OREGON,
Second Edition, *Philip Jones & Jean Henderson*
BICYCLING THE BACKROADS™ OF NORTHWEST WASHINGTON,
Fourth Edition, *Bill & Erin Woods*
BICYCLING THE BACKROADS™ SOUTHWEST WASHINGTON,
Third Edition, *Bill & Erin Woods*
The complete *Bicycling the Backroads™* series, offering detailed information on cycling tours throughout the Pacific Northwest.

Outdoor Books by the Experts

Whatever the season, whatever your sport, The Mountaineers Books has the resources for you. Our FREE CATALOG includes over 350 titles on climbing, hiking, mountain biking, paddling, backcountry skiing, snowshoeing, adventure travel, natural history, mountaineering history, and conservation, plus dozens of how-to books to sharpen your outdoor skills.

All of our titles can be found at or ordered through your local bookstore or outdoor store. Just mail in this card or call us at 800·553·4453 for your free catalog. Or send us an e-mail at mbooks@mountaineers.org.

Name _____

Address _____

City _____ State _____ Zip+4 _____-_____

E-mail _____

562-X

Outdoor Books by the Experts

Whatever the season, whatever your sport, The Mountaineers Books has the resources for you. Our FREE CATALOG includes over 350 titles on climbing, hiking, mountain biking, paddling, backcountry skiing, snowshoeing, adventure travel, natural history, mountaineering history, and conservation, plus dozens of how-to books to sharpen your outdoor skills.

All of our titles can be found at or ordered through your local bookstore or outdoor store. Just mail in this card or call us at 800·553·4453 for your free catalog. Or send us an e-mail at mbooks@mountaineers.org.

Please send a catalog to my friend at:

Name _____

Address _____

City _____ State _____ Zip+4 _____-_____

E-mail _____

562-X

BUSINESS REPLY MAIL
FIRST-CLASS MAIL   PERMIT NO. 85063   SEATTLE, WA

POSTAGE WILL BE PAID BY ADDRESSEE

THE MOUNTAINEERS BOOKS
1001 SW KLICKITAT WAY STE 201
SEATTLE WA 98134-9937

BUSINESS REPLY MAIL
FIRST-CLASS MAIL   PERMIT NO. 85063   SEATTLE, WA

POSTAGE WILL BE PAID BY ADDRESSEE

THE MOUNTAINEERS BOOKS
1001 SW KLICKITAT WAY STE 201
SEATTLE WA 98134-9937